Globalisation and Regional Security

Globalisation and Regional Security

India and Australia

Edited by

Dennis Rumley
D. Gopal

SHIPRA

ISBN : 81-7541-327-1

First Published in India in 2007

Globalisation and Regional Security: India and Australia

Published by :
SHIPRA PUBLICATIONS
115-A, Vikas Marg, Shakarpur, Delhi-110092 (India)
Tel. : 91-11-65277210, 22500954, Fax : 91-11-22458662
Email : info@shiprapublications.com
www.shiprapublications.com

Preface

Ever since, issues concerning national security and mutually of interests assumed critical significance between India and Australia in the academic community in both the countries, the editors felt the need to reflect specifically on the theme of globalisation and its implications for the security of India and Australia. They endeavoured to achieve this along with a group of Indian and Australian scholars who are known to be sympathetic to enhancing the India-Australia relationship generally, and who on occasions have participated in different forums to present their views on these matters. This volume is an outgrowth of a seminar organised by the Australian High Commission in Delhi and Indira Gandhi National Open University (IGNOU) in 2002. The editors are grateful to all the contributors both for their insightful contributions and for their patience in seeing this volume come to fruition.

The editors record their thanks to former Australian High Commissioner to India. Ms Penny Wensley and Prof. H. P. Dikshit, Vice Chancellor, Indira Gandhi National Open University for their continued support and encouragement.

May 2006

Dennis Rumley
Perth, Australia

D. Gopal
New Delhi, India

Contents

PERSPECTIVES ON AUSTRALIAN SECURITY

GLOBALISATION, REGIONAL SECURITY AND INDIA-AUSTRALIA RELATIONS

1

Introduction

DENNIS RUMLEY AND D. GOPAL

The present volume has four principal aims. First, it emphasises the increasing mutuality of regional security interests of both India and Australia consequent upon globalisation and the end of the Cold War. Second, it contributes to the regional debate over the changing nature of security associated with increasing globalisation. Third, the volume highlights some of the principal directions a new regional security agenda might take. Fourth, some of the ways in which India and Australia might play a role in a new regional security agenda are identified. The book comprises four main sections – globalisation, security and the Asia-Pacific region, perspectives on Indian security, perspectives on Australian security, and globalisation, regional security and India-Australia relations.

The Emergence of a New Security Agenda

The post-Cold War concern with a range of "new security challenges" is associated with a profound debate not only over the meaning of the term security but also of the nature of national, regional and global security policy (Stares, 1998). As has been pointed out elsewhere, the case has been well put against the "traditionalists", who want to restrict discussions of security solely to politico-military issues, compared to the "wideners" who want to extend the concept to include economic, social and environmental aspects of security (Alagappa, 1998; Buzan, Wæver, and de Wilde, 1998). The present volume belongs unequivocally to the latter orientation, since, in the post-Cold War period, these issues have become increasingly securitised (Rumley and Chaturvedi, 2005, 3).

To some degree, since the end of the second world war and until relatively recently, both India and Australia, for different reasons, have been regionally disengaged or even isolated in terms of their principal security relationships. The end of the Cold War and its association with increasing globalisation has necessitated a new security outlook on the part of both states in terms of the nature and types of perceived threats. In addition, these changes have precipitated a new outward orientation that threats are no longer conceived solely within a national frame of reference, but also within a non-state, regional and even global context (Thakur and Newman, 2004). Thus, both the nature and the scale of threat have changed while the question of human security has become increasingly significant (Commission on Human Security, 2003). These changes, in turn, have been associated with a developing concern on the part of both states over mutual regional security interests, especially in the Indian Ocean Region (IOR) and in the wider Asia-Pacific region. In short, both India and Australia have been subject to the emergence of a "new security agenda" which all states inevitably have to confront due to globalisation (Coker, 2002, 8). Three overall trends, in particular, have also contributed to the emergence of this new agenda – first, is the emergence of globalised networks which have increased state vulnerability to non-state actors and to a range of transnational threats; second, technological developments in weaponry have generated new threats and have brought states closer together; third, globalised information networks have contributed to increased demands for action and have had an associated impact on international law. As a result, solutions to the new threats generally require regional and even global mechanisms for cooperation and coordination (Allison, 2000).

However, collectively confronting new security challenges due to globalisation is never easy since its impacts are generally uneven and sometimes contradictory (Table 1). It has been argued, for example, that the gap between the so-called 'globalised' and the 'marginalised' or 'unglobalised' is the most important of all cultural divisions, and that this gap will increasingly become a source of conflict during the present century (Coker, 2002, 21). A recent influential and controversial book differentiates between a globalised "functioning core" and a "non-integrating gap" and draws an extremely arbitrary boundary between those states that are seen to be actively integrated into the global economy – that is, the "functioning core", and the remainder that constitute the "non-integrating gap" (Barnett, 2004). While the core states "adhere to globalisation's emerging security rule set", the states of the gap apparently do not (Barnett, 2004, 25-6). The gap states are also characterised as being "poor", and as places where life is "nasty", "brutal" "short", and "solitary" (Barnett, 2004, 161-166). Thus, in the Asia-Pacific region, while all of the ASEAN states (including Singapore) and Sri Lanka are seen to be located within the non-integrating gap, others, such as North Korea, are portrayed as being part of the functioning core.

Table 1: Some Contradictory Impacts of Globalisation

Greater freedom	Human rights violations
Creates wealth	Creates inequalities
Generates human insecurity	Makes some feel more secure
Enabling	Disempowering
Certainty	Uncertainty
The 'globalised'	The 'marginalised'

In the Indian Ocean Region, only three states-Australia, India and South Africa-are included in Barnett's "functioning core". In short, if we accept this aspect of Barnett's characterisation, then all three states will increasingly have mutually significant security interests due to globalisation during the present century. As has been pointed out that the transnational economic and geopolitical space which has resulted from globalisation requires "organized responses" (Lévy, 2002, 130). Given their regional location in this space, both India and Australia are in a unique position to take on a leading role in collaboratively developing and implementing a new regional security agenda.

Globalisation, Security and the Asia-Pacific Region

The first major section of the book – globalisation, security and the Asia-Pacific region – contains four essays which elaborate some of the general characteristics of the processes of globalization and some of their theoretical and practical security implications for the region and for regional states. In Chapter 2, Suparna Karmakar presents a fundamentally economic perspective of security concerns and she analyses the globalisation challenges faced by states in the Asia-Pacific region. This discussion of the processes of growing global economic integration argues that the fostering of economic growth is the most preferred, if not the only, mechanism by which national and regional economic and political security can be maximised. It is clear that there are both positive and negative aspects of increasing integration in trade and finance. From the point of view of the current book, new national and regional security concerns, for example, arise out of the uneven regional impact of globalisation. One of the essential challenges facing Asia-Pacific governments is to be able to facilitate processes whereby trade and investment are channeled into wealth creation and towards the improvement of some of the basic standards of living of their citizens. In recent years, despite the so-called Asian "economic crisis" of the late 1990s, regional states have increasingly been seen as attractive hosts for capital and have become important drivers of global economic growth. However, in order to mitigate any instability arising out of increasing global economic integration, Karmakar calls for a reduction in regional "dependence" on the West and for regional states to devise a set of "inward-looking policies" recognising the interdependence of regional security and the regional attractiveness of investment and trade. On the one hand, the latter are necessary for security-enhancement; on the other hand, the region needs to be seen as a safe place in which to invest.

Kamal Nayan Kabra, in Chapter 3, conceptualises globalization essentially as the strengthening of a North-centric world-wide capitalist economy. While the advantages of an early start tended to be restricted to a small number of industrialised countries that shared the overall gains, world systems approaches suggest the inevitability of the peripheralisation and dependency of the "late arrivals". However, Kabra argues against theories which accept the determinism of the inevitability of dependency. Furthermore, the author points to the inadequacy of approaches which seek to explain economic relationships solely on the basis of external factors, on the one hand, while assigning a passive role to domestic considerations, on the other. In the 'exceptional' case of Australia, Kabra argues that while "development by invitation" may have been one determinant, peripheralisation and dependency did not eventuate primarily due to a combination of domestic factors, including natural resource endowment, socio-economic factors and national policies. This is all the more interesting given that the structure of Australia's export income is similar to that of Indonesia. In Australia's exceptional case, however, a policy-making approach which emphasised "robust self-reliance" was an important overriding consideration and "genuine development" was a result of collective self-empowerment. The author uses an interesting counterfactual approach to demonstrate the differential economic developmental pathway taken by Argentina due to a contrasting configuration of its domestic social, economic and policy structure.

These findings are significant in terms of the theme of this volume since economic and security dependency are often two sides of the same coin. In Australia's case, there has been some debate to the extent to which national security policy has moved from a situation of "dependency" to one of "self-reliance" (Rumley, 1999, 170-2). Some commentators, for example, have argued that Australia has always been a part of a dependency relationship (Bell, 1991). However, official post-Cold War policy rhetoric has indicated that "the foundation of the government's defence policy is self-reliance" partly in response to the changing nature of security threats (Department of Defence, 1994, 13).

In Chapter 4, Sharad Joshi takes up this theme and discusses a range of contemporary, mainly non-military, security threats – terrorism, transnational organised crime, the proliferation of nuclear weapons, human security and environmental security. The author argues that, while these threats are essentially outcomes of globalisation, the state still has a key role to play in maximising security. Sharad Joshi contends that the awful events of 9/11 clearly indicated that terrorism had become a defining characteristic of the global security environment. While terrorism has long been a regional characteristic, more attention has been recently directed towards it; due to linkages between local movements and the transnational network. Indeed, transnational criminal groups involved in drug trafficking, money laundering and people smuggling, among other things, in certain cases have threatened the traditional security function of the state. The regional proliferation of nuclear weapons, on the other hand, has raised new doubts over the efficacy of deterrence and the continued relevance of the Non-Proliferation Treaty. Sharad Joshi argues that human security is now a critical problem due to the preoccupation of regional governments with maintaining control at all costs. Consequently, human rights abuses and associated repression raise serious doubts over the long-term stability of the state. Insecurity as a result of environmental degradation is primarily an outcome of unsustainable development. Environmental degradation, in turn, threatens individuals, communities and states due to the conflicts associated with the local, regional and global consequences of pollution and competition over resources scarcity (Thakur and Newman, 2004, 9).

Pankaj Kumar Jha, in Chapter 5, discusses some of the theoretical and practical arguments over the regional and national impact of the end of the Cold War and globalisation on the security discourse and policy for Southeast Asia in general and for Singapore, more particularly. The author differentiates between "traditional security" and "people-centred security" and elaborates the so-called "clash of security paradigms" between the realists and the liberal-institutionalists. Some of the implications of these differences for national and regional security are explored, especially in the context of increasing globalisation and the nature and character of economic development. In this regard, Pankaj Kumar Jha identifies an important "economic security dilemma" – that is, increased wealth due to market-oriented development policies is security-enhancing, while, at the same time, provides the resources to increase a state's military capability, which is likely to have the opposite effect. Furthermore, contrary to the expectations of some, it is argued that regional economic interdependence has been an effect rather than a cause of benign security relations. The author concludes that, on the one hand, in order to maximise its future security, Singapore should enhance its involvement in cooperative arrangements both with extra-regional powers and other ASEAN states. In particular, it is argued that Singapore needs "to curb terrorism at all costs". On the other hand, while Singapore should implement strong internal security laws to maximise national stability, it also needs to be more mindful of questions of human security in order to avoid a self-defeating security strategy.

Perspectives on Indian Security

Clearly, the end of the Cold War period coupled with increasing globalisation has presented some very significant new security challenges to the Indian government and to Indian society and economy. On the one hand, the end of the Cold War necessitated a rethinking of traditional alliances since the policy of non-alignment possessed fundamental and obvious conceptual problems. On the other hand, globalisation and the opening up of the Indian economy also necessitated a shift towards the world's most important economic powers while at the same time causing India to become more independently self-reliant (Gopal and Rumley, 2004). These changes have also been associated with India's acquisition of nuclear weapons and its move towards great power status. While the combination of these factors has resulted in India being confronted with a new global security environment, the country has had to face an ongoing set of regional and domestic security challenges. The second major section of the book contains three essays designed to give some insight into the emergence of the new security agenda in India following the end of the Cold War and as a result of globalisation. In chapter 6, Pushpita Das presents a comprehensive overview of the main elements of concern in the stability of the South Asian region. She discusses the nature of inter-state relations, democracy, enthno-nationalism, the regional arms race, terrorism and the role of extra-regional powers and their impact upon national and regional security. Das underlines the two central geopolitical realities of the South Asian region – that is, it is Indo-centric and that it is a region which is beset by mutual suspicion and hostility. Secondly, the author describes the democratic process in the region as "still incipient and struggling". She argues that this process still remains hostage to a range of destructive forces despite the fact that it is the most desired form of governance. Nonetheless, most South Asian states are victims of rising communalism, religious fundamentalism and linguistic and ethnic fanaticism. Das argues that the regional rise of ethno-nationalism poses a significant threat to the stability and integrity of regional states and the resultant conflicts, have contributed to a regional arms race. Regional conflicts, to a significant degree, have been made more complex by the involvement of extra-regional powers, especially the United States, China and Russia. The author argues that the combination of underdevelopment, sectarianism and marginalisation has contributed to the emergence and perpetuation of terrorism in the region. As Das points out, while regional conflicts divert scarce resources away from economic development and human security, market forces are increasingly likely to determine regional and global relations.

Darvesh Gopal, in Chapter 7, examines more closely the central security concerns of India in the post-9/11 period and calls for a new cooperative approach in dealing with non-traditional security threats. In doing so, Gopal first outlines a broad sketch of the essential parameters of global security that have been emerging in the post-Cold War period. He then provides a detailed analysis of India's regional security concerns, its internal security issues and an assessment of some of the related transnational and human security concerns before offering some suggestions on how Australia and India can cooperate, more effectively, in dealing with the new security environment. Gopal reiterates the point that the current security environment has necessitated a change in the way security is defined; both to encompass new threats and to identify relevant actors. However, as he stresses, this by no means implies a lessening of the importance of conflicts that arise out of traditional sources. Rather, the contemporary security environment has become far more complex as 'traditional' and 'non-traditional' concerns overlap and interconnect. Thus, India's traditionally regional (for example, relations with Pakistan) and internal (for example, provincial State insurgencies) security matters have increasingly intertwined with transnational problems of terrorism, drug trafficking and organised crime. Gopal argues that a new security strategy is required to effectively deal with this new security environment. He therefore offers a number of concrete suggestions for greater cooperation between India and Australia in dealing with the issues of maritime security in the Indian Ocean.

In Chapter 8, Vivian Louis Forbes discusses the growing awareness and strength of relationships among India, ASEAN and Australia. The author highlights the positive and negative factors that are inherent and suggests avenues along which Governments and policy-makers should proceed in order to achieve their stated goals and objectives for the ultimate benefit of the people of all states and for the good of the region. The Chapter discusses the historical and geopolitical context of relationships before providing a broad overview of some of the main goals of India's contemporary foreign policy. India's 'Look East Policy', conceived in 1991, was a policy formulated as a definitive innovation and the logic was that the Government should engage the increasingly vibrant ASEAN economies as part of economic and geopolitical change. The economic rationale at that time was to try and link India's liberalising economy with the globalising markets of Southeast Asia. Formerly, there was a perception that the tradition of India's historical connections and cultural links with that region of Asia was becoming a mere memory of the past. However, the enhancement of regional economic security was developed further with the BIMST regional initiative and has been broadened with an increase in India's regional naval role. The 'Look East Policy' has a wider horizon south of the Equator in that Australia is also encompassed in its vision of regional cooperation. India and Australia have worked together constructively on key international issues and bilateral trade has begun to increase substantially, especially this century.

Perspectives on Australian Security

In the late Cold War period, many Australian security analysts still believed that Australia was one of the most secure countries in the world for two main reasons: first, Australia was located in a relatively benign geopolitical environment; second, Australia is located some distance from the major centres of global conflict. In addition, Australia is surrounded by vast expanses of water that inevitably would make a conventional attack extremely difficult and costly. In any event, since regional states possessed a relatively limited capability for any attack, such an eventuality was seen to be highly unlikely in the medium-to-long-term. However, in the post-Cold War period, and particularly since 9/11 and 12/10, what has become clear is that conceptualising national security solely through a realist lens in quite inadequate and is even misguided. The new security threats to Australia, which are primarily non-state and 'non conventional' are global in their reach. Such threats, nonetheless, would likely emanate primarily from a regional neighbourhood that was increasingly perceived as an "arc of instability" due to a combination of problems of globalisation, political viability and governance, economic instability, ethnic tension and religious fundamentalism (Rumley, Forbes and Griffin, 2006). Since failing or failed states in Australia's region can provide a safe haven for the new security threats, a fundamentally different set of policy settings is required to deal with the real causes of insecurity. What is now needed, therefore, is a set of policies which reach out to aid and strengthen the capacity of regional states and which are centred on human development, rather than a mere reliance on traditional policies which are 'defence' oriented, which centre on military spending and which recreate a state fortress designed to repel regional state military threats. In short, therefore, non-traditional security threats are more likely to require *regional* rather than *national* responses which are human-centred rather than state-centred.

Globalisation and Rregionalism: Australia and India

The geopolitical, social, environmental and economic impacts of the processes of globalisation not only impact unevenly on states and sub-state jurisdictions and localities. These also have a differential impact upon *regionalism* – that is, spatial collectivities of contiguous states constructed to deliver some mutual security, environmental or economic benefit. This impact can take various forms. For example, globalisation may well engender the felt need on the part of some states to construct a regional entity, as was the case with the Indian Ocean Region Association for Regional Cooperation (IORARC). Such regional entities are in part a response to state concerns over the economic impacts of globalisation, but in general terms, they are unlikely to become very strong groupings in the absence of well-established intra-regional bilateral linkages.

The overarching regional grouping in the Asia-Pacific, the Asia Pacific Economic Cooperation (APEC) grouping, which currently includes Australia, but not India, was initiated at the end of the Cold War period when economic regionalism began to override ideological regionalism. However, the more recently-constructed East Asian Summit (EAS), which was inaugurated in Kuala Lumpur in December 2005, marked a major shift in the enlargement of East Asian regionalism. One of the several reasons for this was that the meeting comprised the group of ASEAN states plus the three Northeast Asian states plus 3 'outside' states (India, New Zealand and Australia). At the 10th ASEAN Summit in Laos in 2004, India was officially inducted into the East Asian regional cooperation process. ASEAN is currently negotiating a Free Trade Agreement (FTA) with India and this should be in place by 1 January 2007. From an Indian viewpoint, its inclusion in the EAS demonstrates some further concrete success of its 'Look East' policy. China has already been in negotiations with ASEAN regarding FTA and its normalisation of relations with India which also helped the latter's case.

Like India, the Australasian states have been 'outsiders' to the East Asian community process. In addition, of course, unlike India, both New Zealand and Australia are 'non-Asian' states. Furthermore, Australia's 'outsider' position was as a result of its apparent reluctance to sign a regional security document-the ASEAN Treaty of Amity and Cooperation (TAC). While the New Zealand Prime Minister, Helen Clark, did not appear to have similar reservations about signing the TAC and thus becoming a part of the EAS process, Australia's hesitation in part reflected something of its perceived regional role. Consent was given by the ASEAN states for New Zealand to be a part of the TAC in July 2005. Outside of Australia and within the region, rightly or wrongly, Australian reluctance to sign the TAC rekindled concern over its possible pre-emption policy as well as diplomatic indignation over "puerile comments about it being America's deputy sheriff in the region" (Alexander Downer quoted in the *Japan Times*, 11 December 2005). From an Australian government perspective, however, being a part of the TAC agreement would have prohibited Australian participation in the East Timor intervention in 1999. The regional perception was that there was some reluctance to give away this type of regional intervention prospect. In the event, in addition to receiving strong regional support for its participation in EAS, Australia signed the TAC on 10 December 2005 and thus became a belated part of the community process (Rumley, 2005, 21-2). As a result, for the first time since the days of Empire, India and Australia became partners in a broader Asia-Pacific regional economic grouping. Recent reports from Japan indicate that there is powerful support for this to develop into an "Asian super trade zone" (Cameron, 2006).

Australian Security Perspectives

In this third major section of the book, three essays deal with different aspects of Australian security in response both to globalisation and to an increase in non-traditional threats. In Chapter 9, Dennis Rumley sketches a broad overview of Australia's regional security challenges from an explicitly geopolitical perspective. He argues that the changing nature of globalisation processes and their differential regional security impacts have yet to be matched by a 'new' Australian regional security paradigm. Rather, Australia is still principally associated with the application of an 'old' security paradigm which emphasises threats which emanate from regional states even though those states are 'neighbours' and among its closest trading partners. Not only are Australia's regional economic ties incongruent with the structure of its defence expenditure, but globalisation has thrown up new security challenges which have yet to be fully incorporated into the policy framework. Of course, Australia is not unique in this regard, since the Asia-Pacific region is in a process of transition from its former Cold War status to one that remains to be designed by regional states. In short, 21st century regional geopolitical realities require the construction of a 'new' security paradigm designed to meet the current regional security challenges. Rumley describes and analyses four principal security challenges from a geopolitical perspective – the trilateral tension which is evident in Australia's regional relations; the differential importance which has been accorded to each of Australia's four main fronts, with lesser importance being given to the Indian Ocean Region; the emergence of an arc of instability to Australia's North and East; and, fourth, the prospects for a "new regionalism" of which both Australia and India will be a part.

H.S. Prabhakar analyses the nature and structure of East Asian regionalism and discusses its relevance for Australia in Chapter 10. The author considers the processes of regionalism and regionalisation in East Asia by focusing on the stances of the various regional states, the leading role which Japan has played and the ways in which Australia has engaged the region via a range of policy adjustments since the end of World War II. One of Prabhakar's central arguments is that the growth of close and mutually beneficial relations between Japan and Australia was inevitable, given the geographical location of both states and the nature of their complementarity and economic development structure. In order to develop his analysis, the author provides a comprehensive discussion of the nature, structure and change of the East Asian political economy, the structure of Japan's regional economic relations, the nature of its economic power and the ways in which Japan has approached the region not just in terms of economic relations and economic development, but also in terms of political and security relations. To date, Prabhakar has seen Japan as being the principal driving force in East Asian regionalism, but he also notes the increasing nature of regional competition between Japan and China over concluding various regional trading arrangements. From an Australian perspective, however, the fact that Japan is Australia's largest export destination and now China has become its second largest market, implies that it will become increasingly integrated into the political economy of East Asia.

In Chapter 11, Anthony Bergin evaluates Australia's approach to combating one of the most intractable of the non-conventional security threats – terrorism. Bergin notes that the threat posed by terrorism is now well understood and that one of the fundamental reasons why Australia has become more of a terrorist target is that the country is perceived to be mainly Western, Christian and a longstanding ally of the United States. Australia's "war on terrorism" is thus a war against militant Islam. Bergin outlines the administrative complexity involved in safeguarding Australia from terrorism. He evaluates the 2004 government strategy for combating terrorism and notes that the approach is one of a four level "layered defence" – offensive action, effective border controls, better agency coordination and improved consequence management. Bergin concludes that, overall, this is a sound approach, although he has some important concerns especially regarding the role of business, the question of public education, the structure of a national terrorist alert system, mass transit security and issues of cost and responsibility. The chapter argues that Australia has taken a leading role in developing a regional approach to combating terrorism. However, Bergin suggests that there is still a need for a more substantive exchange of information and better coordination among the various new regional counter-terrorism centres. However, more fundamentally, there is a need for Australia to increase its level of cooperation with regional states to address the factors which cause terrorism, while, at the same time, strengthening efforts in domestic counter-terrorism preparedness and response.

Globalisation, Regional Security and India-Australia Relations

It has been argued that there is some evidence to suggest that there is an evolving geopolitical convergence between India and Australia in the 21st century. This new "strategic convergence" is an outcome of a combination of post-Cold War geopolitical reorientation, an increasing realisation of mutual and overlapping security interests and a willingness to engage more directly in bilateral and regional security forums (Gopal and Rumley, 2004). The nature of the convergence is also reinforced by the processes of globalisation, by the changing nature of security threats and by a widening of the concept of security itself. As a result, for example, improved market access is contributing to increased bilateral trade, mutual security concerns are much less state-centred and questions related to energy security collectively highlight the substantial prospects for and benefits to be gained from much closer Australia-India ties. In this evolving bilateral context, there exist considerable opportunities for increasing India-Australia cooperation, especially in terms of collectively responding to the new security environment. The final section of the book contains four essays which aim to elaborate some of these issues and opportunities.

Ganganath Jha, in Chapter 12, argues persuasively in favour of stronger policy cooperation and dialogue between India, Australia and the ASEAN states. A greater degree of dialogue and mutual trust, he suggests, will inevitably lead to a higher level of understanding of regional state motives, ideals and values. As a result, such a strategy will not only enable misperceptions and policy contradictions to be overcome and thus promote a perception of consistent policy settings, but it will also facilitate a much more effective approach to resolving many of the region's security problems. Ganganath Jha suggests that Indian and Australian interests in ASEAN are, in fact, complementary, and he offers examples of more effective solutions to regional problems in cases where the two states have acted cooperatively. Indeed, the author argues that Australia and India can collectively contribute to building a regional consensus within ASEAN against terrorism and ethnic disputes. He suggests that the India-Australia Partnership (AIP) is growing slowly even though there is considerable scope for expanding trade and investment relations, especially in the areas of energy and communications technology. The AIP could potentially work very effectively across a range of non-traditional security issues in ASEAN, especially in terms of peacekeeping, nuclear proliferation and terrorism. Such collaboration may also help in overcoming situations where Australia has been perceived as acting inconsistently. Ganganath Jha concludes that, although Australia is economically and territorially closed linked to ASEAN, its "mindset" has yet to completely come to terms with the geopolitical realities of Asia.

In Chapter 13, Madhu Bala discusses the widespread adoption of Information Technology (IT), both for India and Australia, and argues for an increase in cooperation between the two states. Furthermore, she emphasises four sets of implications for the relationship between the diffusion of IT and security. First, the author notes that persistent poverty in the developing world is mainly a function of a lack of widespread information and knowledge. Bala argues that the diffusion of IT can be seen in part as a shortcut to prosperity and hence greater security. A second implication is that the widespread adoption of IT, among other things, is resulting in a paradigm shift involving a transformation of the existing social and economic relations into information relations. This evolution of this shift, in turn, is a major cause of instability. A third implication arises out of the use of information and knowledge as a result of the widespread adoption of IT. In particular, the adoption of IT raises significant questions about the secure use of, sometimes sensitive, information and the rapid movement of knowledge and money, especially in terms of the prospects for a new form of insecurity – cyber crime. The fourth implication for security is the one which Bala emphasises the most – that is, the potential for an increase in cooperation based on the nature of the complementarity between India and Australia in a wide variety of IT areas which will result in closer and more secure ties between the two states.

Chintamani Mahapatra in Chapter 14 argues that, despite any outstanding differences, an India-Australia "partnership" can enable both states to play a more constructive role in international affairs, especially in terms of maintaining peace and stability. The author discusses the changing nature of the relationship since Independence and evaluates the possibilities for future cooperation. As Mahapatra indicates, it is a cause for considerable surprise that the relationship between Australia and India is not closer, given the clear commonalities and complementarities across a wide range of areas. During the Cold War period, Mahapatra argues that, despite being determined by political/ideological differences and conflicting geopolitical orientations, India's relations with Australia were neither friendly nor adversarial. This implied that, with the end of the Cold War, there was considerable scope for an improvement in mutual ties. In particular, a realisation by Australia of past "neglect", and the process of economic reform in India have been two important impulses for change. Thus, the 21st century has been marked, for example, by a significant increase in high-level Ministerial and diplomatic exchange, the emergence of a mutual security dialogue and a rapid increase in trade from a relatively low level. These shifts are indicative of a new geopolitical convergence of interests across a range of traditional and non-traditional security concerns. Mahapatra concludes that there are at least six broad overlapping areas in which an India-Australia partnership might develop further in the 21st century –defence, terrorism, combating drugs trafficking, political cooperation, educational exchanges and economic cooperation.

In the final Chapter, Dennis Rumley and Darvesh Gopal present a conceptualisation of some of the elements that might be incorporated in a new regional security agenda. Overall, increasing interdependence due to globalisation implies greater inter-state cooperation and an increase in the importance of non-traditional security threats. The logical outcome of the interaction of these processes is a decline in inter-state conflict. Regional states, such as Australia and India, are in an important position to facilitate such outcomes by initiating a new regional security paradigm. The authors consider the question of what is a regional security threat and review various ways in which threats are constructed. They describe the nature of conventional security threats in the Indian Ocean Region and evaluate the principal extra-regional security interests of the United States and China. Rumley and Gopal discuss the structure of regional economic *insecurity* before identifying a range of other well-known 'non-conventional' security threats – environmental security, terrorism, money laundering and transnational crime. They discuss, in greater detail, the regional variation in the quality of *human* security since this is regarded by the authors as the principal source of regional insecurity. Underpinning all of this is an argument in favour of an increase in the "democratisation of security" around the Indian Ocean Region in order to maximise 'real' security. While Indian Ocean regionalism is relatively weakly developed, the broad array of non-traditional security threats provide a unique set of opportunities for the enhancement of regional cooperation intimately involving both India and Australia.

REFERENCES

Alagappa, M. (1998), 'Rethinking security: a critical review and appraisal of the debate', in M. Alagappa, ed., *Asian Security Practice: Material and Ideational Influences*, Stanford University Press, pp. 27-64.

Allison, G. (2000), 'The impact of globalization on national and international security', in Nye, J.S. and Donahue, J.D., eds., *Governance in a Globalizing World*, Washington DC: Brookings Institution Press, pp. 72-85.

Barnett, T.P.M. (2004), *The Pentagon's New Map: War and Peace in the Twenty-First Century*, New York: Berkley Books.

Bell, C., ed. (1991), *Agenda for the Nineties: Studies of the Contexts for Australian Choice in Foreign and Defence Policy*, Melbourne: Longman Cheshire.

Bennett, J. (2004), 'Globalization and human development: the cases of Pakistan and India', in Thakur and Newman, *op. cit.*, pp. 19-46.

Buzan, B., Wæver, O. and de Wilde, J. (1998), *Security: A New Framework for Analysis*, Boulder: Lynne Rienner.

Cameron, D. (2006), 'Japan moots Asian super trade zone', *The West Australian* newspaper, 5 April, page 32.

Coker, C. (2002), 'Globalisation and insecurity in the twenty-first century: NATO and the management of risk', ISSS, *Adelphi Paper*, 345, Oxford University Press.

Commission on Human Security (2003), *Human Security Now*, New York.

Department of Defence (1994), *Defending Australia*, Canberra: AGPS.

Gopal, D. and Rumley, D., eds. (2004), *India and Australia: Issues and Opportunities*, New Delhi: Authors Press.

Japan Times (2005), 'Asia-Pacific briefs', 11 December.

Lévy, B. (2002), 'Globalization, hemispheric economic integration and beyond: governance and security issues', in Smith, E.V., ed., *New Perspectives on Globalization*, New York: Nova Science, pp. 113-134.

Rumley, D. (1999), *The Geopolitics of Australia's Regional Relations*, Dordrecht: Kluwer.

Rumley, D. (2005), 'The geopolitics of 21st century Asia-Pacific regionalism', *The Otemon Journal of Australian Studies*, Vol. 31, pp. 3-25.

Rumley, D. and Chaturvedi, S., eds. (2005), *Energy Security and the Indian Ocean Region*, New Delhi: South Asian Publishers.

Stares, P.B., ed. (1998), *The New Security Agenda: A Global Survey*, Tokyo: Japan Center for International Exchange.

Thakur, R. and Newman, E., eds. (2004), *Broadening Asia's Security Discourse and Agenda: Political, Social, and Environmental Perspectives*, Tokyo: United Nations University Press.

GLOBALISATION, SECURITY AND THE ASIA-PACIFIC REGION

2

The Economics of Globalisation

New Challenges and Opportunities

SUPARNA KARMAKAR

One of the most noticeable tendencies in the world economy over the past few decades has been its rapid increase in global economic integration. The world economy has witnessed a growing internationalisation with rising volumes of international trade and increasing levels of foreign investment flows, particularly that of direct investment; the latter primarily initiated by transnational corporations and often seen as a vehicle for international transfers of technology, managerial expertise and finance.

In an increasingly integrating world, the fate and fortunes of all economies are inextricably and irreversibly intertwined, and even a political action by a single country intended purely to have a bilateral impact has been observed to have profound ripple effects on the socio-economy of the rest of the world, courtesy globalisation. At no other time has this been made so explicit as now, when the economic risks and advantages are seen to be globally synchronised and transmitted through the unfolding saga in the Middle East and the poor economic health of the G7 countries. This Chapter, therefore, tries to unravel the complex web of the international political economy and outlines an economic perspective of the security concerns and the globalisation challenges faced by the region.

In what follows, we will trace the recent developments in the region and superimpose them in the international context, and then attempt to draw some conclusions and make projections with respect to the future prospects and concerns of economic and socio-political security in the Asia-Pacific region. For although a relatively recent Asian Development Outlook (2002) expected the recovery of developing Asian countries to continue and strengthen, the short-term uncertainty about the sustainability of the world economic expansion in view of the US presence in Iraq is tempering this enthusiasm. As will be discussed in detail later, rising oil prices and turbulence in the financial sector are amplifying the risk of a return to global recession. Developing Asia's recovery, given its excessive dependence on the performance of its external sector, is highly vulnerable to such an event, which also has significant implications for regional security concerns.

Gains from Increasing Global Integration in Trade and Finance

The rapid growth in global trade in the 1970s increased the need for free capital flows to finance trade and hedge exchange rate risks. The breakdown of the stability of the exchange rate system, dismantling of capital controls in developed countries and the emerging derivatives industry were the major factors behind the massive flow of global capital across the world, particularly noticeable since the mid-1980s. Since then, trade and financial integration have increased exponentially for both developed and developing countries. Interestingly, however, trade integration has been higher for developing countries, while financial integration is seen to be much more extensive in the developed countries.

Nevertheless, it must be remembered that globalisation is a mixed bag; there are benefits to garner, and prices to pay. Hence, the impact of globalisation has been uneven across regions, countries and sectors, depending on what the respective countries could manage to eke out of the process of global integration. Some countries and regions have been able to become more integrated into the world economy and benefit more with growing magnitudes of inward and outward FDI flows and other types of cross-border transactions, while others have been left relatively untouched.

In this process, new sources of FDI and technology have played an important role. For example, in the last two decades of the 20th century, Japan emerged as one of the most important sources of FDI flows after the US and the EU, as Japanese corporations were forced to relocate production abroad in order to stay competitive in the face of rising domestic real wages and the appreciation of the yen vis-à-vis the dollar during the first half of the 1980s and to mitigate its domestic recession in the 1990s.

In spite of the developments in economic and financial integration among economies and the resultant benefits, however, the basic policy challenge facing governments of most of the developing countries still remains as to how best to channel the elemental forces of trade and investment towards wealth creation and the improvement of the basic standards of life of its population. And the countries in the Asia-Pacific region are no exception. Since the 1980s, moves to rapidly liberalise trade and FDI have strongly influenced policy-makers in developing countries in their thinking about the above-mentioned challenge of rapid integration with trade partners.

The Appearance of the Asia-Pacific Region on the International Radar — The Asian Miracle, Crisis and the Subsequent Recovery

For nearly a quarter century since the early 1970s, the East Asian economies grew at phenomenal rates, leading some observers to dub the period as a so-called "Asian Miracle", and putting the region firmly on the global radar (World Bank, 1993). The rapid growth, however, came to an abrupt end with the 1997 Asian financial crisis, and many of the high-performing countries in the region fell into painful recession, and the fabled miracle, if indeed there had been one, seemed to be over.

Clearly, the Asian financial crisis was unforeseen by most and thus it took everyone by surprise. Though the decline in growth in the region (even abstracting from the effects of the financial crisis) was being predicted by some economists for some time prior to the event, even economists of this genre (who had argued that high growth had resulted largely from gains in efficiency and productivity) did not see the Asian financial crisis coming. According to one study (Young 1995), economic growth in the region appeared to have come from a better utilisation of the factors of production, namely capital and labour, rather than productivity improvements; in contrast, there are also studies that indicate overall productivity improvements arising out of the adoption of technology-intensive production processes. However, in order to attract foreign investment through which new technology would be transferred into the economy, governments had to encourage a higher capital compensation and lower labour compensation than economically justified. As a result, as is now evident, there was excessive capital investment and the creation of excess capacity in most sectors, which was very difficult to depreciate, particularly in the real estate sector. After several years, the worst seems to be over, but there is still some way to go before the cloud clears completely.

Notably, a significant development of the last couple of decades has been the active role of the Asian developing countries, particularly in East and Southeast Asia, as host countries for foreign capital, and more importantly, as drivers of global growth. Not only were they unaffected by the earlier debt crisis which hit the Latin American countries in the early 1980s, but also their economic performance had been good enough to successfully attract a significant amount of global capital flows, and that too primarily in the form of FDIs. China's performance in the last decade remains a classic example in this respect. Furthermore, in terms of developing interlinkages, the whole of the Asia-Pacific region is today seen to be integrated with synchronised business cycles and the intra-regional trade is growing rapidly, thus offering an enlarged market to the development and venture capital funds. This has not only helped to increase the financial integration of the region, but has also opened new vistas to transnational companies for exploiting the comparative factor advantages and benefits from the international division of labour.

Another development has been the increasing accumulation of reserves largely denominated in dollar assets, in several countries in the region. Asia, therefore, once the down-and-out debtor to the world's developed states, is increasingly turning financier to some of the world's best companies, the biggest banks and the richest states of the world. Financing the US deficit to a large extent, Asia is easily the United States *de facto* banker. In particular, Japan, China, Taiwan, South Korea, Hong Kong and India are running high surpluses that are essentially held as dollar reserves, and US Treasury debt as well as corporate securities, and this is helping to hold up the Dollar against other currencies, in particular the Euro. Further, it is expected that the Asian appetite for US$ and Euro-denominated debt will be growing in the near future, primarily because of the poor health of their domestic banking and financial systems, and the bearishness of their private sectors.

In addition to the general global slowdown, the whole world has been reeling under the spectre of climate variability and drought. Being more dependent on agriculture, the Asia-Pacific region has also borne its fair share. The poor inclement weather conditions impacted on the fiscal deficits of all the countries in the region as well as on rates of unemployment. Imports of consumer goods have also been impacted, particularly in the food grains and live animal imports items/sector. For example, the severity of drought in Australia has forced the farmers there to import food grains, both for the consumption of humans as well as livestock. Vegetable prices have also gone up considerably as a result of lower supplies due to the drought.

Nevertheless, as mentioned earlier, the Asian region still remains the premier driver of global economic growth. In particular, China has been a major growth engine. China's contribution to the world demand and economic growth is vital; for though its share of world GDP is around 12 per cent, its share of world GDP growth is at an awesome high at 33 per cent. China's large pool of farm labourers in the hinterland plus the retrenched SOE workers have helped it to contain real wage appreciation; meanwhile, since its exchange rate is fixed to the dollar, the exchange rate advantage stemming from the devaluation of dollar is adding to its competitiveness. Contrary to the popular perception, though much of the foreign investment in China is aimed at exports, even more is intended to satisfy domestic demand; this implies a huge growth opportunity for its trade partners. Since intra-regional trade is intensifying, the whole of the Asia-Pacific region is emerging as the dominant trading partner for the country. Therefore, the Asia-Pacific, as a whole, is now increasingly looking to China, for greater trading opportunities and more comprehensive regional integration, and already, demand from China has driven the growth of many a sector in India.

An interesting aside, however, is that, in spite of the slowdown observed in the developed West and particularly in the US, Asia still looks to the US for economic resurgence, since developing Asia is yet to recover fully from the Crisis of 1997 and regain the growth momentum experienced in the decade earlier to that. Traditionally, the region has had a significant exposure in the US market and a high dependence also in terms of the export destination. However, most of the afflicted countries have now gotten over the initial turbulence following the breakout of the Asian Crisis, and after several years, are slowly recovering. The weakening of the dollar is another serious cause for concern for the export competitiveness of the products from the region in a generally weak external demand situation, and is bothering the finance ministries of most economies in the Asia-Pacific region. It must be remembered that exports have been about the sole bright spot in recent years and have helped the revival of the economies in the region from the 1997 Asian crisis.

In fact, in recent years, this region has been growing at a reasonably healthy pace, and growth in the region has helped to mitigate the effects of 9/11 and the slowdown that has been dogging most of the developed world for the last few years. Hence, the need of the hour is that the right strategy be adopted to mitigate the impact of the global recession on the economic performance of the countries in the region. Dependence on the West needs to be reduced, and the economies in the region must work in a concerted fashion to regenerate and integrate the latent dynamism of the region in order to emerge as the economic powerhouse of the world. For, contrary to what is expected, President George W Bush's 670 billion USD stimulus package might be slow to impact the US recovery and even slower to revive Asian exports. Further, for the export-led growth economies of Southeast Asia (ASEAN), uncertainties have heightened with the spectre of continued US involvement in Iraq and North Korean nuclear brinkmanship. The whole region's growth prospects are hanging in the balance as a consequence of the above developments.

Budget and Current Account deficits have been rising exponentially in the US (currently at 5% of GDP), prevailing low interest rates and the fear of war have taken a toll on the might of the world's only transaction currency and raised concerns about its stability. Unless the depreciation of the USD is arrested, the fabled Asian competitiveness will be severely blunted and currencies will have to fall further, thereby making the exchange market volatile. Corporate investment has been hit by increased global risk perceptions and firms all over have been increasingly leaving their investment plans on the drawing board. Consequently, even the developed Asian economies like Japan and South Korea are now being forced to stimulate investments to ride out a buffeting from global risks and counter the resultant dampening consumer spending and business activity. This gives another incentive to the region for devising inward-looking policies, if only to reduce the volatility emanating out of increased global economic integration.

The ranking of the Asian countries as desired investor destinations had been declining since the 1997 crisis, especially since the 9/11 and the Bali bombings. The state of the stock markets has also been quite shaken, given the global recession and bearish market sentiments, and they are yet to recover from the Asian crisis decline. However, given the subdued market sentiment and the economic growth in the rest of the world, the region still remains one of the most profitable areas for international investors. In fact, lately, there have been noticeable signs of improvement in the US investments in technology stocks world-wide (www.fundsupermart.com) and it is not surprising that the Asia-Pacific region is emerging as an important destination for such investments. Recent reports from different investment banks and rating agencies also indicate that investors from all over the world are quite bullish about the region (Spencer and Sanyal, 2002). The EU, in particular, is keen to push EU-ASEAN talks, since while many European businessmen are still transfixed with China, many are getting increasingly disillusioned by the country's business practices. In comparison, ASEAN's prospects, with a market of 500 million, suddenly look more attractive than in the early years of the China rush.

Prospects for Long-term Growth in the Asia-Pacific Region

The long-term growth prospects of the region are what will finally determine how much of the potential of the region will be realised. Economic growth in Asia is poised to outpace the rest of the world for the fifth straight year, although ongoing in Iraq and continued lacklustre performances in the major industrialized economies represent risks to the forecast. The generally upbeat outlook for Asia, excluding Japan, is due in large part to a wide range of economic reforms put in place following the 1997-98 regional financial crisis, analysts said. In addition, Asia will benefit from efforts by governments to stimulate domestic demand, as well as China's growing role as a driver of economic activity in the region (Yonan, 2003).

Strong export growth, primarily to the U.S., was the main reason that Asia was able to rebound from the 1997-98 financial crisis so quickly. Asian economies slumped again in 2001 as a recession in the U.S. triggered a synchronized global downturn. And this time around, the Asian recovery has been more gradual because of the lack of strong external demand. Unfortunately, despite efforts to diversify, the Asia-Pacific economies still depend to a large extent on exports to the industrialized world, and Asia still remains one of the most trade-sensitive parts of the world.

As recovery continues in the region, however, there is a growing hope that these economies will be able to return to their pre-crisis levels of robust growth. However, a wide variety of external environment and policy variables will affect growth prospects by changing the long-run potential income and rate of productivity growth. The historically important determinants of long-run per capita income growth — (1) initial income, (2) human resources, (3) investment rates, (4) exogenous shocks and terms of trade movement, and (5) institutions and policy variables (government consumption, rule of law, and openness) — are still relevant and will play a significant role in the sustained growth in the region. Regressions carried out by several economists indicate that most of the above-mentioned controlling variables still remain significant determinants of long-term growth (Barro and Lee, 2000; Park and Lee, 2002).

As mentioned earlier, the sustainability of the growth momentum is the main concern for many. What is, however, reassuring, is that the main drivers for growth in the region in the past have been high rates of saving, human resources, trade openness and the maintenance of responsible institutions, and, in terms of these fundamentals, the region still has strong potential for sustained growth and is probably going to turn out as the propeller for global growth. Reflecting the worsening global economic environment, the growth momentum of exports from the region has been softening; however, the heartening fact remains that though the recovery in the region cuts across sectors, of late, it has been particularly evident in manufacturing, with services playing a complementary role. Additionally, we observe that the prime drivers of growth in the region now are: (a) the growth of Chinese domestic demand; (b) the growth across the region in tourism, particularly from mainland China; (c) the development of the region's nascent pension-fund industry, and, lastly, (d) the region's massive savings in dollar-assets that are fuelling the growth and sustaining the deficit in the United States.

Furthermore, as discussed earlier, extending sub-regional attempts at regional cooperation that have been initiated under ASEAN and SAARC to the whole of the Asia-Pacific will help exploit the full potential of regional economic integration. At the pan-Asian level, the diversity in the levels of economic development and capabilities are wide and will help in providing for more extensive and mutually beneficial linkages. The diversity in the economic structures of the economies provides its own indigenous capacity and markets for dynamic industrial restructuring within the region on the basis of 'flying geese' patterns, and promises an economic dynamism that could parallel the EU, with international reserves bigger than the EU and NAFTA combined (Kumar, 2003).

And this is notwithstanding the fact that the region is likely to emerge as the most lucrative and safe investment destination either for direct investors or foreign institutional investors. Forecasts for the so-called equity risk premium in the developed country markets (the return in excess of the yield on government bonds demanded by investors to compensate for the extra risk of holding equities) currently ranges from a traditional 5 per cent to as little as 2.4 per cent a year. Several academic research papers and investment banking forecasts also peg the outlook for equity and bond returns in the short-term between 2 per cent and 4 per cent (*Economist*, 21 March 2003). Such a thin premium may look on the low side to many investors, given that share prices could tumble again and that more corporate misbehaviour may be uncovered, and provides the rationale for the diversification of assets into previously uncharted sectors and countries. With the real rate of return in the region easily being almost double of the expected returns in the developed country markets, it is easy to see why investor interest in the region has been increasing over the last few years. This certainly bodes well for the investment-starved least developed countries in the Asia-Pacific region.

Conclusion — Through the Looking Glass

One of the concerns regarding the composition of the growth of merchandise exports from the developing world in part rests on the fact that taking trade statistics at face value can hide more than it reveals. A recent UNCTAD report finds that an increasing number of products, including high-tech exports, are assembled from parts and components produced in different locations (UNCTAD, 2002). With the notable exception of some Asian newly-industrializing economies (NIEs), the goods traded by developing countries remain dependent on the exploitation of natural resources and the use of unskilled labour. And the more worrying aspect is that the markets for these goods are becoming crowded, threatening exporters with terms-of-trade losses and retarded productivity growth, which could disrupt development prospects. In view of the prevailing global economic conditions, this calls for a rethinking of the growth strategies adopted by the developing countries in the region, particularly those that aim for export-led growth.

However, all is not lost. Opportunities and threats are but two sides of the same coin, and the onus is on the country to innovatively convert the threats into opportunities. The crisis which gripped East Asia during 1997-99 underscored the urgency for cross-sectoral reform just as the strong revival of virtually all of the economies in the region convinced the doubters that the East Asian miracle had by no means run its course. The Asia-Pacific's future, as one of the world's most dynamic, resilient and interdependent economic regions could be further consolidated, if it follows through on an institutional reform agenda and embraces technology and innovation – and with it, investments in education and knowledge (World Bank, 2003). This has the potential to breathe new life into the region's development prospects and speed the transition of a number of countries into the ranks of developed states. This is the future of innovative growth, growth which requires a move away from the traditional factor-intensive productivity-driven growth to innovation-led development:

> This transition from factor-intensive to productivity-driven growth, and from imitative to innovative growth is undoubtedly going to be bumpy. Implementation will be difficult. And yet, the opportunities are there. East Asian countries are already starting from a position of strength – with the adequate supply of resources, the manufacturing skills, the educational and research infrastructure, and the base of financial and business services. Most are increasingly open and competitive economies. East Asia is poised for another major step forward. It will be fascinating to see the extent to which the vision is transformed into reality (World Bank President, James D. Wolfensohn, at the release function of the World Bank study in Tokyo).

As mentioned earlier, the United States is now on shaky ground and its economic revival looks uncertain. The EU is having problems with maintaining the stability pact and the conditions member countries have had to accept there from. The requirement of containing the budget deficit at a certain share of GDP has been creating difficulties for member countries. Japan is also no longer the world's second economic power and powerhouse for the Asia and Pacific, dominating the region with capital, technology and merchandise, as it did a couple of decades ago. Thus, as long as global outsourcing remains a key to survival for multinational companies, the developing countries in the Asia-Pacific region will, in our opinion, occupy an increasingly important role in this business model. Private companies in the region and abroad will demand it, and the countries' WTO commitments will obligate it. The sheer necessity for survival will ensure that investors will move private capital to those countries that provide responsible governance with manageable levels of public debt, as well as opportunities for future growth.

China, with its dizzying pace of growth, vast internal market with demand fueled by public investment, low-cost production to capture world markets, and a steady opening up to foreign investment and manufactures, is the only country not so affected by the recession in the OECD countries, and has been the effective engine of growth for the world at large. China's growth potential, however, is still dependent on the fiscal stimulus of public investment, particularly on infrastructure, being given by its government and the growth of the world economy, though that should not belittle the achievements of the country in the last decade and its future potential.

In addition to China, another country (sub-region) to look out for in the next quinquennium is India, a second China-in-the-making in terms of the opportunities waiting to be realised and potential to be exploited.

In India, the viability of the outsourcing model has been demonstrated in the IT services industry. In large part, through the return of foreign-trained Indians, globally competitive software and business services industries have emerged. India is also gradually integrating into the world economy, both in terms of trade and financial flows. That the Indian middle class may still be too small, or too poor, to justify production on a globally competitive scale is not the point neither it was China's a decade ago. However, just as foreign investment has played a key role in China's economic development, so too can it play an important role in India's future as opportunities emerge.

There is also a need for countries to strike a balance between insurance and efficiency. In a globalised economy all countries need social safety nets, whether formal or informal, to help those adversely affected by the change and such as nobody loses out on the benefits of a dynamic economy. Globalisation and change implies its share of pain. However, overall technological change and global growth are good, and that there will be more people to win than lose. The only way to garner the gains of globalisation, as the World Bank report urges, is that the industrializing economies in the Asia-Pacific go beyond the *imitative* phase of development, and into the *innovative* phase, moving up the product value chain and extending their reach into services – both of which call for a deliberate focus on innovation as the major source of growth. To conclude, the key driving force for the global economy in the next few years is most likely to emanate from India and China, and the demand there from. The fostering of growth is the only, if not the best, foil for both economic and political security in this world, or for the Asia-Pacific region, for that matter.

REFERENCES

Asian Development Bank, *Asia Economic Monitor* – Asia Recovery Information Centre, several issues.

Asian Development Outlook (2002), Update, Part 1, Asian Development Bank, Manila.

Barro, R. and Lee, J.W. (2000), 'International Data on Educational Attainment: Updates and Implications', *Working Paper*, Center for International Development at Harvard University.

Dow Jones (2003), *Asia-Pacific Market Outlook.*

Kumar, N. (2003), 'Relevance of an Asian Economic Community', paper presented at the International Conference on Building a New Asia, New Delhi.

Park, Y.C. and Lee, J.W. (2002), 'Financial Crisis and Recovery-Patterns of Adjustment in East Asia, 1996-99', *ADB Institute Research Paper*, No. 45.

Radelet, S. and Sachs, J. (1997), 'Asia's reemergence', *Foreign Affairs*, Vol. 76(6), pp. 44-59.

Radelet, S. and Sachs, J. (1998), 'The onset of the East Asian economic crisis', mimeo, March, (http://www.hiid.harvard.edu/).

Radelet, S. and Sachs, J. (1998), The East Asian Financial Crisis: Diagnosis, Remedies, Prospects, mimeo, April, (http://www.hiid.harvard.edu).

Sen Sunanda (1999), 'Economic Turmoil in Asia: A Reinterpretation', *Economic and Political Weekly*, Vol. 34(30), pp. 2071-80.

Spencer, Michael and Sanjeev Sanyal, (2002): *Will India Challenge China?*; communication from some leading investment bankers in the US visiting India at a private meeting with ASSOCHAM.

Stiglitz, Joseph E. (1996), *Some Lessons from the East Asian Miracle*, The World Bank Research Observer, Vol. 11(2), pp 151-77.

Stiglitz, Joseph E. Stiglitz and M Uy (1996), *Financial Markets, Public Policy, and the East Asian Miracle*, The World Bank Research Observer, Vol. 11(2), pp. 249-76.

The Economist, several issues.

UNCTAD (2002): *Trade and Development Report*.

World Bank (1993), *The East Asian Miracle: Economic Growth and Public Policy*, Oxford University Press, New York.

World Bank (2003): *Innovative East Asia: The Future of Growth*.

World Bank-IBRD (2003): *Global Economic Prospects and the Developing Countries*.

Yonan, Alan Jr., *Dow Jones: Asia-Pacific Market Outlook* for 2003.

Young, A. (1995), 'The Tyranny of Numbers: Confronting the Statistical Realities of the East Asian Growth Experience', *The Quarterly Journal of Economics*, Vol. 103 (3), pp. 641-680.

3

Domestic Factors in the Process of Globalisation

The Australian Experience

KAMAL NAYAN KABRA

Globalisation, from among its several meanings, can relatively justifiably be taken to represent the gradual emergence and strengthening of a world-wide capitalist economy broadly over the last half of the preceding millennium. It can be described as the growth of extensive and intensive international linkages in almost every sphere, more particularly in the economic and political spheres under the impact of a series of economic, political, cultural and technological changes, culminating sequentially in industrial revolutions in many countries, mostly in the West and the colonial subjugation of most of Africa, Asia and Latin America. Given the initial conditions, the advantages of an early start and associated power, the processes of globalisation came to be dominated by the pioneering industrialised countries who came to rule over scores of ancient and new countries. A small section of these industrialised countries became its prime movers and beneficiaries who shared these gains and dominance with their compatriots under the growing creed of nationalism and democracy, spread effects of growing national wealth, opportunities flowing from expanding economies and unsurpassed mastery over global resources. However, the international linkages were asymmetrical and involved tremendous losses and sacrifices by the economies and peoples which were interlinked largely at the behest of, and on the terms dictated by, those states leading the drive towards the internationalisation of industrial capitalism.

State Peripheralisation

On the basis of this well-known description and analysis, a generalised proposition has been advanced, suggesting the inevitability of the peripheralisation of the late arrivals under the tutelage of the core capitalist economies. This view implies rather dim and remote prospects of escaping an asymmetrical position for the dominated, former colonised states. What this meant is that without at least some countries becoming the "cannon fodder", the core capitalist countries neither could acquire nor maintain their superior and steadily growing prosperity and power. This has been interpreted as the inevitability of the peripheralisation for at least some countries. (Wallerstein, 1979). However, it is well known that some countries, such as Australia and Canada, for example, *did* escape peripheralisation. This is supposed to have occurred either as a result of a very much more acute peripheralisation of some other countries, or, that these non-peripheralised successful catching-up countries were cases of "development by invitation" (Senghaas, 1985, 155), courtesy, of course, of the successful industrialisers of the earlier vintage.

We intend to examine, extend and elaborate the associative-dissociative autocentric development theory of Dieter Senghaas, with reference to Australia, contrast it briefly with the experience of Argentina, and draw some conclusions relevant in the current context when the forces of asymmetric North-centric globalisation are on an offensive to impose their interests on the world, especially by incorporating domestic power centres in the South. Do we see shades of voluntary colonisation in these trends as the TINA (there is no alternative) complex overtakes people-centric development?

What is implied by the world systems theory is that the ongoing processes of global capitalist development rule out the possibilities of what Dieter Senghaas calls "autocentric" development – that is, self-reliant, inward-looking, independent development for all-owing to the overpowering influence of the external over domestic factors and forces. It seems to be the position of some that the domineering debilitating influence of the external economic and other linkages renders the domestic configuration virtually powerless and ineffective. This kind of deterministic position, assigning a passive role to domestic factors, such as national policies and priorities, socio-economic configuration, mobilisation, natural resource endowment, national response and adjustment to global socio-economic and geopolitical changes, nationalistic spirit and capabilities, evidently exaggerates beyond reasonable proportions the impact and role of the external, global environment and factors. It is true, the latter may, and, in fact, did create massive obstacles and went a long way in stifling the national potential development of many a countries. One does not have to underestimate the impact of the sheer existence, policies and power of the industrialised, better-off countries in undermining the development prospects of late-comer countries. It is also reasonable to hypothesise that colonial legacy, the compradors and the allies of the powerful aliens do come in conflict with and may well overpower the inward-oriented development processes. Similarly, the imperative of the use of external linkages with the worse-off countries to serve the needs of the core countries continues to remain operative. As a result, global capitalist centres press for and impose an asymmetrical global order. However, it would be unreasonable and defeatist to prejudge the outcome against the efficacy of domestic forces. It does not seem reasonable to write off on *a priori* grounds the positive, decisive role that the nation-state can play in conjunction with a set of effective policies on the home turf, to undo the deleterious effects of one-sided globalisation. The historically positive evidence of Australia, Canada and New Zealand, for example, and the counter-factual evidence of the experience of Argentina, seem to lend support to our view.

Globalisation and the Australian State

States can, and have overcome such massive structural-institutional hurdles. There do exist policy packages capable of asserting national interests, needs and aspirations in the development process. As a result, there are cases when it became possible to overcome the interference by the global metropolitan capital based in the industrialised states. The successful cases, like those of Canada and Australia, are special ones in the sense that the conflict between the inward and outward oriented approaches was not virulent and combative, for many reasons such as the continued importance of primary goods exports, the common ethnic origins of the settlers who populated Australia, the role of foreign capital, the strong balance of payments position which led to the opening up based on the capacity to import (and not just the *propensity* or *pressure* (like via free trade) to import, and surely by resisting one-way free trade, the domestic institutional systemic set up, and the nature of Australian economic linkages with the Western and non-Western world. All of these were, in fact, facilitating factors which were not available in the past to many countries of Asia, Africa and Latin America, and may not be available even now.

In the following, we intend to provide a narrative of the processes by which Australia, while significantly exposed and related to the cross currents of the global economy, successfully developed its economy in terms of national resources, needs and aspirations, especially vis-à-vis the rest of the world. (Senghaas, 1985, 149). It was not caught in the dependency syndrome and did not permit its external sector links to overshadow internal national interests, needs and pattern of development. The constellation of forces which took hold in ensuring such a pattern were identified as the Labour Party (the first Labour Party in the world to acquire power in Australia in 1909), the trade unions, national bourgeoisie, new middle classes. (Senghaas, 1985, 148-9). It means a demonstration of the possibility of not closing one's doors on globalisation (delinking) and yet being able to protect and promote one's national interests, of course, as perceived and pursued by the dominant stakeholders. It becomes an argument for selective de-linking and re-linking in the framework of an inward-looking, nationally-determined policy framework and internal balance of power. This was made possible by not adhering to any externally-dictated or ideologically pre-ordained set of policies and institutions, along with an active response to the domestic political economy – that is, self-reliant in policy processes. This experience suggests the overarching, primacy of domestic factors over the external ones, suggesting that neither peripheralisation nor a closed-door, nor autocentric, self-reliant pattern of development are inevitable, inexorable necessities, nor are export-orientation and import-substitution necessarily mutually exclusive. It also tends to suggest that globalisation in the sense of active participation in international economic interaction does not necessarily mean courting a subservient, dependent, externally-dictated position. Apparently, it cannot be achieved by leaving things to take care of themselves, but requires a sharply focused and nuanced national level approach. It all depends on how the game is played, by mediating the role of global economic and geopolitical conjuncture, domestic economic structure, resource endowment, the legacy of external account vulnerability or viability and the domestic political economy as constraining or facilitating factors.

Self-Reliant Industrialisation

The complex of factors mentioned above were generally favourable for Australia to pursue what Senghaas characterised as "associative-dissociative development" (1985, 32-3) which may well be regarded as equivalent to linking-delinking or selective linking. It is a country with a short historical experience, as a 'modern' state and economy, which, despite its geographical isolation and sparse, scattered population (mostly of settlers from the West) could capitalise on its initial situation of being among the most prosperous countries in the mid-nineteenth century to become a success story of industrialisation. The growth of the economy was facilitated by its rich natural resources endowment and massive and regular export earnings from primary products via their backward and forward linkages (strengthened by fairly widely spread sharing of the gains from exports) and final demand and fiscal linkage, (Senghaas, 1985; 153). As a result, the Australian economy was able to go in for a high wage, high land price economy. This led to the creation of a large and growing home market. The export boom did see some volatility on account of the changing fortunes of the world economy (like business cycle phases and the two Wars), local production conditions (especially occasional weather-induced harvest volatility) and competition from other activities. However, even after substantial diversification of the Australian economy, structural changes, away from goods production in the rich industrialised economies and changes in the pattern of world trade (with new leading activities and actors), the absolute amount of earnings from agro-exports maintained their salience for Australia. However, far more significant, in addition to a very high land-people ratio and the continued flow of migrants, even after the end of the penal economy, were the increases in farm productivity, exports of gold and the use of export earnings for the diversification of the economy. This occurred especially by means of a policy of import-substitution, regular and sizeable inflow of foreign investment combined along with labour immigration, the use of new modern technology, and the growth of mining, all of which increased the relative role of the industrial sector. Australia, in spite of the continued importance of primary (agricultural and pastoral) exports, developed into a well-diversified industrial economy. An internally well-integrated economy facilitated coping with external disturbances and shocks. Continuous growth up to the First World War (4.7 per cent per annum during 1861-1891 and 2.4 per cent during 1891-1914) too was a factor which was both the result of and a contributory factor to the diversification and industrialisation of Australia. It was not a passive response to the relationship with the world economy, but an attempt to strengthen the domestic economy by import-substitution (in a highly export-oriented economy), first, in the sphere of light manufacturing and subsequently to move towards the indigenous creation of the sinews of self-reliant industrialisation by going in for the basic and heavy capital goods industries (Cain, 1970). Such basic, core industries accounted for 25 per cent of the net industrial product in 1977.

The export strength gave the Australian economy a good, sound balance of payments (BOP) position. True, foreign capital flows came in, but were not courted by adopting special measures in order to acquire BOP support-a factor which generally weakens the international bargaining power of the recipient vis-à-vis the investor. In fact, gold production and export earnings enhanced the capacity to import. In other words, the combined inflows of capital and skilled labour were market-determined and were not policy-induced. Regulated additions to labour supply helped maintain high wage rates, which in conjunction with high land prices helped create and expand a large and growing home demand.

We do not portray the Australian experience of globalisation as an ideal to be emulated as a role model but as one which shows the possibility of avoiding the dependency or peripheralisation trap. It would be obviously faulty not to take cognisance of some of the exceptionally favourable factors with which Australia was blessed. Apart from its natural endowments, small and sparse population, common ethnic origins with the successful early industrialisers who peopled Australia were substantive favourable factors. In addition, it shared with those countries a common ideological cultural perspective equivalent to the colonies which fed into the growth and prosperity of the Europeans. Australia had her internal counterpart of the colonies in the indigenous population. One can say that the last two hundred years saw the peopling and settlement of Australia simultaneously with its growth and industrialisation but without making it an appendage to any economy with which it was associated. The industrial sector of Australia was characterised by many plants and a small number of firms. They adopted restrictive practices to protect and promote a highly concentrated industrial structure which thus came to lack effective competition and led to the emergence of large corporations and frequent mergers (the four largest firms controlled a high proportion of industries). The concentration was further helped by geographical isolation, protectionism, but free entry of foreign capital was not disturbed. There was also a sizeable unconcentrated manufacturing sector as well (Brown and Hughes, 1970). The internal economic structure had its independent aspirations and interests which it protected and promoted independently for building up an internationally competitive industrialised economy. In this process, there did arise some conflicts of interest between the pastoral economy and the industrial sector, especially concerning immigration and land prices. However, the industrialisation interests came to prevail. In addition, pastoral and other primary activities (themselves steadily industrialised) have remained larger than the manufacturing for long during the 20th century. The inter-war years saw a slow-down and recession; partly owing to external influences. Manufacturing (based on factory data only; non-factory secondary output too was significant) came to account for a little below 30 per cent of GDP by the middle of the 20th century. More or less equal contribution of manufacturing to employment and output signifies a critical balance in the economy, something lacking in many late-industrialising, poor, ex-colonies which adopted mimetic growth.

Internal Power Balance

Australia maintained her pursuit of national goals under the impact of its internal power balance. Though per capita GDP growth was slower for a better part of the 20th century than that seen in many rich countries, its initial high level associated with the natural resources bonanza of the 1860s helped its presence in the top per capita income league. This factor, coupled with high wage rate, high land prices, export earnings (by 1959, even the share of manufactured goods exports was about 12 per cent of total exports) and gold production giving a healthy and viable balance of payments position and simultaneous inflows of migrant labour (in controlled numbers) and foreign capital enabled Australia to substitute first the imports of consumer goods and then move on towards machinery, equipment and basic and heavy capital goods for building up the basis for domestic industrialisation. Comparatively high rates of return, attributable to a highly concentrated, non-competitive industrial structure, dotted by large corporations attracted foreign capital, in spite of high labour and land costs. As early as 1903, import-competing industries contributed 44 per cent of the industrial output. All along, the salience of primary sector exports, helped by high wool prices, continued, though the impact of volatility in world markets, like the recession during the 1930s, did assert its impact. Thus, from about 12 per cent share of manufacturing during the 1920s (less than that of the pastoral economy), Australia could, by the late 1940s/early 1950s, reach an internationally competitive level of industrialisation and later on became an economy with service sector prominence as in major post-industrial economies as even foreign capital started entering in mainly the service sector.

The Counterfactual Case of Argentina

As a counterfactual, the case of Argentina, in which despite a good deal of similarity with Australia (in terms of resources base, primary sector export orientation, some degree of import substitution, a number of initial conditions, including the level of per capita income) after the early 19th century, the development path diverged and led to the peripheralisation of the former. The different evolution of the two countries has received a good deal of attention by development historians and economists (for extensive references, see Senghaas, 1985; 258). The main differences between Argentina and Australia are noteworthy. They are with respect to the position and experience of Argentina having low wage and low land prices and thus a low cost economy with limited home market, "internal disseverance of Argentine society" (Senghaas, 1985, 147) which reduced its capacity to withstand external shocks, imports giving displacement competition to domestic production, uneven distribution of the gains from primary exports owing to the latifundia-dominated agrarian structure, shallow or light import substitution, control of the MNCs over basic and capital and engineering industries, non-pursuit of a policy of "purposive industrialisation policy by means of protectionist measures" by Argentina (Senghaas, 1985; 149), powerful position of the agrarian oligarchy, and the failure of the Radical Party, which came to power in 1916, to live up to its nationalistic policies. The result is that Argentina joined the ranks of the poor, late-industrialised countries asymmetrically related to the ex-colonial powers.

Conclusion

The upshot of this brief, sketchy, stylised overview analysis above is to argue against the inevitability of dependency and placing the entire onus for this state of affairs on the external factors, which despite their power and sweep, cannot operate without domestic sins of commission and/or omission and on the contrary, can be effectively resisted and overcome by a domestic alignment of socio-economic forces, factors and policies. Of course, natural resource endowment and initial level of the economy and conditions are important. However, as the counterfactual case of Argentina has been used to show in a number of writings, these potential advantages can be squandered by a domestic configuration not alive to the possibilities and domestic policies based on the potential of autocentric development of associative-dissociative variety. Is this not only lost but it may well turn into its opposite? A robust self-reliance in policy-making, learning from the experience of everyone (not becoming excessively North-centric) but responding decisively to the interests of one's fellow citizens is a prime the condition for collective self-empowerment: that is, genuine development.

REFERENCES

Brown, Pat and Hughes Helen (1970), 'The Market Structure of Australian Manufacturing Industry, 1914 to 1963-69', in Forster, *op. cit.*

Butlin, N.G. (1970), 'Some Perspectives of Australian Economic Development, 1890-1965', in Forster, *op. cit.*

Cain, N. (1970), 'Trade and Economic Structure at the Periphery: The Australian Balance of Payments', in Forster, *op. cit.*

Dyster, B. (1979), 'Argentine and Australian Development Compound', *Past and Present,* August, n. 84.

Forster, C., ed. (1970), *Australian Economic Development in the Twentieth Century*, London: George Allen Unwin.

Senghaas, D. (1985), *The European Experience: A Historical Critique of Development Theory,* Leamington Spa: Berg publishers. (Translation from German)

Wallerstein, I (1979), *The Capitalist World Economy*, Cambridge.

World Bank, *World Development Report* and *World Economic Indicators* (various issues), Washington, D.C.

4

Globalisation and National Security Threats in the Post-Cold War Asia-Pacific

SHARAD JOSHI

The decade or so since the end of the Cold War has seen several changes in the geopolitical structure of the Asia-Pacific region, and indeed the rest of the world. This chapter examines the gamut of threats to the security of states and peoples in the region. Some, like proliferation and territorial conflict, have persisted since the Cold War era. Other issues, like human security, are relatively new concepts that have come about as a result of changes in the definition of 'security' and the move away from the Cold War superpower rivalry paradigm. The chapter first discusses the changing nature of the regional security environment consequent upon globalisation and then analyses in turn a range of resultant contemporary regional security challenges – terrorism, transnational organised crime, proliferation/nuclear weapons, human security and environmental security. While the majority of these contemporary mainly non-military security threats are a product of globalisation, it is argued here that the state still has a major role to play in maximising security, especially human security.

The Changing Security Environment

To understand how the concept of security relates to Asia today, we have to examine how the role and powers of the state itself have changed. The forces of globalisation have ensured that the state no longer has the ability to maintain absolute control over its boundaries. Technological and communication advances have revolutionized the way people are able to conduct their businesses and contacts across international boundaries. With the advent of technologies, that enable the transfer of financial resources across the world at the touch of a button, the state's control over such processes has greatly diminished. For the state, this is potentially a source of instability and insecurity. With the steady opening up of borders around the world, economics and security are inextricably linked. The state has become constrained in setting economic policies. The state can be forced to adopt unfavourable rules and regulations to prevent financial resources from flowing out. Its ability to collect revenues can be adversely affected. When its economic power is under threat, the territorial sovereignty of the state itself is under threat (Kobrin, 1997, 1998). The increasing mobility of finance and the decreasing state control also lays entire regions exposed to greater risks of financial crimes and crises (Kobrin, 1997). This was most amply demonstrated in Indonesia during the financial crises in the late 1990s. Financial turmoil provided a catalyst for political upheaval and violence, which has lingered on to this day. Technological and communication advances are just one example of how security issues that states have to face today have changed. Financial processes and issues are very much a part of the security domain because of the effect that they can have on the internal stability of countries and regions.

During the Cold War, security threats were seen through the prism of superpower rivalry. This was one of the main reasons why non-military security threats were obscured. Only state-centric issues were considered as security issues, which was the basis the Cold War security framework. However, it is now accepted that states themselves can be a major sources of insecurity and threats, especially (as in the 1990s) when ethnic and religious violence is involved. The civil war in Yugoslavia was a prime example where the state's repressive apparatus was used to slaughter its own people. The breakdown of the communist bloc also led to a reordering of national boundaries in that region. One distinguishing feature of the post-Cold War era has been the spate of ethnic and religious conflicts, which is not just a phenomenon restricted only to Europe. Nationalistic feelings are on the rise all over, and they are made more potent by the addition of ethnicity and/or religion to the issue. Communication advances mean that people are now more aware of what is happening across the globe, and can thus react to events that may not be in their immediate vicinity.

Other security dimensions are also prominent. The natural environment is one of them. Conflicts over resources are going to be more and more common in future. Environmental changes such as degradation of water resources and agricultural land, declines in food production and deforestation are already major security issues for states and could easily spark off a conflict (Homer-Dixon, 1991; 77). Such environmental changes would induce populations to migrate to other areas, which would bring them into conflict with other groups already there, bringing an ethnic dimension to the problem (Homer-Dixon, 1994; 6-7). Environmental changes are likely to have both national and international effects. Countries that suffer from resource depletion and degradation are more likely to experience armed conflict (Hauge and Ellingsen, 2001; 302). Related to this is the issue of demographic change. States in which population growth is not accompanied by increased opportunities for economic development risk political violence (Goldstone, 2002). Organised crime has existed since time immemorial, in one form or another. However, it is only now in recent years that it has taken on a transnational character. What is different is that organised crime can now operate beyond state boundaries, and pose a risk to the viability of entire governments, as the experience of countries like Italy, Mexico and Russia show (Serrano, 2002, 29). This is what makes it a security risk. In some cases, the state and transnational organised crime develop symbiotic relationships, as in Russia (McFarlane, 2001a, 209). In some other countries organized crime has filled a political and social vacuum in the event of the collapse of the state. Such transnational criminal groups frequently have their own paramilitary armies, or have close collaboration with insurgent groups.

A considerable broadening of the definition of 'security' has occurred with the emergence of *human security*. According to the United Nations Development Programme, this term means 'freedom from fear and want', and, according to this definition, human security is composed of seven components: economic, food, health, environmental, personal, community, and political.

This preceding discussion shows that the concept of security has changed to accommodate different issues and also different actors. In the process, it has also modified the role and capacity of the state. There is now a 'power shift' in terms of the capacity of the state (Matthews, 1997). The state now has to share power and responsibilities with a host of actors, ranging from NGOs, to MNCs, to local governments and to international organisations. Changes in issues have corresponded with changes in the actors that could best deal with such problems. A different, but not contradictory viewpoint is that the state is now moving toward transgovernmentalism to maintain its sovereignty (Slaughter, 1997). This means that states are transferring some of their powers to international institutions that are better equipped to deal with the new security agenda. With this background, the rest of the chapter examines security issues that the Asia-Pacific region is facing today beginning with terrorism. Some issues, like proliferation, fall into the category of traditional issues, while others, like environmental security, are clearly a product of the post-Cold War era.

Terrorism

The attacks on the World Trade Center and the Pentagon on September 11, 2001 signalled to the world that terrorism would be the defining feature of the global security environment for the near future. The Asia-Pacific region, which has long experienced the horrors of terrorism, suddenly found more attention bestowed on it because of the links between local movements and the transnational terrorist network, manifested most prominently by Al Qaeda (Smith, 2002). For example, the presence of the Taliban in Afghanistan, the support for terrorist activities by Pakistan which ensured the linkage between terrorism in South Asia and its global variety, and indeed the shift in the center of gravity of international terrorism to Asia from its erstwhile headquarters, the Middle East (Mohan, 2002; 205). Terrorism in South Asia has its roots in the Afghan civil war of the 1980s, when the United States backed radical Islamic groups to expel the Soviet occupiers and the Communist backed regime in Kabul. The Pakistani government was an integral part of this operation (Chellaney, 2001; 96). By 1989-90, militancy in Kashmir had begun and the Pakistani Inter Services Intelligence (ISI) agency transferred men, material, and expertise to the Kashmir sector. Pakistani support to terrorism/separatism in India has been attributed to its desire to keep the latter bogged down in the subcontinent, and also by a desire to avenge the breakup of Pakistan in 1971 that led to the creation of Bangladesh (Stern, 2000).

However, the interdependent connection between fundamentalist terrorist groups in Pakistan, their ideological mentors and financiers in the Taliban-ruled Afghanistan and Saudi Arabia, led to 9/11. Therefore, the regional dimensions of terrorism in South Asia have been elevated to a global level through connections among terrorist networks. This is made amply clear in the 'interchangeability' of terrorists and expertise among regional groups such as the Lashkar-e-Taiba and the global ones like Al Qaeda (De Borchgrave, 2001). Meanwhile, violence in the region has not decreased. The attack on the Indian parliament by the elements of Jaish-e-Mohammed (JEM) and Lashkar-e-Taiba (LET) in December 2001 (Kumar, 2001) persuaded the Indian government to launch a round of coercive diplomacy, which involved the mobilisation of troops at the border with Pakistan, a level not seen since the 1971 war. This mobilisation ended inconclusively with New Delhi scaling back troops in October 2002.

In early 2002, as a result of pressure from the United States and India's mobilisation, Pakistani President, General Pervez Musharraf, was obliged to announce changes in his country's policy of support for separatism in Kashmir. This involved banning groups such as the LET and JEM and arresting their leaders (Mir, 2002). However, within a few months, the leaders of these two groups were released (Haqqani, 2003). Furthermore, the banned groups had been regrouping under new names (Sharma, 2002). It is clear that beyond such cosmetic changes, not much has been done in South Asia to reverse this infiltration by terrorists. In Southeast Asia, the turmoil of the late 1990s has continued into the next century, with an increase in political and terrorist-related violence. The international community and especially the United States discovered that this region was a fertile breeding ground for extremist violence. Porous borders, weak governments, large sections of deprived population and the presence of armed extremist movements have made the region quite susceptible to Al Qaeda operations (Simon, 2002, 315). Connections between Al Qaeda and Southeast Asia were significant even before 9/11. Ramzi Yousef, responsible for the first attack on the World Trade Center in 1993, lived in the Philippine capital of Manila for a while (Economist, 17 October 2002). In fact, in 1995, while in Manila, he was involved in an aborted plot to blow up eleven U.S. commercial planes (Mylroie, 1995). Also, Yazid Sufaat, a Malaysian national, hosted at separate points of time two of the hijackers involved in the September 11 bombings and the person responsible for the bombing of the USS Cole in 2000 (*Economist*, 17 October 2002). These are but a few instances of the links between Al Qaeda and the Southeast Asian extremist elements.

These interactions have continued after September 11 in an increasingly vicious cycle of violence. The worst incident was the bomb blast on the Indonesian island of Bali that killed nearly 200 people. The group responsible for this, Jemaah Islamiyah, is connected to Al Qaeda (*Economist*, 22 November 2002). Besides this global dimension, terrorism in Southeast Asia also has localized ethnic and religious roots. Several countries in the region have been affected by political violence that have separatist credentials and then developed ethnic/religious characteristics (Chalk, 2001, 242). This has been true of southern Thailand, where there is a Malay Muslim population, Mindanao in the Philippines and Aceh in Indonesia (Chalk, 2001). Furthermore, the Afghan civil war of the 1980s, which seemed to have been a training ground for extremists from different parts of the world, also provided Southeast Asia with a steady stream of veterans. These veterans then turned their energies toward fomenting Islamic revolutions in their own homelands (Simon, 2002; 315). This situation is further complicated by the reported involvement of some states in encouraging such disturbances. Prominent among these is Malaysia, which has allegedly given support to extremist organisations in the Philippines and Thailand (Jones and Smith, 2001; 280).

Since 9/11, the most prominent and publicized of these groups in Southeast Asia has been the Abu Sayyaf gang that has been responsible for a wave of violence in the Mindanao region of the Philippines. This has prompted the despatch of more than a thousand American troops to the region to assist the Philippine government (*Economist*, 1 August 2002). However, potentially the more dangerous group there is the Moro Islamic Liberation Front, a separatist group in the Philippines that has close ties with Al Qaeda (Spaeth, 2002). While it is true that terrorism in Southeast Asia has gained in prominence since 9/11, it should also be considered that some of these states might be using terrorism as a pretext for clamping down on separatist movements. The difficulty of distinguishing between local and international terrorist groups and also between terrorist and separatist movements adds to the confusion (*Economist*, 1 August 2002). Actions by governments in the region have to be seen in light of the desire of states across the world to be seen as supporting the United States in the global fight against terrorism. What better way to do this than to be a partner in the war and have common goals and enemies?

India's response to 9/11 was in the same vein. Its support for the U.S. was quick. However, more than that, New Delhi also termed the subsequent attack on the Indian parliament as part of global terrorism. Combating terror has thus become a buzzword for states across the region. However, in the Asia-Pacific, the complicated mixture of international terrorist groups, ethnic separatism, religious extremism and shortsighted government policies make the situation increasingly dangerous.

Transnational Organised Crime

Transnational organisationed crime (TNC) is one of the best examples of a non-military security threat in the Asia-Pacific region. Some groups involved in activities such as drug trafficking, trafficking in women, and corruption, have taken on the form of parallel governments in some cases and areas. Such groups often have their own paramilitary forces that further threaten the sovereignty of governments (Dupont, 1997; 41). Transnational organised crime groups in the region have assumed varying forms. They are characterised in general by loose, temporary alliances as opposed to the traditional hierarchical organisations seen in the Italian mafia. However, certainly the Japanese yakuza (Japanese criminal organisations) and some Chinese triads are exceptions to the rule (McFarlane, 2001; 200). In spite of such temporary alliances, their activities have infiltrated most sectors of politics, society and business.

Chinese organised crime groups, based on the mainland, Hong Kong and Taiwan, are the most influential in the Asia-Pacific region. Activities such as heroin trafficking are extremely lucrative. Using Hong Kong as a distribution centre, heroin is supplied to the United States, Western Europe and Australia (McFarlane, 2001a, 202-3). Though Chinese triads are prominent in heroin and opium trafficking, they are also diversifying into the trafficking of humans, financial crime, and arms smuggling (Brunker, 1999). Such activities have become a serious security and law and order problem for the governments involved. The liberalisation of economies has also provided increased opportunities for financial crimes for TNC groups. The prominence of Hong Kong as a major financial centre has made it very attractive for money laundering and other illicit financial activities (McFarlane, 2001). The yakuza of Japan are deeply entrenched not just in the business sector but also in the political sector of the country. Their involvement with the police and other organs of the government has helped to maintain law and order in the country (McFarlane, 2001; 204-5). The yakuza generally have conservative positions that coincide with the views of numerous right-wing elements of the polity.

Financial crimes perpetuated by such criminal organisations have a major effect on the economic, political and social stability of a state. They harm financial institutions, economic processes, undermine governments and divert revenue away from the state (McFarlane, 2001; 212). The political turmoil in Indonesia accompanied by separatist activity has its roots in the economic crisis in the region (Rosenberger, 2001; 115). A crucial element of this financial criminal network is the political establishment itself. Senior government officials at the highest levels in Japan, Indonesia, and South Korea have been implicated in financial misdemeanors that have had serious repercussions for their countries (McFarlane, 2001a, 211). This clearly shows how criminal organisations have infiltrated governments in the region at various points of time and have infused instability into the polity. The influence of the Russian mafia in the region is also considerable. It has a high degree of involvement in economic activity in Russia (BBC News, 21 November 1998). Their connections to Japanese organised crime groups have involved smuggling of stolen motor vehicles and even nuclear materials (McFarlane, 2001; 207).

However, the one state that has infiltrated organised international criminal activity (rather than the other way round) is North Korea. In fact, it has been termed a 'criminal state' (McFarlane, 2001b). Its precarious economic situation has persuaded it to indulge in the illegal international trade of a wide range of materials, including illicit drugs such as heroin, cocaine and methamphetamines (Sullivan and Jordan, 1999). It has been recently alleged that North Korea is the only government in the world that is actively involved in international crime as a pivotal component of its foreign policy and economic strategy (Stewart, 2006; 2). From their "Bureau 39" headquarters in Pyongyang, Communist Party officials are believed to be involved in running an international criminal network which yields in excess of $US500 million for Kim Jong-II. This criminal operation is so large that the United States now refers to North Korea as the "Soprano State" (Stewart, 2006, 1).

However, the most direct threat to the physical security of a state is seen in the case of South Asia, notably India. Here the involvement of the underworld is, of course, present in traditional sectors such as real estate, drug trafficking and gun running. However, more than that, groups such as the Dawood Ibrahim gang have been responsible for fomenting communal violence in the country. They were also responsible for a series of bomb blasts in Bombay in 1993 that killed hundreds of people (Verma and Tiwari, 2003). They also pose a threat to the regional stability through the hawala system, which allows illegal transfers of money. This system of monetary transactions has been invaluable in providing resources to terrorist networks.

Transnational organised crime has indeed come of age. Its role has expanded from making profits to actually influencing government policy, and, in many cases, directly combating governments. The links between TOC and terrorism in the Asia-Pacific region can have deadly consequences. Even worse is the existence of states that are directly or indirectly involved in such activities.

Proliferation/Nuclear Weapons

Though the global fight against terrorism and the tensions in the Middle East (for example, Iraq, Israel-Palestine) occupy the top priority for global powers and decision-makers, the North Korean proliferation issue arguably poses a much more imminent threat to global and regional security. The brinkmanship that Kim Jong Il has indulged in has brought the threat of nuclear conflagration closer than ever. In October 2002, it was revealed that North Korea had conceded that it had a programme for enriching uranium for nuclear weapons. This had been in violation of the 1994 agreement with the United States under which North Korea was obliged to freeze its nuclear program. Then, in December, Pyongyang announced that it would resume plutonium production and asked the International Atomic Energy Agency (IAEA) inspectors to leave the country (Jeffery, 2002). Finally, in January 2003, it withdrew from the Non-Proliferation Treaty.

According to the United States, North Korea has probably produced a few nuclear devices but is hampered by inadequate detonation mechanisms. By mid-2003, North Korea could produce one nuclear weapon per year. After the completion of additional nuclear weapons facilities, it could produce 55 nuclear weapons annually Center for Defense Information, 2003). It has also been developing and testing missiles for delivering its nuclear payloads. Pyongyang already has about 100 short-range (800-1300 km) No-dong missiles that can cover all of South Korea and most parts of Japan. It is also developing the longer range Taepo Dong I (1500-2200 km) and Taepo-Dong – II (6000 km) missiles (Center for Defense Information, 2003). The threat from North Korea is manifold. The worsening economic situation in the country has made the regime use its nuclear programme to blackmail South Korea, the United States and Japan in providing it with food and fuel supplies. This had been going on for the last decade. However, after its violation of the 1994 treaty, it will be difficult to persuade anyone that North Korea would fulfill its commitment to any future deal (*The Times*, 26 December 2002).

In the event that a new deal between North Korea and the United States and its East Asian allies is not reached, the prospect of aggression by Pyongyang in the region is not a far-fetched possibility. Even with an unfavourable military balance, North Korea could initiate violence short of all-out war (Gilinsky and Sokolski, 2002). A full-scale conflict on the Korean peninsula would be catastrophic, leading to at least a million casualties (Cha, 2002; 44). North Korea's nuclear ambitions can also lead to a massive arms race in the region with South Korea, Japan and Taiwan rethinking their options (Loeb and Slevin, 2003). As it is, the symbiotic connection between North Korea and Pakistan, in the development of their nuclear and missile arsenal, has already been revealed. In exchange for the ballistic missiles, Pakistan gave invaluable sensitive information on uranium enrichment to North Korea (Task Force on US Korea Policy, 2003).

Pakistan forms part of the other problems of proliferation in the Asia-Pacific region. As stated previously, Pakistani nuclear technologies have found their way to North Korea, which worsens the already precarious balance in the region. However, the more immediate issue in the region is the possibility of war between India and Pakistan. The Kashmir issue is as serious as ever, with violence in the region continuing unabated for more than a decade. In that period, the two sides have come close to full-scale war at least four times. The first was in 1988, at the time of Operation Brasstacks, a massive Indian army exercise that threatened to snowball into war. The second, with clearly nuclear dimensions was the crisis in 1990. The third was the Kargil conflict in 1999, which was a localized affair. The last, and most serious one, was the mobilization of troops by India after the attack on the Indian parliament in December 2001. Though troops were scaled back in October 2002, the core issues are still as strong as ever. In the absence of any solutions to the Kashmir issue, the prospect of a nuclear confrontation is always there. Since India's conventional strength is far greater than Pakistan's (IISS, 2002), the former would consider a nuclear first-strike in the event of a loss in a conventional battle.

On the other hand, one argument is that the condition of nuclear deterrence would prevent a major conventional war that could have nuclear dimensions, and that Indian forces would take care not to push Pakistan over the threshold (Sandhu, 2002). However, another mobilization of forces on the lines similar to that undertaken after December 2001 may not end in a withdrawal. Increasingly there is a feeling in New Delhi that a conventional conflict would not spiral out of control into a nuclear setting, especially since the major aim for Indian forces would be to destroy guerilla camps being used by terrorists, and not to hold on to any territory (Subrahmanyam, 2002).

In a crisis, the possibility of miscalculation is ever-present. Even a conventional conflict would run the risk of nuclear confrontation; as it happens, nuclear weapons and the missiles to deliver them are already deployed in both armies. Between India and Pakistan the flight time for missiles is very small, which makes the chances of preemption by either side quite possible (Chanrasekaran, 2002). The Asia-Pacific region is probably the most dangerous when it comes to the risk of nuclear tensions. The seeming intractability of disputes that underlie the Korean peninsula and the Indian subcontinent makes the possibility of future use of nuclear weapons there more likely.

Human Security

Human security in the Asia-Pacific region covers the various problems of the people of the region that cannot be seen through the prism of the traditional security agenda of states. Indeed, in most cases the state is part of the problem rather than the solution. The Asian economic crisis of the late 1990s led to a human security problem encompassing the economic, political and social life of the countries of the region. For example, economic turmoil in Indonesia led to the political violence and the fall of the Suharto regime. Repression of protestors and ethnic violence were part of the general spiral of violence into which the country degenerated (Ganguly, 2000; 252).

Human security has become such a crucial problem in the region because of the preoccupation of governments, with maintaining their sovereignty and nationhood at all costs. This has meant that whatever notion of security was adopted, it had to be state-centric (Burke, 2001). In the process, the rights and needs of the individual were not deemed important enough. In a bid to consolidate regimes, human rights have been relegated to the back seat in states such as Pakistan. Even in democratic countries like Bangladesh, political instability has led to political violence and economic slowdown.

Human security problems such as underdevelopment, rising population, lack of education and political and ethnic violence all feed into one another and make the position of the state more and more untenable. In its search for security and stability, several states in Asia have, in fact, increased insecurity and instability. Though governments and non-governmental organizations have begun to focus on the needs of the individual, the situation is still precarious. Ethnic and religious violence in the region, in places such as East Timor, Indonesia and the Indian subcontinent, besides of course, causing loss of human life and property, also divert the attention of governments away from their development agenda. The role of the state itself in Asia is sometimes an obstacle to the well-being of the people (Acharya and Acharya, 2002). Corruption in places like Indonesia and China has taken away much needed resources. The lack of political will on the part of some governments is an additional problem.

Another deep-rooted issue is the insistence by some Southeast Asian governments that economic development has to take priority over individual needs. They insist that human rights has a different meaning in Asia, and that according to economic progress, culture, and political system, each country could have its own interpretation of the concept (Anwar, 2003; 538). In the name of cultural differences, this argument could easily justify repression, torture, and political imprisonment. It also leads to the stifling of public debate over government policies that would directly impact on the lives of the people. For example, the Three Gorges project in China involved resettling over a million people, and could have disastrous consequences for millions of others. However, in the absence of any opposition to the government, such factors are ignored (Jones, 1998; 126).

States in the Asia-Pacific region have to focus on this new dimension of security if they are to maintain stability in their country. The biggest problem here is the lack of adequate resources. Economic liberalisation has led to the state reducing its role in the economy and developmental activities. This brings in much needed foreign investment, but it is questionable how much of this trickles down to the poorer sections of society. Furthermore, in this age of globalisation, the realisation of widening inequity promotes a feeling of resentment among people, which then can translate into political tension and violence.

Environmental Security

Several Asian states, especially those in Southeast and East Asia, have made significant progress in the economic field. However, in this race for development, a big price has been paid – that of the natural environment. Environmental degradation and resource depletion are by products of unsustainable development in the region. Industrialisation and urbanisation in the region have led to air and water pollution, scarcity of resources, degradation of land, deforestation, and an increase in industrial waste. Economic development has led to a massive increase in the demand for water. Lack of sewage treatment and the dumping of agricultural and industrial waste in rivers and coastal waters have further strained the situation (Jones, 1998; 127). Scarcity of water and its poor quality have had a direct impact on the health of people, with several outbreaks of serious diseases.

The presence of five of the seven most polluted cities in the world in Asia (Beijing, Jakarta, New Delhi, Calcutta and Shenyang) shows the level of air pollution plaguing the people of these countries (*Economy*, 1998, 47). This has come about because of the high level of automobile use, the inefficient use of energy, and the reliance on coal for more than half of the energy needs of Asia. Just as in the previous section there was a trade-off between human and economic security, here the trade-off is between environmental and economic security. Development is probably the most pressing issue in Asia, and in the absence of this, the danger of social/political disorder and violence is always there. However, development policies have often threatened environmental security. Clearly, in the long run, environmental insecurity will also provide the same kind of political upheaval that comes from underdevelopment and economic deprivation (*Economy*, 1998; 48).

Ecologically unsustainable development in the region has led to environmental scarcity, leading to environmental insecurity. This insecurity then affects other dimensions of security – political, economic development, and human (Weather Bee, 2001; 143). The linkage between resource depletion and insecurity is quite clear. Resource depletion leads to an intense competition for resources, which leads to instability. Furthermore, it is not just the quest for economic development that is straining the natural environment; the growing population in Asia is compounding the situation. The relationship between the environment and conflict is more direct in South Asia. Rapid deforestation has severely damaged the Himalayan catchment area that is leading to lower agricultural production and the inability of areas to support communities (Elliot, 2001; 443). A population of more than a billion makes the natural environment potentially a serious security threat in the subcontinent. Environmental decline exacerbated by the population problem could trigger the next conflict there (Myers, 1993; 102-3).

Conclusion

As this chapter makes clear, the Asia-Pacific region faces numerous security threats and challenges, some new due to globalisation and some a hold over from the state-centric Cold War days. Though other actors like NGOs have entered the fray, it is also quite clear that the state still has a major role to play in governance and politics. 9/11 was touted as a perverse product of globalisation and symbolic of the decline of the state. However, its aftermath showed that it is the state that is responsible for the security of its inhabitants, and it is the state to which the people turn. Having said that, it is also true that states in the region are guilty of adopting short-term policies, especially in fields such as human and environmental security. These are the critical areas where long-term strategies are imperative. Unfortunately, the short time horizon of many governments and the perpetual quest for regime survival indicates that such security threats are likely to remain, and, in fact, exacerbate.

REFERENCES

Acharya Arabinda and Amitava Acharya (2002), 'Human Security in Asia: Conceptual Ambiguities and Common Understandings', http://www.robarts.yorku.ca/pdf/

Anwar Dewi Fortuna (2003), 'Human security: an intractable problem in Asia', in Muthiah Alagappa, ed., *Asian Security Order: Instrumental and Normative Features*, Stanford: California: Stanford University Press.

BBC News (1998), 'The rise of the Russian mafia', November 21, 1998, http://news.bbc.co.uk/1/hi/specialreport/11008/03/98/russian mafia/70095.stm

Brunker Mike (1999), 'Asian gangs are brothers in crime', MSNBC August 1999, http://www.msnbc.com/news/165145.asp?cp1-1

Burke Anthony (2001), 'Caught between national and human security: knowledge and power in post-crisis Asia', http://www.preventconflict.org/portal/main/research/Burke.pdf

Center for Defense Information (2003), 'Factsheet: North Korea's nuclear weapons program', January 23, http://www.cdi.org/nuclear/nk-fact-sheet-pr.cfm.

Cha Victor D. (2002), 'Hawk engagement and preventive defence on the Korean Peninsula', *International Security*, Vol. 27, No.1, Summer.

Chalk Peter (2001), 'Separatism and Southeast Asia: The Islamic factor in Southern Thailand, Mindanao, and Aceh', *Studies in Conflict and Terrorism*, Vol. 24, No. 4.

Chandrasekaran Rajiv (2002), 'For India, deterrence may not prevent war', *The Washington Post*, January 17.

Chellaney Brahma (2001), 'Fighting terrorism in Southern Asia: the lessons of history," *International Security*, Vol. 26, No. 3, Winter.

De Borchgrave Arnaud (2001), 'Connecting terrorism's dots," *The Washington Times*, December 27.

Dupont Alan (1997), 'New dimensions of security," in Denny Roy, ed., *The New Security Agenda in the Asia-Pacific Region*, London: Macmillan Press.

The Economist, various issues.

Economy Elizabeth (1998), 'The Environment and development in the Asia-Pacific Region', in James Shin, ed., *Fires Across The Water: Transnational Problems in Asia*, New York: Council on Foreign Relations Press, 1998.

Elliot Lorraine (2001), 'Regional environmental security: pursuing a non-traditional approach," in Andrew T.H Tan & J.D. Kenneth Boutin, eds., *Non-Traditional Security Issues in Southeast Asia*, Singapore: select Publishing.

Ganguly Sumit (2000), Nuclear proliferation in South Asia: origins, consequences and prospects," in Shalendra D. Sharma, ed., *The Asia-Pacific in the New Millennium: Geopolitics, Security, and Foreign Policy*, Berkeley: Institute of East Asian Studies, University of California.

Gilinsky Victor and Henry Sokolski (2002), 'A time for demanding', *The National Review*, November 6.

Goldstone Jack (2002), 'Population and security: how demographic change can lead to violent conflict," *Journal of International Affairs*, Fall.

Haqqani Hussain (2003), "Pakistan Frees Terrorist Leaders," *Asian Wall Street Journal*, January 7.

Hauge Wenche and Tanja Ellingsen (2001), 'Beyond environmental scarcity: causal pathways to conflict," *Journal of Peace Research*, Vol. 35, Issue 3.

Homer-Dixon Thomas F. (1991), 'On the threshold: environmental changes as causes of acute conflict," *International Security*, Vol. 16, Issue 2, Autumn.

Homer-Dixon Thomas F. (1994), 'Environmental scarcities and violent conflict: evidence from cases," *International Security*, Vol. 19, Issue 1, Summer.

IISS (2002), 'Pakistan and North Korea: dangerous counter-trades" *IISS Strategic Comments*, Vol. 8, Issue 9, November.

Jeffery Simon (2002), 'North Korea restarts nuclear program', *The Guardian*, December 12.

Jones Sidney (1998), 'The impact of Asian economic growth on human rights," in James Shin, ed., *Fires Across The Water: Transnational Problems in Asia*, New York: Council on Foreign Relations Press.

Jones David M. and Mike L. Smith (2001), 'The changing security agenda in Southeast Asia: globalization, new terror, and the delusions of regionalism', *Studies in Conflict and Terrorism*, Vol. 24, No. 4.

Kobrin Stephen J. (1997), 'Electronic cash and the end of national markets," *Foreign Policy*, Summer.

Kobrin Stephen J. (1998), 'Back to the future: neomedievalism and the postmodern digital world economy," *Journal of International Affairs*, Spring.

Kumar Davinder (2001), 'Tracing a puppet chain', *Outlook*, December 31.

Loeb Vernon and Peter Slevin (2003), 'Overcoming North Korea's 'tyranny of proximity',' *The Washington Post*, January 20.

Matthews Jessica T. (1997), 'Power shift," *Foreign Affairs*, January/February.

McFarlane John (2001a), 'Transnational crime and Asia-Pacific security', in Sheldon W. Simon, ed., *The Many Faces of Asian Security*, Lanham, MD: Rowman & Littlefield Publishers.

McFarlane John (2001b), 'Globalization and human security: transnational organized crime', United Nations Conference on Disarmament Issues, at Ishikawa-Kanazawa, August.

Mir Amir (2002), 'The general's fundamental shift', *Outlook*, January 28.

Mohan C. Raja (2002), 'Catharsis and catalysis: transforming the South Asian subcontinent', in Ken Booth and Tim Dunne, eds., *Worlds In Collision: Terror and the Future of Global Order*, New York: Palgrave Macmillan.

Myers Norman (1993), *Ultimate Security: The Environmental Basis for Political Stability*, New York: W.W. Norton.

Mylroie Laurie (1995/6), 'The World Trade Center Bomb: Who Is Ramzi Yousef? And Why It Matters?', *The National Interest*, Winter.

Rosenberger Leif (2001), 'The changing face of economic security in Asia', in Sheldon W. Simon, ed., *The Many Faces of Asian Security*, Lanham, MD: Rowman & Littlefield Publishers.

Sandhu Kanwar (2002), 'Can Indian forces deliver the killer blow', *The Hindustan Times*, January 9.

Serrano Monica (2002), 'Transnational organized crime and international security: business as usual?', in Mats Berdal & Monica Serrano, eds., *Transnational Organized Crime and International Security: Business as Usual?*, Boulder, CO: Lynne Reiner Publishers.

Sharma Kartikeya (2002), 'Rumble in the valley," *The Week*, May 12.

Simon Sheldon (2002), 'Southeast Asia', in Richard Ellings and Aaron Friedberg, eds., with Michael Wills, *Strategic Asia 2002-03: Asian Aftershocks*, Seattle: National Bureau of Asian Research.

Slaughter Anne Marie (1997), 'The real New World Order', *Foreign Affairs*, September/October.

Smith Paul J. (2002), 'Terrorism in Asia," *Harvard Asia Pacific Review*, Spring.

Spaeth Anthony (2002), 'Rumbles in the jungle', *Time*, March 4.

Stern Jessica (2000), 'Pakistan's jihad culture', *Foreign Affairs*, November-December.

Stewart, C. (2006), 'Dirty secrets of the Soprano state', *The Weekend Australian* newspaper, 11 March, pp. 1-2.

Subrahmanyam K. (2002), 'Indo-Pak nuclear conflict unlikely', *The Times of India*, January 2.

Sullivan Jordan Kevin and Mary Jordan (1999), 'Famine, nuclear threat raise stakes in debate over N. Korea', *The Washington Post*, March 13.

The Task Force on US Korea Policy (2003), 'The nuclear crisis on the Korean Peninsula: avoiding the road to perdition', *Current History*, April.

The Times (2002), 'Nuclear Blackmail', December 26.

Verma Tiwari Arvind and R.K. Tiwari (2003), 'Organized crime: a perspective from India," in Jay S. Albanese, Dilip K. Das and Arvind Verma, eds., *Organized Crime: World Perspectives*, New Jersey: Pearson Education.

Weatherbee, D.E. (2001), 'Environment, development and security in Southeast Asia', in Sheldon W. Simon, ed., *The Many Faces of Asian Security*, Lanham, MD: Rowman & Littlefield Publishers.

5

Asia-Pacific Security in the Age of Globalisation

Singapore's Perspective

PANKAJ KUMAR JHA

The Chapter evaluates some of the theoretical and practical arguments regarding the regional and national impact of the end of the Cold War and globalisation on the security discourse and policy for Southeast Asia in general and for Singapore more particularly. In order to do this, the chapter is divided into three main sections – globalisation and the post-Cold War security debate, regional aspects of Asia-Pacific security, and Singapore's perception of Asia-Pacific security. It is concluded on the one hand, that, in order to maximise its future security, Singapore needs to be involved in cooperative arrangements both with extra-regional powers and other ASEAN states; especially with regard with international terrorism. On the other hand, while Singapore needs to implement strong internal security laws to maximise national stability, it also needs to be more sympathetic to the questions of human security in order to avoid a self-defeating security strategy.

Globalisation and the Post-Cold War Security Debate

Security implies boundaries, both real and metaphorical, but these boundaries vary in space and time. Analysts differ over what objects are to be secured-individuals, nations, states or ethnic communities. They also disagree on how much emphasis is to be attached to external as opposed to internal threats to security. Others differ over the terms national, international and global security. Security has traditionally been associated with protecting state citizens against violence, war and the use of force, but a growing number of analysts now argue that these are not its only defining characteristics. Analysts from competing intellectual traditions define security differently. The term "traditional security" was coined by revisionists who sought to distance themselves from the security perspective that was dominant during the Cold War. Some describe it as state-centric, externally-oriented and military based. In contrast to the traditional security perspective, security ought to be viewed as being people-centered. This people-centered definition is predicated on the assumption that *people* are the foundations of political communities and states. Moreover, in an era in which human rights and democracy have become recognised as global entitlements, no definition of security should ignore these values. As people's values, rules, norms and institutions evolve, the definition of security must also evolve. People-centered security in achievable only in conditions where sovereignty is also defined in terms of the people's needs, rights, interests, values and hopes.

In the current globalizing context, there is a unique blending between the security and the economic objectives of a state. Globalisation relies increasingly on a kind of trust-the unsentimental expectation that people individually and collectively will behave more or less according to their rational self-interest. The terrorists make use of that trust to achieve certain objectives. This basically ensures that terrorism in deeply connected with globalisation and that it will extend itself by using the technological developments associated with globalisation. In fact, the Southeast Asia regional organisation (ASEAN) in its 7th summit issued a declaration on joint action to counter terrorism with the view that act of terrorism is a profound threat to international peace and security and requires concerted action to protect and defend all peoples and the peace and security of the world.

The attack on the U.S. defence headquarters and the World Trade Centre in New York by hijackers on 11 September 2001 highlights how global changes have transformed the nature of security threats. The nature and intensity of such a level of attack impinge on different facets of the motivation of the attackers. The subsequent comments and opinion on this have illustrated how the analysts and decision-makers were myopic about their view of terrorism. However, this attack has also ushered in a new era in terms of strategic thinking. In fact, the Western alliance, NATO (North Atlantic Treaty Organization), invoked its principle that an attack on one of them is an attack on all. There has been increasing concentration on state building and economic development, which have been the central rationale for security discourse, especially the broader issues of the popular appeal and legitimacy of these two processes and if they are to be sustainable over the long term. This agenda rests on an attempt to shift the centre of gravity of security debates away from traditional policy circles to the broader segments of the non-governmental community. These has also in a sense been a deepening concern over the framework of discussion apart from the organisational and governmental level interaction, and Track Two diplomacy has been gaining wider acceptance.

Globalisation as such does not inherently change the external context within which the state operates, but reflects also in the very nature of states. From a security perspective, such a flow of external forces determines how the state manages its security (internal and external) problems. In this age of globalisation, the forms of threat have become diverse, which in turn has complicated the way states should respond to them. Globalisation has been accompanied by an even greater threat of transnational crime. Thus, a more globalised and integrated world will not automatically provide a sense of security to the international community. Globalisation is, in a way, facilitating terrorism by making borders more porous, by ensuring that information and communications are more capable and less expensive, and by enabling the transnational movement of funds.

The basic framework of discussion of security debates in Southeast Asia and the Asia-Pacific region generally has provided an area where tensions become articulated. The notion of comprehensive security has long been the starting point of discussions regarding security issues in the region. Its focus on the idea that effective state building in all its military, economic and social dimensions was the pre-eminent way to ensure domestic and regional security and stability in the area not only catered to the most pressing concerns of decision-making bodies but also justified their near complete monopoly of the security discourse. The concept of co-operative security subsequently emerged as a centrepoint, spurred on by the need to broaden the problematique of security to integrate the vast array of issues (for instance, transnational problems, ranging from the growing economic interdependence of the region to illegal migration and environmental degradation) which has been marginalised in that discourse, but it always has the potential to jeopardise the state building project at the heart of the regional security agenda.

The concept of regional security gained importance when it was put forward in the 1994 UNDP Report on Human Development; to emphasise the need to focus on the development and well-being of the individual if security was to be a sustainable goal in the post-Cold War era. Currently, exclusively debated in the Asia-Pacific region, this notion directly critiques certain conventions within the regional security discourse: where there is a focus on the state, it advocates a fundamental concern with the individual; where there is an open-ended process of discussion, it proclaims on abiding commitment to the democratisation of security.

In so far as economic-security relationships were the subject of scholarly and policy-maker interest during the Cold War, the focus was much more on different aspects of domestic security. In order to counter communism, economic development was seen as a weapon. The Marshall Plan and developmental aid to Third World states, including many in the Asia-Pacific region, had undertones of a security objective. This incentive of development was seen as a balancing factor to tilt the power situation in favour of Western states. In the changed scenario, "engagement" and "monitoring" of different nuclear powers, along with economic interdependence, have been the main concerns of all states. Thus, the security has become a multi-pronged approach at the global level.

Furthermore, the economic variable has played an important role in the collapse of the Soviet Union, German unification, and thus the end of the Cold War gave prominence to the thought that economic-strategic thinking should dominate global policy-making and interstate relations gained currency. The growing linkages between international economic developments and security have now become focused on the Asia-Pacific, where rapid economic growth has increased interdependence and increased military spending by the small states in the region. Several important developments have augmented increased concerns about security, including:

1. The emergence of China as an economic power
2. Trade frictions between the US and Japan and their impact on security.
3. The increased military spending by countries such as Singapore and Brunei.
4. The effects of North Korea and China with increasing liberalisation at the international level.
5. The role of the military in a number of Asian countries such as Indonesia and Pakistan.
6. The rise of Islamic separatist groups in countries like Indonesia, Malaysia and the Philippines.

Development in the Asia-Pacific region has been based on regional conceptions of security which, while they have differed from state to state, have tended to see economic development, political stability and social welfare as or more important than military power in preventing conflict.

The role of economic development as a major contributor to security has been a particular focus in East Asia, and has been fundamental to offsetting the external threats (often linked to domestic instability) in the region. Critics of broadening the concept of security in new directions, for example, include environmental problems, crime-related problems, terrorism and similar activities, have argued that so doing creates conceptual confusion and that the term "insecurity' becomes a grab-all category into which just about every human ill, from war, to environmental degradation and AIDS gets indiscriminately lumped together.

Theoretical discussion of the links between economics and security has tended to embrace two quite different world views-the "realist" and "liberal" – in a so-called "clash of security paradigms" (Stares, 1998; 12-17). In each category there is a spectrum of views but, in general, realists adopt a state-centric view of the world. Realist theory treats states as unitary rational actors condemned by the imperatives of an anarchic world system to seek security either by balancing the power of other states, or seeking dominance over them. Power is the key variable in realist analysis and power relations are seen as playing a critical role in the non-military interactions between states, including those of institutionalized cooperation.

Realists tend to see economic resources as important, in part because they are necessary for increasing military power, but also because they are levers of power in their own right. Liberals believe that realists accord too much significance to the pursuit of military power security and underestimate the extent to which states may successfully use non-military, non-coercive means in seeking security.

Realists tend to see international economic interactions, like security interactions, as zero-sum games. States are seen as pursuing relative gains in both the economic and security realms. Realists believe that cooperative international institutions reflect the power balances of the international system and that the role of cooperation in enhancing security is extremely limited, except in the case of alliances. Realists are skeptical that growing economic interdependence will reduce conflict. Conflicts which disrupt economic linkages between states also hamper the economic growth which such linkages generate; and economic growth has become perhaps the single most important objective of modern states, and the legitimising basis of many governments.

Structural realism claims that the destabilizing consequences of changes in the distribution of economic-military power between states continue to influence North American international relations theory and much of the literature on Asia-Pacific security. Even critics who are skeptical about many structural realist claims agree that economic change may have important security consequences. Few would doubt that shifts in economic power among the major regional powers – Japan, China, Russia and (potentially) Korea – could have important security implications for the region. Similarly, the continued economic growth of India and Indonesia will almost certainly increase the political and security significance of these states during the twenty-first century.

In the Asia-Pacific region, an "economic security dilemma" arises because the increased wealth that derives from a commitment to market-oriented development policies is seen both as fostering security enhancing democratic institutions and interdependence. On the other hand, it also provides the resources to enhance military power in possibly destabilizing ways. Continued growth in regional economic military capabilities will have major long-term implications for the global, as well as the regional, military balance.

With regard to APEC, its member countries account for about a quarter of the World Gross Domestic Product (GDP), compared with about 10 per cent three decades ago. On current projections, they are likely to account for a third of global GDP in the early decades of the twenty-first century. The military competence of the countries in the region is changing as a result of increased economic growth, but as the growth is not even among the regional states so the resultant effect is that the intra-regional balance equation is changing.

In this region, the most important shift in the regional balance of power has been the emergence of China. However, with regard to the economic interdependence and security concerns, there is certain level of understanding. Interdependence has both positive and negative security effects. On the positive side, it creates disincentives to wage war because disruptive conflicts threaten the economic linkages that generate wealth. Beneficiaries of such linkages form domestic constituencies with a vested interest in peace. Interdependence also creates channels of communication and information that can help dispel misperceptions and misunderstandings. The negative effects of interdependence, particularly in terms of trans-Pacific relations, have often been marked by disputes, mistrust, charges of unfairness and threats of sanctions. Interdependence, in other words, may enhance security traditionally defined (that is, as the absence of interstate wars), while at the same time providing new instruments of coercion for the powerful to wield against the weak.

Regional Aspects of Asia-Pacific Security

Interdependence in the Asia-Pacific region has tended to be an effect, rather than a cause of benign security relationships. Once established, however, interdependence may "develop its own constituencies" and thus reinforce the positive security relationships which facilitated its emergence in the first place. Multilateral institutions may enhance security and the emerging Asia-Pacific multilateral institutions of ASEAN and APEC and the related "Track II" networks as embodying a form of interdependence from which a sense of shared values may emerge.

The collapse of the Soviet Union, and the end of the Cold War led the US to consider withdrawing its dominant military presence from the region. This opened up the possibilities for the creation of new multilateral security arrangements without upsetting the existing US bilateral security arrangements and forward deployment strategy. The perceived US withdrawal from the region (especially after the closure of the Philippine bases) made them interested in finding an indigenous solution to their security requirements, but one that would take into account the relevant outside powers. They needed to keep the US engaged and interested in the region so that the ambitions of the other upcoming powers, like Japan and China, could be kept in check. An assertive China (with its military modernisation and naval expansion), an ascendant (though "power shy") Japan, and a "withered Russia" tended to impact on the security of the wider Asia-Pacific region and thus necessitated the setting up of the ARF.

Greater economic prosperity in the ASEAN region has also meant an increased allocation of state budgets for defence and a rapid modernisation of the military. This has paradoxically led to a feeling of increased regional insecurity. Besides, the ASEAN states, realising that their security could not be divorced from the security of the rest of the Asia-Pacific region, decided they must lead in the formation of such a security mechanism.

Instead of allowing other powers like Australia, Canada or Russia to implement their proposals, ASEAN decided to seize the opportunity. However, military factors *per se* do not exercise an overwhelming role in such decisions. Security has become an extended concept. There often are several other security-related objectives such as dealing with international terrorism, maritime disputes, sea piracy, narcotics trafficking, the spread of AIDS, ecology (environmental pollution) and information warfare.

In the changed post-Soviet and post-Cold War scenario the focus has shifted to new threats which include: China, the volatility of the Korean peninsula and a potentially reassertive Japan. The US has been assured additional facilities at Singapore's Changi Naval base as it seeks to engage China in order to limit it economically and militarily. The Clinton Administration, which had some reservations about multilateral security cooperation in the Asia-Pacific, dropped its objections to a multilateral security dialogue in the region. The US has come to acknowledge that multilateral dialogue must supplement its links at the bilateral level and thus it welcomed the formation of the ARF. Though the Secretary of State Warren Christopher himself was unable to attend the inaugural meeting (due to preoccupation with "Middle East" negotiations), his juniors, Deputy Secretary of State Strobe Talbott, Assistant Secretary of State for East Asia and Pacific Affairs, Winston Lord, and Under Secretary of State for Economic, Business and Agricultural affairs, Joan Spero did attend. The US wanted the ARF to play a pro-active role in tackling regional conflict situations.

The growing economic linkages and the increasing importance of the Asia-Pacific region in the global economy made ASEAN opt for a stabilising factor to promote that growth. Because of economic reasons, the ASEAN states had as much an interest in having a security mechanism in place as did outside powers. As the ASEAN economies are so dependent on trade, it became imperative for them to ensure that the movement of goods was free and unimpeded.

The 1997 economic crisis altered the way ASEAN looked at security and it began to be looked at from a holistic perspective. Since the military modernisation process underway in Southeast Asia was put on hold, arms procurement from the major powers was also adversely affected. The defence budgets of Southeast Asian countries were curtailed. This required putting on hold previously concluded arms procurement deals, and a reduction in military exercises and training programmes with the major powers.

Certain issues animate the ASEAN states and the major powers to an almost equal degree. Some issues which affect their security interest and on which they could cooperate include:

- The Security of sea lanes, straits and passages
- Search and rescue
- Disaster relief
- Confidence building
- Curbing Drugs and narco trafficking.

The ARF will have to find new ways to tackle the problems of terrorism and drug trafficking which could be traced to the economic meltdown. Terrorist activities have increased as regional governments have found themselves unable to focus their attention on these issues on their borders because of their preoccupation at home.

China, like the United States, has agreed to participate in the ARF and the Asia-Pacific Economic Cooperation (APEC) grouping, but not to the extent where either group will compromise Beijing's ability to conduct individual bilateral security relations throughout the region. China's overriding security objective remains to avoid compromising its sovereign interests and to preserve its current political system at a time when most other communist governments have disappeared. This distinctively nationalist orientation appears largely at odds with multilateralism, which the Chinese regard as a security formula largely Western in origin. Addressing his counterparts at the inaugural ARF meeting in Bangkok, during July 1994, Chinese Foreign Minister, Qian Qichen, cautioned that any process of multilateral dialogue must take into account the reality that Asia-Pacific countries differ greatly from each other in terms of their historical conditions, cultural origins, political systems, religious beliefs, values and levels of development. Accordingly, Qian argued, different values and norms could best be overcome by strengthening bilateral relations with other states and by rigidly observing the principle of equality in all negotiations, as China had done in exercising its independent foreign policy. Qian called for the simultaneous development of bilateral and multilateral security dialogues in the region, thereby indirectly rejecting the premise that a multilateral security regime alone presented the best opportunity for ensuring regional stability. A common strand running through both China's and the United States' resistance to multilateral security regimes in the Asia-Pacific is the mutual Sino-American fear of losing the leverage afforded by both countries' size and power relative to other Asia-Pacific security actors.

Realists argue that with any reduction in US military power in the region, China and possibly Japan will vie for the regional predominance and that either Asian power may become the "deviant state" that prevents effective regime formation and maintenance. Those fearing Chinese hegemony cite China's economic potential as increasingly complementing and inevitably strengthening its already formidable military strength. Beijing continues to display irredentism in regard to unsatisfied territorial claims and appears determined to protect core Chinese culture and national institutions from outside penetration and contamination. Concern about

Japan's future intentions relate to Tokyo's increased apprehensions that the US will abandon its post-war commitments to Japan's defence, leaving Tokyo on its own to confront and necessarily dominate a still hostile set of regional neighbours.

China has shown increasing signs of becoming a more responsible regional and global power as it gains strength, joining multilateral regional institutions instead of opposing them. Japan has also become increasingly "regime oriented" staking out what it regards as a special relationship with ASEAN and moving visibly to coordinate strategy with China and South Korea for constraining North Korean nuclear aspirations.

Singapore's Perception of Asia-Pacific Security

Singapore currently has a population in excess of 4 million of whom 76.8 per cent were Chinese, 13.9 per cent Malay and 7.9 per cent Indian. Profiting from the booming regional economy, Singapore has consolidated its reputation as a leading financial centre largely as a result of the swift and professional actions of Singapore officials to contain the crisis like the collapse of the British banking group, Barings PLC, in London in 1995. At the ASEAN summit in December 1998, Singapore supported the adoption of substantial measures to increase regional trade and attract foreign investors, and, in July 1999, the ministers of foreign affairs of the ASEAN member countries accepted a proposal by Goh Chok Tong, then Singapore PM, to send joint investment missions to attract capital back to Southeast Asia. At the ASEAN summit, held in Singapore in November 2000, the Republic again stressed again the need to re-establish ASEAN's strength. There was some resentment, particularly on the part of Malaysia, at Singapore's moves to conclude bilateral free trade pacts with New Zealand, USA, Australia and other countries, ahead of the ASEAN arrangement scheduled for 2003.

The Asian economic crisis strained relations between Singapore and the Republic's immediate neighbours. At the National rally in August 1998, however, Prime Minister Goh emphasised Singapore's dependence upon Indonesia and Malaysia, and the Republic continued to hold reserves in Indonesian and Malaysian currencies, provided humanitarian aid to Indonesia, proposed a loan to support the Indonesian currency, and in September 1998, offered to discuss bilateral trade finance guarantees. Singapore continued to maintain friendly relations with both the People's Republic of China and with Taiwan. By 2001, earlier problems over the progress of the Sino-Singaporean Suzhon joint venture, from which Singapore had contemplated withdrawing, had been overcome, and

Singapore continued to encourage investment and commercial links. The maintenance of good relations with USA continued to be of crucial importance to Singapore. The actions taken by the Singaporean Government to mitigate the Republic's domestic financial problems following the onset of the regional economic crisis in 1997 won praise in the US press. Goh Chok Tong was the first Southeast Asian leader to meet President George W. Bush in Washington in June 2001, when he urged a permanent US interest in Southeast Asia.

Singapore was appalled at the terrorist attacks on New York and Washington DC, on 11 September 2001 and immediately pledged its support for the US effort to create a world-wide alliance to counter terrorism, urging in particular that Muslim and developing countries should be drawn into the coalition. Since the Republic was heavily dependent on the US economy, and already facing considerable problems, the crisis threatened a more prolonged downturn in its fortunes.

Singapore and Terrorism

In fact, Singapore has been quite apprehensive of its security concerns as since the mid-1980s there has been a robust military modernisation and expansion programme by the ASEAN states which was temporarily put on hold (by most of the countries, except Singapore and Brunei), during the Asian economic crisis in 1997 and 1998. As Singapore is located between the two strong states of Malaysia and Indonesia, so its security concerns, vis-à-vis Islamic terrorism and economic growth aspects, are high priorities. The problems faced by Indonesia remain precarious, as the issue is no longer Indonesia's political and diplomatic support for the US-led war on terrorism. Gradually Indonesia and other Southeast Asian countries are being drawn more deeply into the "war" as evidence begins to surface that the region may emerge as a major breeding ground for international terrorism. Southeast Asian governments will need to deal decisively with domestic radical groups that may be linked to international terrorist networks. Initially, they have downplayed the threat posed by those groups.

It might not be difficult for the Philippines government to pinpoint the Abu Sayyaf rebels in the Southern Philippines as having close links to Al Qaeda. President Arroyo has made a deal with the United States, allowing US troops, including special operation forces trained in counter terrorism, to be sent to the Philippines to help destroy Abu Sayyaf. In December 2001, the governments of Singapore and Malaysia arrested 28 alleged terrorists, believed to be linked to Al-Qaeda. This was followed by another arrest in the Philippines in January 2002. These arrests have also led to the allegations of the involvement by Indonesians and groups based in Indonesia, particularly Abu Bakar Baasyir, the leader of the Mujahideen Council of Indonesia (Majelis Mujahideen, Indonesia). However, Malaysia and Singapore still have the notorious Internal Security Act with which they can more easily arrest people.

Terrorism, by striking at civilian targets, is essentially a threat to human security. The scale and scope of operation by the new terrorists also makes them a threat to state security. The war on terrorism is a new kind of war. In dealing with the new terrorists, the state, acting to protect itself and its citizens, may resort to policies and measures or rules and practices, that in themselves could threaten human security. Individuals suspected of subversive intent can be held without charge. The cruelty and danger that the new terrorists pose has mobilized wider public opinion against terrorism and has engendered something of an "anything goes" mentality.

The threat of new terrorism can be contained only through hard counter-terrorist measures, such as law enforcement and intelligence cooperation. Singapore has set up a new national security secretariat within its defence ministry to coordinate anti-terrorism initiatives between its security organizations. The Singapore government has announced that the terrorist it arrested in December 2001 had links to Osama Bin Laden and was planning strikes against American targets in Singapore. Singapore and Malaysia have used their Internal Security Act (ISA) to arrest those suspects. In view of the public concern and panic expressed following the release of the news of the arrests, the Singapore government was prompted to issue a statement to calm the public and there may be less urgency to revive the agenda.

The arrests in Singapore and Malaysia, seem to have foiled the "ground Asia Strategy" of Jemaah Islamiyah. The group aims at establishing Daulah Islamiah, an Islamic state that would include parts of Malaysia, Indonesia and the Philippines. Jemaah Islamiyah was established in 1995 and has members in Indonesia, Malaysia, Singapore, Brunei and the Philippines. The arrests in Singapore and Malaysia have also exposed the links between the groups operating in different countries. It is reported that an Indonesian cleric, Abu Bakar Baasyir, played a key role in guiding the terrorist cells in Singapore and Malaysia (*The Asian Wall Street* Journal, 17 January 2002).

On 1 October 2001, a 15-page document in Arabic titled "Operation Jihad in Asia" was discovered in Solo, Central Java. The document is said to contain detailed operation plans to bomb US embassies and installations in Jakarta, Singapore and Malaysia, in December 2001, and that the plan was ordered by Osama Bin Laden.

For Singapore, the city-state's future is uncertain because of the volatile international climate and so it has begun to explore the possibility of locating Singapore-owned factories on nearby Indonesian and Malaysian territory. In 1990, the idea expanded into a proposal to include the adjacent parts of Indonesia (the Riau archipelago) and Malaysia (the State of Johor) to form a special economic zone, known as "Sijori". Sijori took off in 1992 when Indonesia allowed 100 per cent Singapore ownership of factories on Batam Island. Also, Singapore has no significant natural resources and it imports oil from Indonesia and water from Malaysia. Both countries could easily blockade Singapore, as the Straits of Malacca are relatively narrow. Singapore even lacks any natural barriers to invasion and Indonesia or Malaysia could easily overwhelm Singapore militarily, just as Japan did during World War II. Thus, the possible options for Singapore are to have good relations with powerful neighbours like China, Japan and North Korea as well as cordial relations with Malaysia and Indonesia.

Conclusion

Singapore has developed largely because of its strategic geographical location, adopting sound economic policy, enforcing political stability, strong administration and also being a beneficiary of the "trickle down effect" which came because of the spillover of economic growth of countries like Japan in the region. Singapore should try to educate public opinion about the presence of a strong military power in its territory, like the US, without hurting the sensibilities of the Chinese population in the city-state. It should also undertake joint intelligence operations and military exercises with both the U.S. and China in case of any emergency. Along with these measures it has also become imperative for Singapore to convince Islamic countries like Malaysia and Indonesia to contain any radical Islamic elements. Apart from these steps, there is also a need for Singapore leaders to have a more 'lenient' view of democracy as otherwise this might lead to increasing emigration of Singaporeans. The need of the hour is to curb terrorism at all costs so that it does not mushroom in the backyard of Indonesia or Malaysia, as such a development would spell doom for Singapore's economy and security in the long run.

REFERENCES

Almonte, Jose T. (1998), 'Ensuring security the "ASEAN Way"', *Survival*, Vol. 39, No. 4, Winter 1997-98, pp. 80-92.

Anwar, Devi Fortuna (1996), 'Changing modalities of Southeast Asian security', Paper Presented at the Defence Services Asia (DSA 96), Conference: "Changing Conceptions of Security in A Changing Pacific Asia, "April 25-26, Kuala Lumpur.

Bandoro, Bantarto (2002), 'Global coalition Against terrorism: security Perspective and ASEAN', *The Indonesian Quarterly*, Vol. 30 (1), pp. 44-55.

Cutler, John. A. (1989), 'Will US political and military policy towards the South and Mid-Pacific hang in the Bush administration?', *Contemporary Southeast Asia*, Vol. 11 (1), pp. 75-91.

Da Cunha, Derek ed. (2000), *Southeast Asian Perspectives on Security*, Singapore: Institute of Southeast Asian Studies.

Da Cunha, Derek (2001), *Singapore in the New Millennium: Challenges Facing the City-State*, Singapore: Institute of Southeast Asian Studies.

Dupont, Alan (1997), 'New dimensions of security', in Denny Roy ed., *The New Security Agenda in the Asia-Pacific Region*, London: Macmillan Press, pp. 31-45.

Dutta, Sujit (1995), 'Security in the Asia-Pacific: key issues and challenges', *Strategic Analysis*, November, pp. 1029-1045.

Emmers, Ralf (2001), 'The influence of the balance of power factor within the ASEAN Regional Forum', *Contemporary Southeast Asia*, Vol. 23 (2), pp. 275-289.

Funabashi, Yoichi (1997), 'Bridging Asia's economics-security Gap', *Survival*, Vol. 38 (1), Winter, pp. 101-16.

Harris, Stuart and Mack, Andrew eds. (1997), *Asia Pacific Security-The Economic and Political Nexus*, Sydney: Allen and Unwin.

Makinda, Samuel M. (2001), 'Security and sovereignty in the Asia-Pacific', *Contemporary Southeast Asia*, Vol. 23 (3), pp. 401-19.

Sallen, Wan Ahmed (2002), 'Terrorism in Southeast Asia: how real is the threat?', *Indonesian Quarterly*, Vol. 30 (1), pp. 38-43.

Saw, Swee Hock (1999), *The Population of Singapore*, Singapore: Institute of Southeast Asian Studies.

Schilling, Walter (1997), 'Changing power structures in the Asia-Pacific region', *Aussen Politik*, Vol. 11.

Singh, Udai Bhanu (2000), 'Major powers and the security of Southeast Asia', *Strategic Analysis*, Vol. 24 (2), pp. 315-341.

Soesastro, Hadi (2002), 'Southeast Asia and global terrorism: implication on state security and human security', *The Indonesian Quarterly*, Vol. 30 (1), pp. 31-37.

Stares, P.B., ed. (1998), *The New Security Agenda: A Global Survey*, Tokyo: Japan Center for International Exchange.

Stubbs, Richard (1995), 'Asia-Pacific regionalisation and the global economy: a third form of capitalism', *Asian Survey*, Vol. 35 (9), pp. 785-797.

Tow, William T. and Gray, Richard A. (1995), 'Asia-Pacific security regimes: conditions and constraints', *Journal of Political Science*, Vol. 30, pp. 436-51.

Vasil, Raj (2000), *Governing Singapore: A History of National Development and Democracy*, Singapore: Institute of Southeast Asian Studies.

Zoellick, Robert B. (1998), 'Economics and security in the changing Asia-Pacific', *Survival*, vol. 39 (4), pp. 29-51.

6

Post-Cold War South Asia

Geopolitics and Crisis

PUSHPITA DAS

South Asia, also referred to as the Indian subcontinent, is defined as a contiguous land mass bounded by the Himalayas and its offshoots in the north and the Indian Ocean in the south and constituting about 2 per cent of the global land mass. South Asia comprises seven sovereign states-India, Pakistan, Nepal, Bhutan, Bangladesh, Sri Lanka and Maldives-and occupies an important strategic position vis-à-vis the northern half of the Indian Ocean (Upreti, 2000; 6). A great deal of diversity exists among all these countries in terms of size, population, economic structure, military strength and power. India, by virtue of its overwhelming size (constituting approximately 76 per cent of the total area of the region), population, resources, economic strength, military capability, and technological advancement occupies the dominant position in the Indian sub-continent. Pakistan and Bangladesh are medium-sized countries, Sri Lanka and Nepal are small countries, while Bhutan and Maldives are microstates (Khan, 2002; 8).

Post-Cold War security debates have shifted focus from issues such as traditional nationalism, sovereignty and balance of power to concepts of internationalism and world state (Buzan, 1997). Terrorism, deterioration in the living environment, atrocities, genocide, discriminations of all kinds and civil war between irregular forces with loose chains of command fired by narrow considerations of ethnicity, religion or regionalism (Subramaniun, 2001) are the destructive forces which are posing a considerable threat to humankind in the contemporary world, and the South Asian region is not untouched by these forces, which are proving inimical to the peace and security of the region.

The principal purpose of this chapter is to provide a broad overview of the main elements of concern in terms of the stability of the South Asian region and to flesh out the key considerations which are emerging in the new security agenda. The chapter is organized into six main sections – inter-state relations, democracy in South Asia, ethno-nationalism, the arms race, terrorism and the role of extra-regional powers with particular reference to the United States, Russia and China.

Inter-State Relations — India and Pakistan

The geopolitical situation of South Asia is influenced by two realities. Firstly, South Asia as a region is Indo-centric. India, by virtue of its sheer size, population, resources, economic strength, military capability, and technological advancement enjoys a dominant position in the Indian sub-continent. Moreover, geography has accorded India a central position and it shares its land and maritime boundaries with all six countries of the region, whereas no other country shares its border with each other. India's strength and position acts as a geostrategic pivot safeguarding the independence of the smaller countries and enhancing their status in the international arena (Kak, 2001; 8). Secondly, there exists both cooperation and an environment of mutual suspicion and hostility among the various countries in the region. To some degree, the size and power of India is perceived as a threat to the sovereignty of regional states. This apprehension has its roots in the colonial legacy when India was used a base by the British to extend its colonial influence into the neighbouring kingdoms in the sub-continent. India's dominating presence and its efforts to prevent any extra-regional powers to secure a foothold in the region is viewed as proof of India's hegemonic designs. The other South Asian countries, on the other hand, welcome extra regional powers with a premise that these powers would not only offset the dominant position of India, but would also safeguard their autonomy and identity. India, for its part, expects the other countries to cooperate with each other and keep South Asia free from the politics of the Cold War. India's foreign policy towards its neighbours has been guided by the "Gujral doctrine", which states that while dealing with the smaller states, India should be generous and need not insist on reciprocity of its gestures (Malhotra, 1997; 225). However, the desire of other countries to form partnerships with extra regional powers is viewed with great suspicion by India because if the smallest of states allows its soil to be used as a base by any superpower hostile to India, it would prove inimical to the India's security interests.

The rivalry between the two most important countries of the region, India and Pakistan, is significantly responsible for the situation of crisis, prevalent in South Asia today. This hostility can be traced back to their inception in 1947, when Pakistan was carved out of India based on the principle of the "two-nation" theory. Religion became the basis of nationhood for Pakistan, whereas territoriality formed the principle for India's (Kalayanaraman, 1998; 489). The partitioning and creation of Pakistan proved highly disadvantageous from an Indian point of view. Pakistan posed not only a significant religious/ideological threat but also a territorial threat to India. Ideologically, the creation of Pakistan put pressure on India to create a mechanism to unify its diverse ethnic and cultural communities and also to contain their separatist tendencies. Pakistan, the self appointed guardian of the Indian Muslims, tried to embarrass India in the international arena by highlighting the communal tensions in India and raising doubts about India's ability to safeguard Muslim interests. It also criticised the secular and democratic ethos of India. Coupled with this, Pakistan made extensive territorial claims on India, especially in the Muslim majority State of Jammu and Kashmir. Kashmir came to occupy a very important position in the sub-continental balance of power. India maintains that Kashmir is an integral part of India and the instrument of accession signed in 1947 by Hari Singh, the then Maharajah of Kashmir, and later ratified by the Jammu and Kashmir Constituent Assembly in 1956, is irrevocable. Pakistan challenged India's claim on the grounds that Kashmir is a Muslim majority area, so it should be part of Pakistan. Pakistan tried to wrest Kashmir by force in 1948 and in 1965. Pakistan was instrumental in instigating and fomenting secessionist movements in Kashmir from 1989. Since then, a Pakistan-aided insurgency has been taking place in Kashmir. A crisis situation leading to a conventional war was reached when, in 1999, the militants and foreign mercenaries supported by the Pakistani regular troops occupied the Kargil heights. Pakistan was forced to withdraw its troops from Indian territory and to cease any cross-border infiltration to avert the crisis and maintain peace in the region.

Pakistan's attitude towards India is that of perennial insecurity. India had from the outset rejected the "two-nation" theory propagated by some "insecure Muslim elite" to partition the Indian sub-continent. Pakistan had always been fearful that India would try to "undo" the partition and assimilate Pakistan within its territory (Ashley, 2001, 227). A crisis of identity, insecurity and small power psyche fueled Pakistan's quest for parity in terms of dominance and power position vis-à-vis India. Unable to match India's superior strength in size, economic and military capability, Pakistan devised a foreign policy of forging politico-strategic partnerships with extra regional powers in order to maintain an artificial parity with India. Pakistan's politico-military alliance with other global powers, especially its defense agreements with the United States and the United Kingdom, as well as its time tested friendship with China since 1963, posed an acute security threat for India (Muni, 1980; Jayasuriya, 1987, 157). To offset this security threat, India also entered into a strategic partnership with the Soviet Union by signing the "Treaty of Friendship" in 1971.

From 1963 to 1971 Pakistan embarked on a large-scale militarisation programme. It was in consonance with the firmly held premise that a strategic partnership with global powers and a military strong Pakistan will not only enhance its own power position, but would also guarantee the intervention of the partners in case of any eventuality. The military debacle of 1971, which led to the secession of the east wing of Pakistan and the creation of Bangladesh, forced Pakistan to review its earlier strategy. Pakistani policy-makers realized that it would be quite difficult to defeat India in a conventional war and also that the partners' help might not be forthcoming in a situation of dire need. Pakistan's strategy changed to preserving its territorial integrity and building a sound defence system based on indigenous capabilities and the acquisition of nuclear weapons. It also devised the strategy of supporting insurgent movements in various parts of India and carrying out a "proxy war" through militants and foreign mercenaries in the state of Jammu and Kashmir, causing massive attrition to the defence forces of India in terms of personnel and materials. The hostility between India and Pakistan has at least three major ramifications in the geopolitics of the South Asian region. Firstly, it has resulted in a massive arms race between the two countries leading to the heavy militarisation of the region. Secondly, it has resulted in the increased incidence of cross-border terrorism, thus posing a threat to the security of the region. Last but not least, due to the prevalence of hostility between the two countries, extra regional powers have been able to find a foothold in South Asia.

India and Bangladesh

India-Bangladesh relations are also characterised by cooperation and conflict depending upon which political party is in power in Bangladesh. There was a substantial improvement in ties, for example, when the

Awami League government was in power. India and Bangladesh resolved the 27 years-old Ganga water-sharing problem by signing a 30 year accord in 1996. The problem of the repatriation of the Chakma refugees from the bordering Indian state of Tripura and the insurgency problem in the Chittagong Hill Tracts were also resolved amicably. The illegal migration of Bangladeshis into India in search of a better livelihood has always been a major cause of concern for the Indian government. The recent standoff between the Border Security Force and the Bangladesh Rifles over the issue of the return of the Bangladeshi migrants has led to a crisis situation, straining relations between the two countries. The anti-India feeling fomented by the political parties in Bangladesh to gain political mileage, the use of Bangladeshi soil as a safe heaven by the insurgents of the Northeastern states of India, the cross-border infiltration and illegal migration of Bangladeshis into India, the growing presence of Pakistan's Inter Services Intelligence in Bangladesh and Bangladesh's desire to form a strategic alliance with the United States are some of the irritants in the smooth functioning of Indo-Bangladesh relations.

India and Sri Lanka

India and Sri Lanka share a cordial relationship. The problem of Tamil secessionism in Sri Lanka, however, does place a strain on the relationship between the two countries. Sri Lanka accused India of abetting Tamil insurgency in the country. The signing of the 1987 accord between the two governments marked the beginning of a new relationship with Sri Lanka. India pledged its support to the Sri Lankan government in fighting the insurgency and sent the India Peace Keeping Force to fight the Tamil militants.

India and Nepal

The relationship between India and Nepal is also smooth, barring a few incidents. Issues like river water sharing, border problems, and the increasing use of Nepalese soil by Pakistan's ISI agency for anti-India activities are putting a strain on the cordial relationship between the two states. Nepal's policy of blackmailing India by tilting towards China also causes conflict in relations between the two countries. The question of porous borders and the Maoist insurgency in the Himalayan Kingdom since 1996 are of great concern to both countries.

India and Bhutan

Relations between Bhutan and India are quite cordial, but the use of Bhutanese soil by the insurgents active in the North Eastern states is a potential cause of irritation between the two countries. The alleged persecution of the Bhutanese of Nepalese origin by the Bhutanese Government and the repatriation of 90,000 refugees who took shelter in Nepal is causing conflict in Nepal-Bhutan relations. Moreover, Nepal alleges that these Bhutanese refugees are involved in insurgency.

Democracy in South Asia

The democratic process in the South Asian region is still incipient and struggling. It is hostage to numerous destructive forces such as the excesses of bureaucratic and military regimes, personality cults and the rise of sectarianism, among other things. In the post-Cold War period, the installation of democracy in many of the South Asian countries indicates that it is the most desired form of governance and democratic processes are gradually gaining strength. India, Bangladesh, Nepal and Sri Lanka have democratically elected governments. Maldives has a quasi-democracy; Bhutan is a monarchy, while Pakistan is under a military regime (Khan, 2002). After gaining independence from the British, the six south Asian states have pursued divergent socio-political policies. India tried to accommodate and unite its multi-ethnic, multilingual and multicultural society by evolving and strengthening secular and democratic institutions. While Indian democracy remained vibrant and robust throughout, the other South Asian states, however, took time to incorporate and strengthen democratic institutions.

Pakistan, on the other hand, followed a diametrically opposite policy and tried to unite its diverse population under one religion – that is, Islam. In the initial years, Pakistan experimented with parliamentary democracy, but it always remained feeble and shaky. The vested interests of the military and the landed aristocracy did not allow democracy to take full root in Pakistan. Although Pakistan has been ruled by military regimes for half of its existence, from 1988-99, Pakistan had democratic governments as a result of national elections in 1988, 1990, 1993, and 1997, and it was hoped that democratic institutions would be gradually strengthened. However, this hope was short-lived, as democratically elected governments could not serve their full terms and were dismissed by the President. In October 1999, the government of Prime Minister Nawaz Sharif was overturned in a bloodless coup led by the Chief of Army Staff, Pervez Musharraf, who suspended the parliament and declared himself

Chief Executive. In 2002, parliamentary elections were held and Musharraff become the President of Pakistan (Gupta, 2002; 1).

Democracy in Bangladesh has also had a shaky and slow start. After its liberation in 1971, democratic and secular institutions were established in Bangladesh only to be dismantled a few years later by the powerful military. In 1975, after the assassination of Mujib-ur-Rehman, the military government usurped all state power and declared Bangladesh an Islamic state. The people of Bangladesh, however, became dissatisfied with the military regime of General Ershad, which was overthrown after violent protest. The regular and peaceful holding of general elections over the years has revived people's faith in democracy and democratically elected governments in Bangladesh.

Nepal was ruled by a monarch until the full democratic process was restored in 1990, and the King withdrew to be a constitutional head of the country. However, Nepal's democracy has been threatened by the Maoist movement since 1996, which has put a strain on the democratic process by indulging in terrorist tactics to articulate its demands, and over the past decade more than 13,000 people have been killed. After an awful intra-family murder, and in an apparent response to the Maoist insurgency, in February 2005, the new King Gyanendra dismissed parliament, assumed absolute power and imposed an increasingly severe series of curfews. Subsequent citizen demands for the restoration of democracy resulted in considerable internal unrest. At the time of writing, after three weeks of intense street protests, the King reconvened the dissolved Parliament and asked the mainstream political parties to form an alliance government and to choose a Prime Minister. As a result, the Maoists declared a three-month ceasefire while reaffirming their demand for a new constitution. In addition, the Maoists have engaged in a "loose alliance" with the mainstream political parties and it is not inconceivable that they might even run candidates in the next general election. The interim Prime Minister is likely to be the 84 year-old Girija Prasad Koirala, who is head of the largest political party, the Nepali Congress. However, given the recent history of Nepali democracy, the situation remains somewhat uncertain.

Sri Lanka had a full functioning democracy right from its inception. However, the insurgency movement of the Tamil Tigers and the frequent burst of Sinhalese militancy have overshadowed the democratic processes in the country. These conflicts have restricted the Government's economic reform efforts and polarized political debate. Simultaneously, continued political instability has equally been the result of Tamil militancy. In

Sri Lanka, religious chauvinism, intensified by the corrosive effects of years of civil war, is powerful and erodes the tolerance that is imperative for maintaining the country's democracy.

Maldives was ruled by the sultanate followed by a Presidential system. It is not a true democracy as the Majlis (the National Assembly) consists of nominated or selected representatives (Khan, 2002; 8).

Bhutan is a monarchy. However, there is a growing sense of disenchantment among the public for the monarchy. As Rangthong Kumlay Dorji, chairman of the Druk National Congress, has said in a symposium in New Delhi that."democracy is inevitable in Bhutan, it is just a matter of time" (Nayyar, 2000).

Ethno-Nationalism

The inherent heterogeneity which characterises South Asia is increasingly reflected in divisiveness in many countries of the region. Almost all South Asian states are victims of rising communalism, religious fundamentalism and linguistic and ethnic fanaticism. The forces of ignorance, intolerance and obscurantism are gradually creating a deep chasm in South Asian societies. The rise of ethno-nationalism poses a serious threat to the stability and integrity of the multiethnic, multicultural societies all over the world. In recent years, the lethal mixture of politics and religion, especially religious extremism and fundamentalism have led to the resurgence of ethno-nationalism, which is fracturing the social fabric of South Asian societies (Qadeem, 2002; 211). Domestically, most of the countries have expended significant resources in containing ethnic and religious conflicts which could have been utilised for developmental projects if peace and harmony had prevailed in the society. India, Pakistan and Sri Lanka are perennially engulfed in ethnic, religious, secessionist and political conflicts, while countries like Bhutan and Nepal have to cope with their internal political conflicts (Baral, 2002).

India is home to multi-ethnic and multicultural communities. Since independence, it has often had to grapple with the centrifugal forces generated by these diverse communities which have threatened the territorial integrity of the country. The insurgent movements in the North Eastern states, the secessionist movement by the Tamilians, the Khalistan movement and the independence movement in Kashmir are manifestations of the assertion of the identities of various communities. In recent years, the rise of an extreme right wing Hindu ideology is increasingly coming in conflict with the secular ethos of the country. These groups seek to alter India's traditional vision of an inclusive, liberal and secular polity with a new monocultural vision centered on the so-called Hindutva ideology. To gain political mileage by propagating Hindutva, these groups resort to various tactics such as mobilising interest groups, rewriting history in the textbooks for mass education and attacking minorities (Tellis, 2001; 235).

Pakistan was formed on the concept of the two-nation theory and has imbibed religion as the basis of its nationhood. This, however, has conflicted with the multiethnic character of Pakistan and it has had to grapple with the problem of ethno-nationalism in the province of Sindh, Baluchistan and the Northwest Frontier Province. The ethnic contradiction finally led to the dismemberment of Pakistan in 1971 and the creation of Bangladesh. Over the years, ethnic conflicts between the Pathans, Mohajirs, Sindhis, Baluchis and Punjabis have assumed serious proportions. Apart from ethnic conflict, the rise of Islamic fundamentalism has led to widespread religious intolerance and oppression of the minorities in Pakistan. Since the early 1990s, many Pakistani cities, such as Karachi (the capital of Sindh), have become battlegrounds for rival Islamic sects (the Sunnis versus the Shias), and widespread sectarian violence now perpetually poses a crisis of legitimacy for the ruling Pakistani Government. More than 1,000 people are reported to have been killed in sectarian clashes in several parts of Sindh during 1998 alone, forcing the authorities to repeatedly declare a state of emergency in this strife-torn Province (Bhanot, 2001).

Although Sri Lanka has an impeccable record as far as social development is concerned, it has failed miserably in the development of a modern state (Senanayake, 1999; 3). The ethnic conflict between the Tamils and the indigenous Sinhala population is not only having serious social repercussions but is also posing a threat to the territorial integrity of the country. A growing trend of intolerance coupled with a shift towards sectarianism based on the Sinhala identity is becoming pervasive in Sri Lankan society (Muni, 2002; 36).

The smaller Himalayan kingdoms of Nepal and Bhutan are no longer peaceful. Ethnic conflict in Bhutan between the Lhotshapes (the southern Bhutanese of Nepali origin), the Shanchops and the Drukpa is gradually worsening and putting a strain on the social structure of Bhutan. It is also adversely affecting Bhutan's cordial relations once shared with neighbouring Nepal. Nepal has also to bear the brunt of an intensified Maoist insurgency since 1996, in which nearly 3,000 people lost their lives (Baral, 2002; 188).

The Arms Race in South Asia

The peace and stability of the South Asian region is adversely affected by a number of major wars and minor conflicts between the various countries of the region. The continued hostility between India and Pakistan has led these two countries to fight a couple of wars over the Kashmir issue. There are other intermittent border clashes not only between India and Pakistan but also with other countries of the region. This environment of hostility and conflict is responsible for forcing the countries of the region to launch a programme of weaponisation to safeguard their territorial integrity at all costs. The beginning of the 1990s witnessed further worsening of relations between India and Pakistan because of the escalation of incidences of insurgency and violence by Pakistan-backed militants in the Indian state of Jammu and Kashmir, coupled with the continuing arms race between the two countries to gain an upper hand in terms of both nuclear and conventional weapons. Both India and Pakistan had displayed their willingness to acquire nuclear weapons to have a "credible minimum deterrence" against their respective enemies. The proliferation of nuclear weapons in South Asia is part of a chain of rivalries among China, India and Pakistan. India, in order to achieve deterrence against China, embarked upon a nuclear weapons programme following its defeat in the Sino-India war of 1962 and the nuclear test conducted by China in 1964. Pakistan, on the other hand, aspired to gain equality with India, which was conventionally stronger than it. Its nuclear weapons programme was as a response to its defeat in 1971 at the hands of India and the nuclear testing by India in 1974. In May 11 and 13 1998, India tested four fission bombs and one thermo-nuclear or "hydrogen" bomb after a self-imposed moratorium of 24 years. Despite strong international criticism and censure, Pakistan followed suit and allegedly exploded 5 nuclear devices. India is believed to have enough plutonium for at least 75 nuclear weapons, whereas Pakistan may have enough enriched uranium for 25 nuclear weapons (Gupta, 2002; 10).

The test firing of the Intermediate-Range Ballistic Missile Agni-II, capable of carrying nuclear warheads up to a distance of 2,500 kms, by India, further heightened the nuclear arms race in the Indian sub-continent, which became quite apparent by Pakistan response. Pakistan also test fired the long range Ghauri-II and short range Shaheen missiles in order to obtain parity with India, and foil its so called "aggressive designs" (Cherian, 1999). The Agni was first developed in the mid-to-late 1980s and tested in 1994. After a gap of four years, following the test firing of the Hatf-III missile by Pakistan, the programme was revived in April

1997. In addition to Agni, India has the Prithvi series of short-range missiles, a submarine-launched ballistic missile, the Sagarika, and a 12,000-kilometer range developed on the lines of the Soviet SA-2 surface-to-air missile. India is reportedly developing an intercontinental ballistic missile, the Surya. In the 1980s, to counter India's Prithvi series of short-range missiles, Pakistan, with the active assistance of China, started developing the Hatf series of short-range missiles. To counter India's long-range missiles, again Chinese assistance was obtained. In September 1993, China provided Pakistan with the components of M-11 missiles. In February 1996, it was reported by the Washington Post, that, in 1995, China sold ring magnets to Pakistan which are used for enriching uranium for developing nuclear weapons (Gupta, 2002, 11). As an answer to India's intermediate range ballistic missiles, Pakistan has developed the Ghauri and Shaheen series of missiles, which would enable Pakistan to strike targets in India. It is widely suspected that whereas the Shaheen might be a copy of the Chinese M-9 missile, the Ghauri is apparently based on the North Korean Nodong missiles, and that a transfer of completed missiles from the DPRK probably took place (Carnegie Endowment for International Peace; 1999).

The unfolding of subsequent events in the subcontinent has affirmed that the nuclearisation process in South Asia has not been able to achieve cordial bilateral relations between India and Pakistan. Initially, the holding of the 10th SAARC summit in Colombo, the bus diplomacy and the signing of the Lahore Declaration displayed an improvement in the relationship between the two countries. The rapprochement was shattered by the Kargil war, which was followed by the return of the military regime in Pakistan in 1999. The Kargil war also shattered the myth that nuclearisation would end the possibility of any conventional war between the two countries. There is also a substantial rise in the defence spending on conventional weapons of not only these two countries but also among other countries of the règion as well. The arms race in the South Asian region is having a negative impact not only on peace and stability but is also causing a strain on the bilateral and multilateral relations among the countries of the region.

Terrorism and South Asia

Terrorism is neither culture nor region specific. It does not recognise any boundaries and any state or region is vulnerable to terrorism attacks (Baral and Mohanty; 2002, 508). It is quite evident that the threats of terrorism have also transcended the boundaries of South Asia and today almost all of its countries have to cope with terrorism of differing forms and hues. The inherent ethnic, cultural and religious diversities in South Asia have always been a cause of instability and turbulence in the politics of the region. Apart from this, the socio-economic and political problems prevalent in South Asia are the root causes of the emergence and perpetuation of terrorism in the region. The relinquishment of a secular ethos and the embracement of sectarianism based on religious and ethnic identity by most South Asia states has seriously disturbed internal social cohesion and political harmony. It has instilled a sense of fear and desperation in the minds of the marginalised minorities and has generated intolerance and violence between both the dominant and the neglected communities. Over the years, different ethnic communities have asserted their identities, articulated their demands and vented their dissatisfaction against the state through various violent modes.

In Sri Lanka, the Liberation Tigers of Tamil Eelam (LTTE) launched a separatist movement demanding a separate state for the Tamil population of Sri Lanka. In India, religion became the main driving force behind the secessionist movements in Punjab and Kashmir. Poverty, hunger, unemployment and the dismal state of economic growth coupled with bad governance, which perpetuates underdevelopment, sowed the seeds of discontent among the general masses. Many violent movements, like the Maoist movement in Nepal, are a manifestation of deep-rooted economic problems of underdevelopment. The insensitivity of the government towards the grievances of the people, coupled with delayed and insufficient action and often ruthless suppression of any form of public protest by the government paved the way for the rise of militancy and secessionism in many states of India.

The violent form of protest, however, cannot sustain itself for long and the militants gradually lose mass appeal. To sustain their movement, the leadership of the insurgent movements then turn towards external agencies, which provide them with economic and political support. In South Asia, many countries have aided and abetted terrorism among their neighbours to achieve certain strategic goals against each other (Muni, 2002; 37). That is why the border areas have become a familiar arena for terrorism in most of these countries and terrorist groups operating in a particular country have links with ideologically similar groups active in the neighbouring country. Pakistan's sympathy towards the Khalistan movement and Kashmir's self determination movement and its support to cross-border terrorism against India are quite well known in this regard. The Inter Services Intelligence of Pakistan, notorious for supporting cross-border terrorism, has found a comfortable base in Nepal and Bangladesh. Bangladesh also shelters and encourages many Indian extremist groups which are active in the Northeastern states of India. Bhutan is trying to cope with the violent Nepali uprising that is suspected of being supported by Nepal. It, in turn, is known to be providing safe haven for the insurgent groups of Northeast India, especially the United Liberation Front of Assam (ULFA) and Bodo militants. India, on the other hand, has been blamed for supporting Tamil militancy in Sri Lanka (Muni, 2002).

Contemporary South Asia has to grapple with the challenges of cross-border terrorism, religious extremism and small arms proliferation, which is financed by narcotics trafficking. The recent trend indicates, with the shift in the area of operation from west Asia to South Asia, that terrorism is becoming more religiously or ideologically motivated rather than being politically oriented (Kapil, 2001; 9). Today, Afghanistan-Pakistan has become the "epicentre of terrorism" in the region. The root cause of religious extremism and terrorism in this region can be traced back to the Cold War politics. The extra-regional powers, especially the United States, are responsible for abetting and exploiting fundamentalist groups to pursue their own global strategic interests in this region. To gain an upper hand in the war of ideologies, Islamic fundamentalists have been pitted against the communists, by making Pakistan a "frontline state" against Soviet expansionism. In Pakistan, successive militarily regimes provided patronage to the religious extremist groups with a view to gaining a political constituency, whereas the religious parties found it expedient to support the military regimes to gain political mileage. With the tacit approval from the United States, the Pakistan government created a widespread infrastructure for the spread of fundamentalism (Qadir, 2002; 14). Thousands of *madarasas* imparting military training on Pakistani soil were used by the United States for propagating *jihad* (holy war) and for training thousands of Afghanis and other volunteers from all over the world in the name of religion, supporting the faith of Islam against the atheistic, anti-religious policies of the USSR. Most brought with them ideas and tactics learned elsewhere, and, in some cases, that included hatred and terrorism (Eastham, 2000). The erstwhile Soviet Union and the United States left Afghanistan after the end of the Cold War, but the Mujahideens, which came from all over the world, did not return to their respective countries. Their plan of action shifted from Afghanistan to various other areas such Kashmir, Chechnya, Bosnia, Xinjiang and elsewhere. In addition, these Mujhahideens found a benevolent patron in Pakistan.

The terrorist attack on United States on September 9 2001 has led to the redefining of terrorism. It is defined as "premeditated, politically-motivated violence perpetrated against non-combatant targets by sub-national groups or clandestine agents usually intended to influence an audience" (Pillar, 2001). In this definition of terrorism, secessionist movements embracing violence are no longer categorised as freedom movements, nor does it holds the state responsible for being the cause of terrorism. Keeping this in mind, the strategy adopted by the United States was to attack countries and regimes supporting and abetting international terrorism. It launched a massive programme named "Operation Enduring Freedom" with an aim to fight terrorism. It zeroed in on Afghanistan as the main centre for terrorism in the world. The Al Qaeda Chief, Osama bin Laden, and his host, the Taliban regime, were declared as the enemies of the United States. India and Pakistan, along with the entire world, condemned the terrorist attacks on the United States. Yet again, because of its geostrategic importance, Pakistan was made the "frontline state" for the fight against terrorism in Afghanistan. The United States offered many concessions to Pakistan for the help it extended for the fight against terrorism. Apart from a change in regime in Afghanistan, nothing substantial has resulted from the "Operation Enduring Freedom". Today, Islamic fundamentalism is becoming an integral part of the politics of Pakistan, which is manifested in the increasing intra-Islamic sectarian riots within the country and jihad against India, in the state of Jammu and Kashmir. Pakistan has nearly 40,000 to 50,000 *madarasas* imparting military training. There is an estimated enrollment of 1 to 2 million students belonging to the *Wahabi* militant Muslim sub-sect. There are around 2,000,000 armed jihadis, which is equal to one third of the 6,000,000-strong Pakistani army (Satish, 2003; 233). Pakistan is exporting these jehadis to wage a proxy war against India in the state of Jammu and Kashmir. It is also courting the leaders of various Islamic fundamentalist leaders like Azhar Masood and Osama bin Laden.

The spread of terrorism had undermined the democratic political structure of South Asia – for example, the virtual collapse of representative government in Nepal, the strain it has placed on the smooth functioning of democracy in Sri Lanka, the invoking of a state of emergency in various states of the Indian sub-continent and the adoption of stringent anti-terrorist acts like POTA by India. Terrorism has also contributed to the increasing communalisation of society and the growth of reactionary right wing politics in the region. It has also had an adverse effect on the economic development of regional states. Many South Asian states have to bear the heavy economic costs in terms of destruction of economic infrastructure, a loss of confidence in the economy, the inability to attract foreign investment, enhanced military expenditure and high transaction costs, all leading to a reduction in economic activity (Dubey, 2003).

Entwined with menace of terrorism, South Asian countries are experiencing a serious issue of the proliferation of small arms and light weapons. This proliferation is linked to the heightened incidence of gun culture associated with the insurgent movements, sectarian violence, organized crime and political movements in the subcontinent. The Afghanistan crisis resulted in a heavy influx of small arms and light weapons in the region, which later got diverted to the other South Asian countries, particularly Pakistan and India. In Sri Lanka, The LTTE and other insurgent groups are acquiring arms from international black markets, and in Nepal, with the growing strength of the Maoist movement, there is a growing demand for small arms and light weapons. The growing incidence of insurgent and terrorist activities is transforming other South Asian countries like Bangladesh, Nepal and Bhutan from a conduit of small arms and weapons to end users of them. In order to contain this growing menace of the proliferation of small arms and light weapons, a south-led organization-South Asian Partnership (SAP) – has been established to form a network for sharing information about the small arms and light weapons among member states ((Arputharaj, 2001).

The Role of Extra-regional Powers in South Asian Geopolitics

The geopolitical concerns of the South Asian region go beyond its geographical boundaries and encompass not only the superpowers but also the adjacent lands – such as Central and West Asia, Afghanistan, China, Southeast Asia, Myanmar and the Indian Ocean rim-which are intimately connected to South Asia by culture, geography, religion and trade. China, with its massive economic and military strength, is the most powerful neighbour and has a significant influence on the geopolitics of South Asia. Due to its rivalry and a long-standing border dispute with India, China presents a challenge to the long-term strategic security of the region. Afghanistan, which witnessed a civil war for decades, has been a major theatre of Cold War politics and a breeding ground for Islamic fundamentalism. The negative impulses emanating from Afghanistan adversely impact on the stability and security of the adjoining areas. Central Asia, with its vast natural oil and gas reserves, is increasingly becoming a hotspot of international power politics. The presence of the Russian Federation in close proximity with the South Asian region and the pockets of US influence in the form of US satellite countries and the presence of a naval fleet in the Indian Ocean, all are factors which play an important role in shaping the geopolitical future of South Asia (Malhotra, 1997, 223).

The regional politics of the Indian subcontinent instrumental in inviting extra-regional powers, namely the United States, the erstwhile Soviet Union and China into the region. The role of these extra-regional powers in shaping the geopolitics of the region, over the years, is quite apparent. The hostility between India and Pakistan forced them to pursue diametrically opposite foreign policies. India, after gaining independence, was anxious not only to safeguard its territorial integrity but also to keep the South Asian region away from the politics of Cold War. It, therefore, imbibed nonalignment as the core principle of its foreign policy – that is, maintaining equidistance from both superpowers and not getting drawn into the rivalry between the two superpowers.

The US Factor in South Asia

The relationship between Pakistan and United States is an outcome of Cold War politics and South Asian regional politics of the 1950s. The United States, along with other Western countries, welcomed the creation of Pakistan. The strategic location of Pakistan in close proximity to the oil-rich Middle East and the communist Soviet Union and China made it the most viable country for the United States to transform into its satellite to contain Communism in South Asia. Pakistan, on the other hand, always strived to alter the status quo in the region and to gain parity with India. Unable to match the size, population, resources, economic and military capabilities and other technological advancement, Pakistan devised the foreign policy of seeking diplomatic support and economic and military assistance from extra-regional powers, especially the United States, which would not only enhance Pakistan's pursuit of gaining parity with India, but would also support Pakistan and intervene militarily on its behalf in case of any threat from India (Burke and Lawrence, 1990). Pakistan's geostrategic position, adjacent to the Soviet Union's soft underbelly and its willingness to forge ties with United States, led the two countries to negotiate a mutual defence assistance agreement. The incorporation of Pakistan into the Western alliance of SEATO and CENTO brought the Cold War to the doorstep of South Asia.

The failure of the United States to support the Pakistani cause, and the suspension of arms transfers to both Pakistan and India during the Indo-Pakistan wars of 1965 and 1971, soured the relationship between the two countries. Moreover, Pakistan's efforts to possess nuclear arms, as a response to India's underground nuclear explosion in 1974, further deteriorated their ties. It was the differing security perception between the two countries that led to the strains in their relationship. The Soviet invasion of Afghanistan in December 1979 provided an opportunity for the United States and Pakistan to renew their ties. The United States again acknowledged the importance of Pakistan to counter Soviet designs in the South Asian region. Pakistan was made the frontline state in the fight against Soviet expansionism and millions of dollars of security and economic aid were given to Pakistan by the US administration.

The end of the Cold War and the disintegration of the Soviet Union ended the importance of Pakistan as a key ally of the United States to combat the USSR. Consequently, United States policy interest towards Pakistan changed. It was no longer guided by the sole purpose of containing communism in the region but by a wider range of issues such as nuclear and missile proliferation, stability in the South Asian region, democracy and human rights issues, economic and market opportunities and efforts to counter terrorism and narcotics. The post-Cold War period in the 1990s saw a weakening in the relationship between the two countries. Pakistan's acquisition of nuclear arms, its support to cross border terrorism, the "Kargil adventurism" and the overthrow of its democratically elected government attracted many stringent economic and military sanctions from the United States. What these developments demonstrate is that, just as Iraq had become expendable and a war with Iraq facilitated the US to militarily move into the Middle East, Pakistan seems to have become dispensable, and, if the US can move in there it can have a direct eye on not just India, but China and Russia; besides Iran and Central Asia with its rich resources. The Pakistan-USA see-saw relationship has been on an upswing following Pakistan's enlistment as a frontline state in the US-led war on terrorism resulting from the September 2001 attacks on New York and Washington.

As far as India is concerned, the Unites States has been trying to forge closer relations with India in the post-Cold War era. It described India as a "responsible power" and praised India's restraint during the Kargil conflict of 1999. India is fast emerging as a major regional power. The United States has also ordered Pakistan to stop cross-border terrorism in India and to dismantle all infrastructure which helped facilitate and sustain Islamic fundamentalism. The United States has also shown considerable willingness to forge a strategic partnership with India with a view to counter balance the growing Chinese influence in the region. India, on the other hand, has displayed its desire to have friendly relations with the United States. India was one of the first countries to denounce the September terrorist attacks on the United States and also offered its military bases to the United States to carry on "Operation Enduring Freedom". It has also tried to impress upon the United States that it has been a victim of terrorism for more than two decades. Unfortunately, India did not quite fit in to the strategic calculations of the United States. It has given no more than lip service to the Indian Government regarding its assurance that Pakistan will stop all cross-border terrorism, especially in the states of Jammu and Kashmir. The United States has also censured India for talking about using force against Pakistan by drawing parallels with the Iraq's invasion. It could be argued that bilateral relations between India and United States have a long way to go.

On the other hand, however, the emergence of India as the greatest global consumer market and also of inexpensive skilled labour is attracting US investors in this region. Geo-economics is thus likely to become an increasingly important factor in the relationship. India has always been a dominating power in this region and has been traditionally opposed to any extra-regional influence in sub-continental politics. It has made efforts to maintain extra-regional influences outside the ambit of the subcontinent to safeguard its own interests. It has stressed the finding of solutions to vexing problems without the interference of any outside power. It has tried to dissuade any country in the region to form a partnership with the superpowers. Thus, to counterbalance the US-Pakistan partnership, it had to forge a bilateral and military partnership with the USSR. However, with the disintegration of Soviet Union, India lost a reliable friend. The successor Russian state showed less enthusiasm in supporting India's causes in international fora like Kashmir and regarding a permanent seat in the Security Council. The emergence of the United States as the sole superpower in the post-Cold War period, however, compelled India to look towards the USA. It has been observed that the Indian Government is not averse to forming bilateral and strategic ties with the United States. India's greater reliance on United States' intervention in sub-continental matters as unwittingly inviting the United States has to be viewed with skepticism. Its appeal to the United States to pressurise Pakistan to stop cross-border terrorism in Kashmir and resume a meaningful dialogue with India can be described as unwittingly inviting the United States to have a greater say in the geopolitics of the South Asian region. The US military presence in Pakistan and Afghanistan has further provided the United States with the additional power to extend its influence in this region vis-à-vis other powers. This might also prove a cause of apprehension and tension in the region in the future. India as an aspiring regional power might thus find its pre-eminent position in this region undermined by the US presence.

In the present situation, the United States' intervention in eliminating the vestiges of Taliban and Al Qaeda nexus was welcomed. The US presence was viewed as necessary for the peace and stability of the region until a stable and popular government is firmly established in Afghanistan. The US interest in the acquisition and control of strategic resources, especially oil and natural gas in this region, is not unknown to the world. The persistence of the US military presence might be viewed as a means to advance its geo-strategic ambitions in this region by the other global and regional powers causing tensions in future years. However, the recent recognition by the United States of India as a nuclear power clearly represents the beginnings of a shift in the relationship.

The Russian Factor in South Asia

With the end of the Cold War, Russia had to come to terms with its modified status as a new nation-state instead of a superpower. Its continued search for a national identity in the international arena has made Russia, as a successor state of the erstwhile Soviet Union, devise new ways to interact with the countries of the former USSR. Its failure to prevent the eastward expansion of NATO also reduced its regional sphere of influence. Faced with this changed situation, Russia tried to compensate its loss of sphere of influence by gaining a strategic depth through forging strategic partnerships with China and India (Srivastava, 1999).

The India-Russia friendship has withstood the vagaries of the ever-changing international geo-political situation. In the initial years, the Soviet government did not appreciate India's commitment to the principle of the non-aligned movement and was hesitant to form any close friendship with India. However, the growing US-Pakistan partnership provided an opportunity for both India and the Soviet Union to reassess their impressions of each other. The signing of the "Treaty of Friendship" by India and the Soviet Union in 1971 was a cornerstone in the everlasting friendship between the two countries. The Indo-Soviet friendship has provided the much-needed strategic balance vis-à-vis the US-Pakistan partnership in the South Asian region. The Soviet Union and India have forged a close military partnership and today Russia is one of the most important suppliers of military hardware to India. Almost 60 per cent of the Indian army's military hardware, 70 per cent of its naval hardware, and 80 per cent of air force hardware is of Soviet/Russian origin (Srivastava, 1999). The defence cooperation between India and Russia augmented India's defence system quite appreciably. With the end of the Cold War, the equation has changed dramatically. India started looking for a greater alliance with the United States and other Western countries, and, as far as Russia is concerned, China rather than India has become more important. However, Russia has acknowledged India as an important regional power and has shown its willingness to upgrade its friendly relationship to that of "strategic relations". India on its part needs Russia for supplying it with military hardware, technological cooperation and the peaceful use of atomic energy and outer space. The convergence of interests regarding the threat from Islamic fundamentalism to both countries emanating from Afghanistan has also reinforced the need for a mutually beneficial partnership between the two countries (Dixit, 2000).

The China Factor in South Asia

China, in pursuance of its desire to be a global power, had embarked upon a policy of massive modernisation, both in the military and economic field. Consequently, with the end of the Cold War and the disintegration of the Soviet Union, it emerged as a potential and alternate power to the Soviet Union in the global scene. China, by virtue of its location as neighbour to many South Asian states, has registered a significant presence in the geo-politics of the sub-continent over the years. China's relation with the countries of the subcontinent is primarily guided by its desire to contain India, which has the potential to challenge the Chinese desire to see itself as an important power in the subcontinent. China, to undermine the dominant position of India in the subcontinent started cultivating friendships with countries which are hostile to India, especially Pakistan and Myanmar. The Chinese relationship with other countries of South Asia was not very close. However, it cultivates a friendship with Nepal and Bangladesh so long as they serve its interest in containing India.

China and India shared an initial cordial relationship, based on the principles of Panchsheel. Their relationship began to deteriorate as a result of heightened border disputes and came to an acrimonious end following the Sino-Indian war of 1962. After a freeze for many decades, relations between India and China gradually started thawing in the 1980s and in the 1990s. The normalising of relations between the two countries led India and China to sign two agreements in 1993 and 1996, to "maintain peace and tranquility along the border" and to strive to develop "confidence building measures along the LAC". A continuation of better relations with China was displayed during the Kargil war between India and Pakistan when China took a neutral stand. It also changed its earlier stand of supporting Pakistan's cause for Kashmir and has emphasised that the Kashmir problem should be solved bilaterally between India and Pakistan.

Pakistan, on the other hand, shared a mutually beneficial friendship with China for over three decades. Even though the first contact between China and Pakistan took place during the Bandung Conference in 1955, the real friendship started after the Sino-India war of 1962. Pakistan's neutral, if not pro-Chinese, stand in the war of 1962 and the United States' offer to provide military aid to India instilled a feeling of betrayal in the minds of Pakistan which led it to turn to China as an ally in the South Asian region (Bhutto, 1963). Pakistan started relying on China to alter the balance of power in the Indian subcontinent. China, on the other hand, felt that, in view of Pakistan's disenchantment with United States, its deteriorating relations with the Soviet Union and the presumed convergence of Soviet-American interests in the sub-continent in favour of India, Pakistan could not only be used as an instrument against India but it would help China to gain substantial leverage against India in the Indian sub-continent. The convergence of mutual interests between Pakistan and China resulted in the flourishing of long-term and fruitful friendship between the two countries (Simon, 1967; 177). The China-Pakistan alliance proved to be militarily quite beneficial for Pakistan and detrimental to the peace and security of the South Asian region. China not only provided diplomatic support to Pakistan for Kashmir's cause but also became a major arms supplier for Pakistan. China not only helped Pakistan built its conventional armoury but also provided it with the technology and components for building nuclear arms.

In a world where South Asia is facing the menace of terrorism, China's supply of conventional and nuclear arms to Pakistan cannot but be viewed with great trepidation. Pakistan's hand in harbouring and fomenting religious fundamentalism and terrorism is a well-known fact. Post-9/11, the larger and more horrifying dimension of these transfers became more apparent, most notably, the possibility of the re-transfer of these lethal weapons and technologies via Pakistan to the Islamic fundamentalists.

China's relationship with other South Asian countries, namely Nepal, Bhutan and Bangladesh, is primarily aimed at weakening India's influence on these countries and making India vulnerable. Nepal, sandwiched between India and China, periodically tried to develop friendly relations with China to offset the dominating influence of India. China was more than willing to extend its support for the Nepalese cause against India. Unlike India, which supported democracy in Nepal, China always sided with the Nepalese royalty. It provided Nepal with both economic and military aid. A Chinese hand is suspected in the Maoist insurgency in Nepal which was launched to undermine the democratic processes in Nepal. China also tried to forge close relations with Bangladesh.

Conclusion

In the post-Cold War era, South Asia has emerged as a geo-political zone of conflict and has succeeded in attracting a great deal of attention from all over the world. Both its past and present socio-political tensions, such as strained bilateral relations between countries, rising ethno-nationalism, terrorism, weak democratic institutions, political violence, nuclear threats and underdevelopment, all have not only kept the region but also the global powers on tenterhooks. In the contemporary world, globalisation and liberalisation are the two most important phenomena which are shaping the future course of world politics. Today, it is the market forces, which are dictating the direction of interstate relationships in a significant manner. The South Asian region, with its massive population resource and vibrant economy, is fast emerging as an important consumer market. This region has the potential of attracting large-scale foreign investment in all sectors, which, in the long-term may well make this region's economy one of the most vibrant in the world. Unfortunately, the South Asian region is plagued by a socio-economic and political crisis. Large-scale underdevelopment and political unrest prove detrimental to any economic investment. It is necessary that all regional states should make an effort to provide a conducive environment for the growth of economic activities, which will usher in greater prosperity to this area. SAARC is one such platform, which not only facilitates greater interaction among member countries but also provides guidelines for working together for the betterment of the region. It is therefore, imperative to strengthen such institutions so that peace and prosperity prevails in this region.

REFERENCES

Arputharaj, James W. (2001), 'The crisis in South Asia', *Frontline*, Volume 18-Issue 18, Sep. 1-14.

Ashley, J. Tellis (2001), 'South Asia', *The National Bureau of Asian Research*, at http://strategicasia.nbr.org/Report/pdf/ShowReportPDF.aspx?ID=6&f=1

Baral, J.K. and Mohanty, J.N. (2002), 'The US War Against Terrorism: Implications for South Asia', *Strategic Analysis*, Vol. 26, no. 4, Oct-Dec.

Baral, Lok Raj (2002), 'Emerging Social Dimensions and SAARC in the Twenty

First Century', in Dipanker Banerjee (ed.), "SAARC in the Twenty First Century, Towards a Cooperative Future", New Delhi: Indian Research Press.

Bhanot, Monica (2001), 'Order, Welfare and Legitimacy in the Regional Context of South Asia: An Ultima Thule', *Regional Center for Strategic Studies*, at http://www.rcss.org/policy_studies/ps_14.html

Bhutto, Z.A. (1963), As Foreign Minister made a detailed statement to this effect in Pakistan's national Assembly. See national *Assembly of Pakistan's Debates*, Vol. 2 (Part II), 17 May.

Burke, S.M, and Ziring Lawrence (1990), *Pakistani Foreign Policy: An Historical Analysis, ed.2*, Karachi: Oxford University Press.

Buzan Barry (1997), 'Rethinking Security After the Cold War', in *Cooperation and Conflict*, Vol. 32, no.1, pp. 23-27.

Carnegie Endowment for International Peace (1999), South Asian missile race, Non Proliferation Fact Sheet, Carnegie Endowment for International Peace April 15 (http://www.ceip.org/programs/npp/factsheet3.htm)

Cherian, J. (1999), 'The Arms Race', *The Hindu*, Volume 16-Issue 9, Apr. 24-May. 07, at (http://www.frontlineonnet.com/fl1609/16090230.htm)

Dixit, J.N. (2000), 'The Putin Dividend', *The Indian Express*, Thursday, October 5, at http://www.indianexpress.com/ie/daily/20001005/ied05031.html

Dubey, Muchkund (2003), 'Anatomy of terrorism in South Asia—I', *The Hindu*, Jan 01, at http://meadev.nic.in/opn/2003jan/1hin.htm

Eastham, A.W. (2000), Principal Deputy Assistant Secretary of State's South Asia Bureau, testified July 12 before the Houe International Relations Committee on the "new locus of global terrorism in South Asia." *Washington Files*, 12 July, at http://usinfo.state.gov/topical/pol/terror/00071302.htm

Gupta, A. (2002), 'Pakistan-U.S. Relations', Issue Brief for Congress, (Congressional Research Service, The Library of Congress), June 4, p. 1, at (http://fpc.state.gov/documents/organization/11073.pdf)

Jayasurya, P.S. (1987), *India's National Security and Foreign Policy*, New Delhi: ABC Publishing House.

Kak, Kapil (2001), 'Geo-Strategic Realities of South Asia", *World Focus,* Special Issue, October.

Kalayanaraman (1998), 'Operation Parakaram: An Indian Exercise in coercive Diplomacy', in *Strategic Analysis*, Vol. 26, No. 4, Oct-Dec.

Khan, Abdur Rob (2002), 'Interfacing Traditional and Non-Traditional Security: Views from South Asia', 11-12, September, at http://www.utdt.edu/cci/papers/papers seguridad/Rob per cent20Khan. pdf

Kumar, Satish (2003), 'Reassessing Pakistan as a Long Term Security Threat', *Strategic Digest*, Vol. 33, no. 3, March.

Malhotra, Inder (1997), 'Security Issues in Southern Asia', *Strategic Analysis*, vol. 20(2), May.

Mossarat Qadeem (2002), 'Cultural Development in South Asian Society', in Dipanker Banerjee, ed., *SAARC in the Twenty First Century, Towards a*

Cooperative Future, New Delhi: Indian Research Press.

Muni, S.D. (1980), 'South Asia', in Mahmmmed Ayoob, ed., *Conflict and Intervention in the Third World*, London: Oxford Publications, pp. 38-77.

Muni, S.D. (2002), 'Challenges of terrorism in South Asia', *South Asian Politics*, Vol. 1, May.

Pillar, Paul. R. (2001), 'Terrorism and US Foreign Policy', Brookings Institute Study, as quoted in S.D. Muni, 2002, p. 35.

Qadir, Shaukat (2002), 'Threats of Religious Extremism in Pakistan and India,', *South Asia Politics*, Vol. 2, June.

Senanayake, Darini Rajasingham (1999), 'Democracy and The problem of representation: The Making of Bi-Polar Ethnic Identity in Post Colonial Sri Lanka', in Joanna Pfaff-Czarnecka, et al., "*Ethnic Futures: The State and Identity Politics in Asia*", New Delhi: Sage Publications.

Simon, S.W. (1967), 'The Kashmir Dispute in Sino-Soviet Perspective', *Asian Survey*, Vol. 7, no. 3, March.

Srivastava, Anupam (1999), 'Indo-Russian Military Technical Cooperation: Implications for Southern Asia', *Iron Eagle Menu, Spring,* 1999, at (http://iron-eagles.tripod.com/articles/indorus_coopera2.htm)

Subramaniun Vidya (2001), 'Black Tuesday and After', *The Times of India*, 12 September.

Upreti, B.C. (2000), 'SAARC: Dynamics of regional Cooperation in South Asia, Vol. II, Areas and Dimensions of Cooperation', New Delhi: Kalinga Publications.

7

India's Security Concerns

Post-9/11 Era

D. Gopal

Some five centuries ago, Niccolo Machiavelli wrote in his masterpiece, *The Prince*:

> Political disorder is like a wasting disease: to start with it is easy to cure but difficult to diagnose; after a time, unless it has been diagnosed and treated at the outset, it becomes easy to diagnose but difficult to cure (Mansfield, 1998; 134).

Nothing could be more apt a description of the current international security scenario and the myriad of issues arising out of it which impact on nation-states across the world. Surprisingly perhaps, the international community in the past has failed to correctly diagnose international terrorism and adequately evolve an appropriate mechanism to meet the challenges. Today, as frustrated individual nation-states take unilateral action and administer questionable policy measures, purported to restore order, international terrorism has acquired an even more critical dimension and intensity.

Given the magnitude of international terrorism in recent years, especially since the tragic events of 11 September 2001 (commonly referred to as the 9/11 event), there is no gainsaying that a new diagnostic approach to unravel the complexity of international terrorism has become critically imperative. Even a cursory glance at the recent incidence of international terrorism suggests the complexity of the phenomenon. Given that terrorist activity sprouts from the existence of an aggrieved group, the events of 9/11 have forced governments all over the world to reevaluate their threat perceptions and policies. So much so, it is now recognized that non-state actors such as the terrorist groups are to be treated as part of the international system. Admittedly, this is a departure from the traditional international security framework where nation-states alone were viewed as the main actors in an anarchic environment.

It is against these transformative changes in the international security framework that an attempt is made here firstly to sketch a brief overview of the global security situation since 9/11 and then to identify the security threats that India faces in the current global environment. A detailed examination will be made of the magnitude and dimensions of these threats to the country's national security and the current debate on possible policy options will be highlighted to meet the country's security challenges, including bilateral initiatives with Australia.

Emerging Parameters of Global Security

Unlike in the past, in what used to be described as the 'realist' world, when security threats and concomitant international interactions have largely been the concern of nation-states, in the present-day global order, terrorist groups (either with the tacit or covert support of a state), non-governmental organisations and religious groups, along with traditional main actors such as nation-states, have come into the foreground, influencing a state's security doctrine and policies. In turn, this has necessitated a metamorphic change in the way the concept of security is defined to encompass the newer threats and at the same time identify the relevant actors. Consequently, national security concerns have transcended its narrow military confines to include environmental disasters, large-scale human migration, refugee spills over international boundaries and even epidemics. One widely-acknowledged approach to deal with these security concerns is what is called 'human security'. Human security, as enunciated by the United Nations:

> "...can be said to have two main aspects. It means, first, safety from such chronic threats as hunger, disease and repression. And second, it means protection from sudden and hurtful disruptions in the patterns of daily life—whether in homes, in jobs or in communities" (UNDP, 1994; 23).

The occurrences of these security threats and their causes have in no way lessened the conflicts that arise out of traditional sources. Rather, dealing with traditional threats has now become more complicated, given the array of newer threats to human security. What is more, the resurgence of religious fundamentalism and its intersection with terrorism and other insurgencies, some of which are covertly sponsored by nation-states, has compounded the threats to national security. Therefore, on what constitutes a national security threat, as one observer puts it, is:

> "...an action or a sequence of events that (1) threatens drastically and over a relatively brief period of time to degrade the quality of life for the inhabitants of a state, or (2) threatens significantly to narrow the range of policy choices available to a state or to private non-governmental entities (persons, groups, corporations) within the state" (Ullman, 1983, 133).

Admittedly, such an approach offers scope for dealing with both traditional and non-traditional security threats. Environmental degradation, refugee outflows and demographic explosions can cause competition for scarce resources, resulting in violence, internal political and social disorder which erupts into civil strife and wars, often along ethnic lines. In turn, resulting civil wars cause further damage to the environment and accentuate problems of refugee spills and attendant epidemics and hunger. Outbreak of diseases such as HIV/AIDS and SARS (Sudden Acute Respiratory Syndrome) not only cripple the economy but also cause havoc on the socio-political fabric of a region or of a state.

While these are the direct consequences of the currently witnessed processes of globalisation, advances in modern technology, especially in respect of communication and transport, have facilitated terrorist groups to plan and launch acts of violence across the world with funds transferred for these dastardly activities through a variety of labyrinthine networks as evidenced in the 9/11 events. In many of these instances, the governments and their law enforcement agencies do not have the necessary means and capacity to meet these challenges (see, for example, Homer-Dixon, 1992; Weiner, 1992; Rudolph, 2003; Curley and Thomas, 2004). These apart, forces of economic globalisation are already impinging adversely on the welfare and employment opportunities for the larger segment of the population, leading to socio-economic upheavals in the less developed countries of the world.

Under these critical circumstances, nation-states perforce have to take policy initiatives not only to meet the new challenges, posed by the inexorable forces of globalisation, but also to enunciate policy prescriptions that anticipate security threats rather than merely react to them. In the past, security forces and law enforcement agencies of nation-states have largely been trained to meet traditional security threats whether it is by repelling territorial aggression or investigating criminal activities. However, at present, given the new security threats, the structure, training and objectives of these state institutions need to be modified. This does not mean that traditional security threats can be ignored. Instead, these institutions need to be equipped with the necessary capabilities to deal with the new security threats as well. Cross-border or international terrorism has to be dealt with by the security forces, which necessarily call for additional training and equipment. Or, special task forces will have to be put in place to meet these unconventional threats (Scholte, 2000).

Improving the security forces and creating mechanisms towards this end are just one response. At the same time, on a broader global level, some kind of a consensus among nation-states is called for in order to respond to the myriad threats, which transcend nation-state boundaries. After all, in recent years, some of the regions in the world such as the north-western regions in South Asia and northeastern parts of Africa became havens for terrorist groups from where they expanded their clandestine criminal activities, ranging from dispensing funds to drug-trafficking and trade. To deal with these threats, some kind of consensual norms of intervention, among nation-states, had to be arrived because of the danger posed by the "failed" states in these regions.

It is against the backdrop of these disturbing developments, an attempt is made in the following two sections to delineate India's security concerns—traditional and non-traditional, and consider its responses. India's security concerns emanate from a variety of sources. It may, however, be added that most of these security concerns are inter-related and enmeshed into each other.

India's Regional Security Concerns — Pakistan

Since Independence, India's security concerns, regionally speaking, continue to be factored on Pakistan and China. India's conflictual relation with Pakistan is based on several disputes, the most critical being the Kashmir issue. For long, the essential elements have remained the same. While India occupies the Kashmir valley and the Jammu area, Pakistan controls what is called *Azad* Kashmir, the northern areas of which Pakistan ceded a part to China. Since 1947, four major wars have been fought between India and Pakistan, the last one being the so-called Kargil conflict in 1999.

Be that as it may, the real danger for India in respect of its security could plausibly arise from the collapse of the Pakistan state into a fundamentalist regime on the lines of the Taliban in Afghanistan. In recent years, religious organisations and political parties based on religious ideologies have emerged as relatively strong groups. Together, sections of the armed forces and Inter Services Intelligence (ISI), too, are intensely "Islamised", leading to a resurgence in militancy and providing a fertile ground for the unprovoked attacks on India (Haqqani, 2004). What is more, political parties, such as the Pakistan People's Party and the Muslim League-liberal, centrist and somewhat conciliatory towards India-today are fragmented and seem unable to bid for a stable government in Pakistan. In these circumstances, the present government under General Parvez Musharraf, by virtue of its control over the military, is better placed. However, its effectiveness to remain in power is essentially predicated on its avowed anti-India posturing (Bennett Jones, 2002; Haqqani, 2003; Haqqani, 2004).

Events since the Agra Summit between the leaders of both India and Pakistan amply demonstrate the emerging pattern in Indo-Pakistani relations. Ever since, at intervals there have existed avenues for working in unison on confidence-building measures — both military and non-military — between the two countries, but so often they are held hostage to progress on talks on Kashmir and related terrorism issues, as both sides, after registering positive progress, revert back to their intractable posturing and position on Kashmir. What is worse, as evidenced in recent years, is that the hardening of the position on both sides has led to acts of heightened hostility such as the amassing of troops along the borders, which in a sense led to the Kargil war in 1999, or terrorist sponsored attacks such as the Pakistani terrorists attack on the Indian Parliament in 2001. In such an unpredictable and tense atmosphere, the nuclear power potential of both countries adds yet another critical dimension. In the event that nuclear weapons fall into the hands of the rogue elements of the army or the militant Islamic groups, they could then be tempted to use them against India. These apprehensions are by no means without any basis (Hersh, 2004).

No doubt in recent years the United States has assumed the role of an unacknowledged interlocutor between India and Pakistan. Does its mediatory role allay India's apprehensions regarding Pakistan? Also, it is often pointed out that the United States has ceased to treat India on an equal footing with Pakistan as it used to do in the Cold War years. Yet, events since 9/11 indicate two noticeable features in the US-Pakistan relationship: one, the need of the United States for Pakistan's strategic and material support in combating *Al Qaeda* and its affiliates both in the region and elsewhere; and, secondly, US pressure on Pakistan to clamp down on militant Islamic groups. Both aspects affect India's security in different ways. Given its prime objective to destroy the *Al Qaeda*-sponsored terrorism, at least for the time being, the US may not choose to avidly support India in its current peace negotiations with Pakistan. Secondly, US pressure on Pakistani militant groups has in no way reduced the cross-border terrorism spearheaded by these groups in Kashmir or elsewhere along India's borders.

It is against this background that one can make predictions regarding the future role of the United States in the South Asian region. It is true that during December 2001 and October 2002, in the standoff between the two countries over the attack on India's Parliament, the US played a proactive role in avoiding a situation that could have degenerated into open hostilities between the neighbours. However, the US concern then was not about simply the fear of yet another instance of an Indo-Pakistan war but more importantly its adverse fallout on its military operations in Afghanistan against the Taliban and *Al Qaeda* (Hathaway, 2002). Presently, the United States' prime global agenda is to deal with the political disorder in Iraq and pitch high for its credibility with the global community in its fight against international terrorism. Under these circumstances, at the maximum the US may opt to play a mediatory role between the two neighbours and shore up the present Pakistani regime. That a balancing act is already underway cannot be gainsaid. Not only has the United States accorded Pakistan the status of a 'major non-NATO ally', but it has reopened talks with it for the resumption of the sale of F-16 aircraft. At the same time, it has indicated its desire to improve military ties with India with its commitment to continue its joint military exercises and offer advanced conventional weaponry to India. In effect, what this implies is, at least for the time being, the US would choose to maintain its relations with India and Pakistan on an even keel. This suggests that there is no palpable change in the US role in the region. Given the potential threats from Pakistan and the equivocal position of the US, India certainly cannot afford to remain complacent in its security dealings with Pakistan.

China

Although boundary disputes between India and China remain inconclusive, yet in past years the two have steadily improved their relations. Besides several rounds of negotiations on the boundaries, in 2003, India officially acknowledged the Tibetan Autonomous Region as part of China while the latter conceded India's sovereignty over Sikkim. Progress in bilateral ties has now expanded to include a quest for markets and partners in the Southeast Asian region. Also, China's inclination to adopt a conciliatory approach in its dealings with other countries, through its diplomatic approach, christened as the "peaceful rise", augurs well for India-China relations (Madeiros, 2004).

Yet there are several security issues that bedevil India-China relations. One major issue relates to the so-called "Pakistan card" that China often plays against India. It is well known that Pakistan has been an ally of China for the past several decades. It is also well known that China has been an integral participant in Pakistan's nuclear and missile programmes. Therefore, in each of its confrontations with Pakistan, one of the major concerns was whether China would intervene militarily to take pressure off its ally, Pakistan. For instance, in the Kargil war, China's stance was somewhat ambivalent, whereas, in the terrorist attack on the Indian Parliament, China made pronouncements which sounded somewhat belligerent, implying that in the event Pakistan was involved in an open military confrontation with India, it would firmly be inclined to support its traditional ally (Garver, 2001; Malik, 2002).

Notwithstanding India's nuclear recent capability, the equation between India and China both in terms of a nuclear arsenal and delivery system is not to the advantage of India. While China has a distinct advantage to carry out a nuclear attack on India, India does not have the capability to deliver its nuclear weapons to any major metropolitan region in China. On the other hand, India's conventional defence, along the borders between the two countries, is strong enough to inflict grave damage on China (Perkovich, 2004; Tellis, 2002; 131-7). If a potential nuclear exchange is wide of the mark, other irritants are likely to persist. Mention here may be made of China's recent initiatives to make an opening into the Indian Ocean by accessing port facilities in Myanmar and Pakistan (Parthasarathy, 2003).Military security threats apart, India has reason to be concerned with the economic security threats likely to be posed by China in its immediate region. Though both India and China are vying with each other for markets in their immediate regions, China is economically far ahead of India. No wonder India is making efforts to gain access to the Association for South East Asian Nations (ASEAN) if only to ensure that China's preponderance does not deny India its stake in the region. Yet another concern for India relates to meeting its energy needs from its traditional sources in the West Asian region. Now, the accelerated economic development of China is certainly going to increase its demand for oil, which already has created competition with India to secure access to oil from Iran, one of the largest producers in world (China Economic Net, 2004). Put succinctly, increasing economic rivalry, be it for markets or for access to secure energy supply, has the potential to derail the progress so far made in other bilateral issues or at least lessen the incentive to seek cooperation on other issues.

Internal Security Issues

There is no gainsaying that the internal security threats have substantially been on the rise in recent years arising out of internal terrorism concentrated in provincial States such as Assam, Kashmir, Manipur, Nagaland and Punjab (abetted by external forces) besides Naxalite insurgencies in Andhra Pradesh, Bihar, Chattisgarh and parts of Madhya Pradesh.

Terrorist violence mounted by ISI-trained outfits such as *Lashkar-e-Taiba, Harkat-ul-Ansar* and *Jaish-e-Mohammed* has remained unabated since the 1990s. However, investigations made since 9/11, have brought to light the clandestine activities of these groups and their global networking for funds, arms and explosives from outside sources. The Indian government's intelligence has established that a majority of these militants are not Kashmiris. Instead, they are associated with radical Islamic groups, which have links with the Taliban. One speculation is that these militant groups moved eastwards seeking haven and safe asylum in Kashmir, following the US-led military campaign in Afghani-stan. Despite Musharraf's assurances following the attack on the Indian Parliament in December 2001 to shut down militant groups operating from Pakistan, as of today there is no perceptible improvement on the ground.

In recent months, as part of confidence-building measures, the government of India had even reduced its troop levels along the India-Pakistan border in Kashmir. However, this policy initiative is not devoid of the risks involved because of the possibility of militant groups or rogue elements of the Pakistani army or the ISI exploiting the situation to their advantage. Here, Musharraf's reiteration that Kashmir is the core issue in the ongoing negotiations between the neighbours only reinforces the resolve of the militant groups to use the resulting India-Pakistan stalemate to their advantage and objectives. In the event terrorist violence increases, the government of India may then be forced to suspend its present troop reduction level in the region (Oberoi, 2004).

A Terrorist-related violent insurgency has been sporadic in the north-eastern and eastern regions of India for long. The latest is an instance when violence became widespread in the provincial State of Manipur following the killing of an activist of the legally banned People's Liberation Army. The immediate demand of the insurgents was the unconditional withdrawal of the Armed Forces Special Powers Act, which provided for the summary killing of suspected culprits. While the government has offered to consider the demand, it nevertheless indicates a broader policy choice that the government has to make when it comes to dealing with such insurgencies.

Acts of terrorism and violent upheavals have occurred in other parts of north-eastern India in the provincial States of Assam and Nagaland. In Assam, the United Liberation Front of Assam (ULFA) is the main insurgency group with its avowed objective for an independent state and has refused to participate in any negotiations with the government unless the issue of sovereignty is included in the agenda for talks. A related political movement is the All Assam Students Union, which seeks the deportation of illegal migrants from neighbouring Bangladesh. Since the ULFA's military camps are located in parts of Bangladesh, cracking down on their activities calls for coordination with the governments of Bangladesh and Myanmar. What is more, as has become evident on the basis of government's intelligence, many of these dissident groups receive funding and training from *Al Qaeda* and the Pakistan's ISI (Hussain, 2003). The Naga rebels, led by the National Socialist Council of Nagaland, have been negotiating with the government over their demand for remapping the north-eastern region to create a 'greater' Nagaland, encompassing part of the neighbouring provincial States. Though a ceasefire with the rebels is currently in force, no permanent solution is on the horizon either.

Yet another source of internal security concern is the Naxalite movement claiming to be fighting on behalf of the oppressed classes. However, in recent years, the movement's activities have developed into criminal and terrorist activities such as abduction and extortion. The recent merger of the two main ultra radical groups – the People's War Group and the Maoist Communist Centre — has created an organisation that has influence over a significant geographical area stretching from Andhra Pradesh in the south and through a corridor up to Bihar and beyond in neighbouring Nepal. This merger has provided the Naxalite movement with strategic depth and space to manoeuvre over the coming years.

In all of these internal security concerns, since the neighbouring governments as well as the Islamic fundamentalist terrorists groups are involved, it calls for deft and well orchestrated handling on the part of the Government of India. In other words, in meeting the challenges posed by these terrorist and insurgency movements, the government ought to devise a four-pronged counter strategy principally aimed at:

(i) curbing violence and restoring civil order;
(ii) putting in place innovative but less repressive legal mechanisms;
(iii) keeping the door open for sustained negotiations; and,
(iv) exerting pressure on external supporters of violence.

Related Transnational and Human Security Concerns

India, like most other countries, is no exception to having to deal with an array of transnational security threats. Of these, the most menacing is the spiralling illegal drug trade, trafficking and attendant violence. The fall of the Taliban in Afghanistan has led to an increase in illicit drug production in that country. The threat to India arising out of the drug production and trade is two-fold: one, India could become an even bigger conduit in the drug trafficking network; and two, the enormous profits from the sale of Afghanistan-produced drugs would possibly be transferred to the Taliban and from there to militant Islamic groups in Kashmir. Added to this is the already on-going drug trade produced by the ethnic armies in Myanmar. The view that northeastern rebel groups such as the ULFA are linked to these activities in Myanmar is plausible given the need for funds for the ULFA military camps in Bangladesh. Maoist groups located in Nepal are already involved in drug production in the areas they control and before long the profits from drug trade are likely to be funneled to their affiliates in mainland India (Ramachandran, 2004).

Organised criminal groups are another source of transnational threat to India. The most publicised of this group is the Dawood Ibrahim known as the D-Company. It is unique because of its influence in many sectors ranging from the real estate and cine business in Mumbai to the drug trade in Afghanistan and to *Al Qaeda* and Taliban groups. D-Company's complicity in the Mumbai blasts of 1993 and its partnership with ISI in transferring funds to a variety of terrorist groups is well established. So much so, the US government has named Dawood Ibrahim as a 'specially designated international terrorist' organisation. Similar crime groups, yet to surface in the media, are apparently active with access to resources both from legitimate and illegitimate business all over West and East Asia.

In recent years, caste and communal violence have erupted causing huge human carnage and property destruction. The Gujarat riots of 2002 were a stark reminder of the fragility of the country's social and religious fabric. Agitations, whether triggered on proposed locations of religious shrines or perceived oppression of one caste over the other, invariably carry with them the potential for violence. Agitations spearheaded by such groups as *Ram Janam Bhoomi* in Uttar Pradesh, *Shiv Sena* in Maharashtra and *Ranvir Sena* in Bihar are some of the prime examples.

Resulting instability has caused internal migration and illegal immigration from outside. These, in turn, affect the already shaky socio-economic framework of metropolitan areas. These and related social upheavals fomented by communal, caste or cultural identities are likely to provide fertile ground for tensions and violence and lend themselves to easy exploitation by external adversaries. At the same time, it becomes incumbent on the state to deal with these internal security issues.

The challenge then is to formulate a security strategy that can deal with the range of threats not only rooted in the traditional state-oriented international system but those that have emerged as a consequence of the newer social, political and global realities. No less important a factor in any such exercise is the resource base that each nation-state can command. Given that the security threats of today are intertwined, as the dividing lines between internal and external security threats are becoming narrower, so it has become imperative for nation-states to combine their resources to design and devise what is termed a 'proliferation security initiative'. With this in mind, in the concluding section below an attempt is made to briefly examine what opportunities exist for India and Australia to devise such a joint initiative.

Australia's Role in India's Security Matters

As has been mentioned earlier, countries sharing in many respects the common historical antecedents, legal-political systems and values, and also at the same time sharing similar security concerns, could collectively address them and jointly devise bilateral mechanisms to meet the challenges. Notwithstanding the different trajectories through which the two countries-India and Australia-have traversed until recently, the events of 9/11 and since have brought them together to explore avenues for cooperation in dealing with their security concerns.

Beginning in 2001, both countries initiated the first-ever strategic dialogue in New Delhi, which they officially acknowledged, was "open, constructive and wide-ranging, and demonstrated shared perspectives and common interests on a number of issues" (Tomar, 2002, 12). The agenda, among other things, included importantly regional and maritime security issues. In the second round of the security dialogue held in Sydney, both sides underscored the need for promoting better mutual understanding in areas key to strategic and defence planning and the development of a 'second track' framework for continuing the strategic dialogue and exchanges. According to one observer, the consensus in the Sydney round of talks was that "efforts are still required at both government and 'second track' levels to enable the bilateral relationship to achieve the level of closeness befitting common interests" (Singh, 2004; 186).

The common interests are obvious as both countries share the Indian Ocean and have a mutual and important stake in protecting the sea-lanes not only for the safe passage of trade vessels but also for controlling piracy, drug trafficking and illegal human cargo. Half of the world's maritime trade after all passes through the Malacca and Lombok Straits, of which the volume of Australia's transiting trade is no less significant. Also, many of the islets in the Indonesian archipelago are suspected of being used as transit points for gunrunners and smugglers including drug traffickers and poachers. Besides, these areas are also notorious for acts of piracy.

While India, for long-maintained its naval and coastguard presence in the Andaman and Nicobar group of islands, in 2001, it decided to set up its tri-services command — the Far Eastern Strategic Command based at Port Blair. Fully operational, the Command includes air force helicopters, naval Fast Attack Craft (FAC) and coast guard vessels under its navy. Units of Offshore Petrol Vessels (OPVs) have since been added. Eventually, India intends to have a full strength army component and an air base in the Andamans. Recognising that these initiatives would give India not only the strategic depth but also the potential to protect maritime traffic bound for Australia and the South China Sea. Australia desires closer cooperation with India to enhance maritime security in the region.

However, it may be underlined that maritime security is multifaceted and involves a wide range of issues, including:

1. hard military security issues such as naval threats and blockades;
2. hard non-military security issues such as arms trafficking, narco-terrorism and piracy; and,
3. non-military security issues such as shipping, fishing, sea-bed minerals, offshore oil/gas resources, illegal immigration, environmental protection and maritime management.

However, basic to all of these is the vulnerability of the sea-lanes of communication (SLOC) as they are crucial to the survival of the littoral countries in the Indian Ocean region. No country can defend the wide radius of these sea-lanes by itself. Furthermore, threats to SLOCs can arise out of external factors such as piracy, the laying of mines, military and territorial conflicts and disputes of some islets as well as out of non-traditional threats such as narco-terrorism, drug trafficking and illegal migration. Therefore, cooperative approaches to the safety and protection of sea-lanes need to be developed on a priority basis.

In doing so, both India and Australia should first reach agreement regarding cooperation in law enforcement on the high seas for guaranteeing norms for international navigation on the high seas. Second, both countries need to initiate the establishment of joint patrol areas and joint development zones. Finally, to reduce uncertainty in the maritime security environment, concrete cooperative approaches by the navies of both countries need to be worked out for the protection of SLOCs to deal with non-conventional threats.

The landmark Memorandum of Understanding on Cooperation in Combating Internal Terrorism that India and Australia had signed, following the third round of the strategic dialogue, amply demonstrates that the two countries are cognizant of the critical importance of Indian Ocean security as basic to their own national security. That the protocol is seen as paving the way for closer cooperation between the security, intelligence and law enforcement agencies between the two is admittedly a qualitative index of the expanding strategic convergence between India and Australia.

REFERENCES

Bennett Jones, O. (2002), *Pakistan: Eye of the Storm*, New Haven, CT: Yale University Press.

China Economic Net (2004), 'China and India Wrestling for Iran's Oil', *China Economic Net*, 22 November.

Curley, M. and Nicholas Thomas (2004), 'Human Security and Public Health in Southeast Asia: The SARS Outbreak', *Australian Journal of International Affairs*, vol. 58, no. 1, March, pp. 17-32.

Garver, J.W. (2001), *Protracted Contest: Sino-Indian Rivalry in the Twentieth Century*, Seattle: University of Washington Press.

Haqqani, H. (2003), 'Pakistan's Internal Divisions', Center for Strategic and International Studies-South Asia Program, 1 December.

Haqqani, H. (2004), 'The Role of Islam in Pakistan', *The Washington Quarterly*, vol. 28, no. 1, Winter, pp. 85-96.

Hathaway, R. (2002), 'The US-India Courtship: From Clinton to Bush', *Journal of Strategic Studies*, vol. 25, no. 4, December, pp. 17-19.

See Seymour Hersh (2004), 'The Deal', *The New Yorker*, 8 March.

Homer-Dixon, T.F. (1992), 'On the Threshold: Environmental Changes as Causes of Acute Conflict', *International Security*, vol. 16, no. 2, Autumn, pp. 76-116.

Hussain, W. (2003), 'Testing the Hot and Cold India-Bangladesh Relationship', *South Asia Tribune,* 7-13 September.

Madeiros, E.S. (2004), 'China Debates Its 'Peaceful Rise' Strategy, *Yale Global Online*, 22 June.

Malik, M. (2002), 'The China Factor in the India-Pakistan Conflict, *Occasional Paper*, Asia-Pacific Center for Security Studies, Honolulu, November, pp. 1-38.

Mansfield, H.C. (1998), Translation of Niccolo Machiavalli, *The Prince*, Chicago: University of Chicago Press.

Oberoi, Surinder Singh (2004), 'Ethnic Separatism and Insurgency in Kashmir', in Satu P.Limaye, Robert G. Wirsing and Mohan Malik, eds., *Religious Radicalism and Security in South Asia,* Honolulu, Hawaii: Asia-Pacific Center for Security Studies, pp. 168-175.

Parthasarathy, G. (2003), 'Axis of Evidence', *The Indian Express*, 14 November.

Perkovich, G. (2004), 'The Nuclear and Security Balance', in Francine R. Frankel and Harry Harding, eds., *The India-China Relationship*, Washington D.C: Woodrow Wilson Center Press.

Ramachandran, S. (2004), 'War or no War, Drug Trade Flourishes', *Asia Times*, 9 October.

Roland Paris, R. (2001), 'Human Security', *International Security*, vol. 26, no. 2, Fall, pp. 87-102.

Rudolph, C. (2003), 'Globalization and Security: Migration and Evolving Conceptions of Security in Statecraft and Scholarship', *Security Studies*, vol. 13, no. 1, Autumn, pp. 1-32.

Scholte, J.A. (2000), 'Globalization and (In)security', in Jan Arte Scholte, ed., *Globalization: A Critical Introduction*, New York: St. Martin Press, pp. 207-260.

Singh, D. (2004), 'Strategic Perspectives of India and Australia: Towards Convergence", in D. Gopal and Dennis Rumley, eds., *India and Australia: Issues and Opportunities*, New Delhi: Authors Press.

Tellis, A. (2002), *India's Emerging Nuclear Posture*, Santa Monica, CA: RAND.

Tomar, Ravi (2002), 'India-US Relations in a Changing Strategic Environment', Research Paper No.20, Department of the Parliament Library, Canberra.

Weiner, M. (1992), 'Security, Stability, and International Migration', *International Security*, Vol. 17, no. 3, Winter, pp. 91-126.

United Nations Development Programme (1994), *Human Development Report, 1994*, New York: Oxford University Press.

8

India's 'Look East Policy'

Factoring ASEAN and Australia as Partners

Vivian Louis Forbes

"We have taken note of relevant reports. We welcome India and relevant countries engaged in friendly cooperative relations... We hope this relationship is beneficial to regional peace and stability."

Chinese Foreign Ministry spokesman Zhu Bangzao, Beijing, January 2001

"The 'Look East policy' has substantially strengthened our linkages with Japan, the member countries of ASEAN and the Republic of Korea. ...Our relationship with ASEAN has taken on new dimensions and we hope to realize its huge potential."

Address by the President of India to Parliament, New Delhi, 25 February 2005

"India is an increasingly influential global and regional player whose interests converge with Australia. We work together constructively on key international issues..."

Prime Minister of Australia, John Howard, Canberra, 4 March 2006

The littoral States of the eastern sector of the Indian Ocean basin collectively have the potential to create a dynamic economic trading bloc and at the same time enhance security to ensure a geopolitically stable region. India's 'Look East Policy' is just one of the many stepping stones towards this end. ASEAN, as a collective group of states with a unique philosophy, and Australia's 'Look West' concept, is the other stepping stones to assist in achieving this aim.

The Government of India seized the opportunity for the country to broaden the scope for brighter prospects of cooperation in all aspects of international relations in both the regional and global contexts when it launched its Look East Policy in 1991. Viewed in a regional context, the Australian Government, in turn, has demonstrated its willingness to foster its relationship with India and ASEAN as equal partners and to make every endeavour to promote the initiatives offered by its regional neighbours. Australia's and ASEAN's economic and foreign policies are relevant to India's security in this globalised era not only because of their potential links to India's more immediate region, but also because of the prospects to contribute to the overall security of the Indian Ocean basin. That there is a great deal of bilateral and multilateral interaction is acknowledged. However, there is scope for much greater substance.

This chapter discusses the growing awareness of the three synergies, highlights the positive and negative factors that are inherent and suggests avenues along which Governments and their respective policy-makers should proceed in order to achieve their stated goals and objectives for the ultimate benefit of the people of all states and for the good of the region. The first section of the chapter is a discussion of the historical and geopolitical context. The second section provides a broad overview of some of the main goals of India's foreign policy. The 'Look East Policy' is then considered in more detail and is followed by a discussion of India-ASEAN relations, the BIMST regional initiative, India's role in regional security and its relations with Australia in the context of this discussion.

Historical and Geopolitical Context — Colonisation and Control

Prior to the arrival of the Portuguese explorers and mariners in the Indian Ocean in 1498, no single maritime group or power (apart from pirates) had attempted to monopolise the sea lanes that connected the ports of subcontinental India with the ports of Southeast Asia and China to the East and the Middle East and the East African littoral on the West. Historical cultural linkages and trading patterns among Australia, India and the countries of Southeast Asia over many centuries have been documented in, for example, Fisher (1964), Hall (1981), Chaudhuri (1990), Osborne (1990) and MacPherson (1993) and on maps such as those in the volumes by Schwartzberg (1978), Forbes (1995) and Suarez (1999).

Peaceful trade had remained the norm in the Indian Ocean basin. There were periods, however, when the coastal rulers of the Malabar coast and Southern India were powerful enough to demand toll taxes from passing ships and Arab and Persian rulers attempted to control the shipping lanes through the Persian Gulf and the Red Sea. However, there had not been any systematic attempt by any single political power to eliminate all others from the oceanic trade that touched the Indian subcontinent. Indian port authorities that demanded high taxes from the administrators of ships that had called into the ports invariably lost out to 'free ports' *i.e.*, ports that demanded very low tariffs from ships using the port facilities. In fact, several of the Indian Ocean ports were politically neutral entities thereby giving free and equitable access to the shippers of varied nationalities and religious affiliations. For a century, the Portuguese managed to exact tribute from most of the regional traders who were active in the Indian Ocean. This was followed by a period of Dutch domination, although there were also pockets (and periods) of competitive trade as other European rivals attempted to outflank the Portuguese (and later the Dutch). The disintegration of the Mughal Empire was followed by the domination of European maritime powers in the trade patterns within the Indian Ocean basin and their associated influence extended into the heartland of Asia as well. In the end, it was the British who seized the opportunity to pacify and administer India for economic reasons, edging out their European rivals who found other territories to colonise in Asia and Africa.

The colonisation of India by the British was followed by the colonisation of Burma (present-day Myanmar), Malaysia and Singapore, parts of the Middle East and a vast part of Africa. China's coastal areas and Indo-China also come under European domination. However, since 1945, the geopolitical map of the Indian Ocean basin delineated drastic changes, as India as well as several countries within Southeast Asia became sovereign states. Each pursued individual policies on all matters including trade, although many of the policies were based on rules and regulations that were formulated on legislation that was inherited from the colonial administrators, notwithstanding subsequent amendments.

In the five decades since attaining independent status, the various Governments of India ensured that their policies and guidance through specific national development plans enhanced India's status and economic, political and technological standing within the international community. Parikh (2006; 15-39) has argued that the Indian economy has a number of strengths and has acquired considerable resilience and predicted that it will sustain the high growth rate until about 2016. He cautioned that such a sustained growth rate will not be achieved easily as policy-makers will need to address the inherent weaknesses of the Indian economy such as providing infrastructure, especially for electricity, fresh water and transport systems; reform the labour laws and the judicial systems – especially the lengthy delays in reaching judgment – and reducing the educational backlog. He also stressed that achieving fiscal consolidation and flexibility may pose political changes especially as multi-party coalitions are likely to be the norm.

A plethora of geo-economic studies has been undertaken by numerous scholars and issued by publication houses in India and Southeast Asia that stress the importance of India's 'Look East Policy', the vibrant economy of some members of ASEAN, and Australia's standing in the emerging global order in the context of trade, security, energy management policies and political grandstanding. These publications include, but are not limited to, Savage and others (1998), Gopal (2002), Chia (2003), Gopal and Rumley (2004), Savage and Mullins (2005), Kumar and others (2006) and Devare (2006).

Regional Geopolitical Challenges

Many years of argument over the status of Sikkim, which is a part of (now administered by) India but has long been disputed by China, ended after a meeting between Chinese Premier Wen Jiabao and his Indian counterpart, Atal Bihari Vajpayee, on 8 October 2003 during the ASEAN +3 Summit meeting held in Bali, Indonesia. India's the then Foreign Secretary, Kanwal Sibal, commented that he would "… characterise this meeting as excellent and remarkable in terms of the cordiality and friendliness of its tone and conduct", after the talks between the neighbours that have fought one border war since the1950s.

It had been noted that China's Foreign Ministry had altered its Web site (in October 2003) to take into account the status of Sikkim and no longer showed the tiny Himalayan (former kingdom) as a separate country. "Yesterday if you looked at a list of the countries in the region, Sikkim used to figure after Singapore," Sibal commented, and added that "It is no longer there… China was looking at the resolution of the boundary issue in a long-term and strategic perspective and in the context of long-term and strategic relations between the two countries".

China's agreement to open trade through Sikkim, during an historic visit by Vajpayee in June 2003, had been already been seen as a concession to Indian rule in that country. An agreement between the two countries also opens up the opportunity for cross-border trade to flourish in Tibet. The concession was India's acceptance that Tibet is an undisputed portion of China.

A further development which encompasses these regional states is the Kumming initiative, which is a Track II attempt to involve India and China in promoting economic activities in the northern border regions of Southeast Asia. However, such rapid developments in the 'national interests' should not be at the expense of degrading the traditional values of the minority communities that reside along the international frontiers.

New Dimension: Relations with China

The Government of India has clearly been improving relations with China. This was evident when respective country's Prime Ministers met in Vientiane for the 3rd India-ASEAN Summit which was held on 30 November 2004. The Chinese leader indicated that the most important item on his agenda for 2005 would be his visit to India in March of that year. Two rounds of talks had already been held between the special representatives of the two countries on the boundary question. The importance of the relationship was also reflected in the visits of two senior Chinese State Councilors and K. Natwar Singh, Minister for External Affairs, during four meetings in a three-month period in Qingtao, Jakarta, New York and Almaty.

During his visit to India, State Councilor, Tang Jia Xuar, recognised the active role that India could play in international affairs and in the Security Council. He is not the only one to do so. ASEAN's Ong Keng Yong observed that China and India should work together and use their economic leverage to persuade the military Government of Myanmar to reform (*Channel News Asia*, 20 April 2006). ASEAN recognises that the Myanmar issues are difficult and hence feels that external partners could influence that Government to adopt a democratic process and incorporate human rights into its Constitution.

India should impart its own dynamism and participate in the Asian economic community, as argued by the Prime Minister, Dr. Manmohan Singh, to constitute part of the arc of advantage and prosperity and stability and for closer economic integration. (Kumar, 2006; 303).

Purposeful, Result-Oriented and Proactive Indian Foreign Policy

The Government of India has adopted a foreign policy that can be characterized as "purposeful, result-oriented and proactive". Real gross domestic product (GDP) growth for the fiscal year ending 31 March, 2005 was about seven per cent, down from 8.5 per cent growth in 2004. Foreign portfolio and direct investment inflows had risen significantly in recent years. They have contributed to the $144 billion in foreign exchange reserves at the end of October 2005. Government receipts from privatisation were about $3 billion in fiscal year 2003-04.

India's external debt was $123 billion in 2004, up from $111 billion in 2003 (Athukorala, 2006, 145-148). Bilateral assistance was approximately $4 billion in 2004-05, with the United States providing about $134.7 million in development assistance. The World Bank plans to double aid to India to almost $3 billion a year; funding that will be used for infrastructure, education, health, and rural livelihood developments. India is the largest single recipient of World Bank lending.

Indeed, on 2 May 2005, The World Bank committed loans totalling Rs. 2,817 crore to partly finance power and municipal reform projects in India. The Bank signed two separate agreements with the Union Government for providing loans of Rs. 1,845 crore (410 million dollars) for power transmission projects of the Power Grid Corporation of India and extending Rs. 972 crore (216 million dollar) credit for a municipal reform projects in Karnataka. The Power System Development project-III is designed to focus on strengthening the transmission system in power deficit regions and increasing inter-regional transmission capacity. In addition to this, it aims at developing the institutional capacity of the Power Grid. The municipal reform project aims at enhancing urban infrastructure and services delivery in the state, along with development of Bangalore city. The project will be implemented over a period of five years. The loan agreement was signed by Madhusudan Prasad, Joint Secretary, Department of Economic Afairs, Ministry of Finance and Michael F Carter, Country Director, World Bank. (*Economic Times*, 2005)

India's population is estimated at nearly 1.1 billion on a land area of about 3.3 million square kilometers and it is growing at 1.6 per cent each year. India has the world's 12th largest economy – and the third largest in Asia behind Japan and China – with total GDP of around $700 billion and growing at a rate of 7 to 8 per cent per annum. Services, industry and agriculture account for 50.8, 27.2, and 22.0 per cent of GDP respectively. Nearly two-thirds of the population depends on agriculture for its livelihood. About 25 per cent of the population lives below the poverty line, but there is a large and growing middle class of 320-340 million with substantial disposable income for consumer goods (Kumar, 2006; 304).

India encompasses a wide spectrum of economic activity, ranging from high technology to subsistence agriculture. Indigenous technological achievements extend to fields such as nuclear energy, space and satellite communications, superconductors and deep sea oil drilling equipment. Recent reforms include liberalised foreign investment and exchange regimes, industrial decontrol, significant reductions in tariffs and other trade barriers, reform and modernisation of the financial sector, significant adjustments in government monetary and fiscal policies, and safeguarding intellectual property rights. However, economic growth is constrained by inadequate infrastructure, a cumbersome bureaucracy, alleged corruption, labour market rigidities, regulatory and foreign investment controls, the 'reservation' of key products for small-scale industries, and high fiscal deficits. The outlook for further trade liberalisation is mixed. India eliminated quotas on 1,420 consumer imports in 2002 and announced its intention to continue to lower customs duties. However, the tax structure is complex with some compounding effects of various taxes.

The rapidly growing software sector is boosting service exports and modernising India's economy. Revenues from the information technology industry reached a turnover of $US16.2 billion in 2004-05. Software exports amounted to $US17.2 billion in 2004-05 and a similar growth is expected in fiscal year 2005-06. Personal computer penetration is nine per 1,000 persons. The cellular mobile market is expected to surge to over 70 million subscribers by fiscal year ending 2005 from the present 67 million users. The country has 54 million cable TV customers (Parikh, 2006; 22-24).

Table 1: Exports from and Imports into India – Total Value

Exports (top) and Imports (lower)			
		Value in US $Million	
	2002-2003	*2003-2004*	*Growth*
Region			Per cent
ASIA and OCEANIA	22726.28	29408.08	29.40
	43.11	46.35	
ASIA and OCEANIA	17937.77	26609.30	48.34
	29.21	34.54	

Source: http://commerce.nic.in/india_trade/region_analysis_mar2004.htm <accessed 13/4/06>

Growth for the year ending 31 March 2006 was expected to be between 7-7.6 per cent. Exports to and imports from Asia and Oceania have been increasing rapidly in recent years (Table 1). Further, during

2006, India could expect to enjoy a unique profile in the international arena as a factor of stability, a model of plural and secular democracy and an economic powerhouse that is destined to play a greater role in the international affairs and especially within the Southeast Asian region on the basis of its 'Look East Policy'.

> *"... I allude to Foreign Affairs; ... in the case of India the phrase includes her relations with the whole of her neighbours and that it carries with it the politics of the greater part of the Asiatic Continent."*
>
> Lord Curzon, Extract from Budget Speech, 25 March 1903 (Curzon, 1906, 405)

The Rationale for Change: The 'Look East Policy'

India's 'Look East Policy', conceived in 1991, was necessary in the era of globalisation and from which many benefits have accrued in a relatively short timeframe. India has advanced economically with market-oriented reforms since the year that the Look East Policy was pronounced. It was a policy formulated as a definitive innovation and the logic then was that the Government should engage the increasingly vibrant economies of the countries of the Association of South East Asian Nations (ASEAN) (Kumar and others, 2006; 1-14). The rationale within the Government's foreign policy establishment at that time was to try and link India's liberalising economy with the markets of South East Asia. On the one hand, there was a perception that the tradition of India's historical connections and cultural links with that region of Asia was becoming a mere memory of the past. However, it was felt in the early 1990s that ASEAN's perception of Indian Government as a non-belligerent state might be conducive to its economic engagement of the South East Asian states (Devare, 2006; 18).

The focus adopted by the Government of India on the finer aspects of that country's links with several East Asian states for over ten days, during 2002, demonstrated a sincere desire to formulate a new foreign policy. When the then External Affairs Minister, Jaswant Singh, returned home after visiting China, Myanmar, South Korea and Thailand, the former Prime Minister of India, Atal Bihari Vajpayee, set out on a tour of Singapore and Cambodia.

The rationale for their separate tours is irrelevant in the context of this discussion; however, any perceivable advantages of the travel logistics stamped their mark on the geo-politics of the Asia-Pacific region for the future. Mr. Singh's diplomatic travel through parts of East Asia appeared to have been planned in the specific context of an inaugural commercial flight between Beijing, and New Delhi. The overall logic of these diplomatic exercises by Mr. Singh and Mr. Vajpayee and their ambitious intentions was to establish India's geostrategic footprint across the different political spectrum of East and Southeast Asia.

Of much greater relevance to the changing dynamics of India's foreign policy in 2002 was the apparent reality that the Government was eager to engage at a mutual level in its relationship with other countries so as to be able to pursue independent objectives towards reshaping the present global order. If this was the most striking aspect of Mr. Singh's latest diplomatic foray, Mr. Vajpayee had, during his visit to Singapore, sought to portray India as a country with a manifest destiny in the entire Asia-Pacific region and not just Asia. This was indicative of an essentially formative vision and one that was to be pursued.

The 'Look East Policy' in the Context of UPA's Foreign Policy

Since the May 2004 elections, the 'Look East Policy' has been given a new dimension by the United Progressive Alliance's (UPA) Foreign Affairs Office, Government of India. In its *Common Minimum Programme* released by the new Government in New Delhi, in May 2004, it stressed that the UPA Government would pursue an independent foreign policy, keeping in mind its past traditions. (*The Hindu*, 2004) This policy would promote multi-polarity in world relations and oppose all attempts at unilateralism. The UPA Government would give the highest priority to building closer political, economic and other ties with its neighbours in South Asia and to strengthen the South Asia Association for Regional Cooperation (SAARC). Particular attention would be paid to regional projects in the area of ecological conservation, water resources and energy security. Dialogue with Pakistan on all issues would be pursued systematically and on a sustained basis. The Government supports peace talks in Sri Lanka that fulfill the legitimate aspirations of Tamils and religious minorities within the territorial integrity and solidarity of Sri Lanka. Outstanding issues with Bangladesh would be resolved. Intensive dialogue would be initiated with Nepal for developing water resources to mutual advantage.

Trade and investment with China would be expanded further and talks on the border issue pursued with vigour. Relationships with East Asian countries would be intensified and traditional ties with West Asia given a fresh thrust. Even as it pursues closer engagements and relations with the USA, the Government of India will maintain the independence of India's foreign policy position on all regional and global issues.

In keeping with the stance adopted at Doha, Qatar in September 2001, the UPA Government will fully protect the national interest, particularly of farmers, in all World Trade Organisation (WTO) negotiations. Commitments made at earlier forums would be adhered to, even as efforts are formulated to ensure that all agreements reflect India's concerns fully, particularly in the areas of agriculture and intellectual property (Hoda, 2006; 94-98). The UPA Government would utilise the flexibility afforded in existing WTO agreements to fully protect Indian agriculture and industry and it will play a proactive role in strengthening the emerging solidarity of developing countries in the shape of G-20 in the WTO (Sally, 2006; 121-44).

The Indian Government's engagement with its neighbours is not limited only to the Government-to-Government level but has consciously encompassed different sections of society and across the political spectrum. The UPA Government is of the opinion that it is important to have frequent and regular contacts and wide-ranging discussions with neighbouring countries at all levels to take forward and to maximise opportunities for mutually beneficial cooperation. That said, the Government has not hesitated to address issues where there may be differences, but has done so in a spirit of friendship and in a constructive search for practical and mutually acceptable solutions. This was the approach taken at the SAARC Summit held in Dhaka in January 2005. The Government remains committed to a collective future of peace and prosperity for the entire South Asian region.

ASEAN-India Relations

The Association of South East Asian Nations (ASEAN) was established on 8 August 1967 in Bangkok by the five original member states-Indonesia, Malaysia, Philippines, Singapore, and Thailand. Brunei Darussalam joined on 8 January 1984, Vietnam on 28 July 1995, Laos and Myanmar on 23 July 1997, and Cambodia on 30 April 1999; finally making up the 'ASEAN 10'. The ASEAN region has a population of about 500 million, a total area of 4.5 million square kilometers, a combined gross domestic product of US$737 billion, and a total trade of US$ 720 billion (ASEAN, 2003).

In 1997, the ASEAN leaders adopted the ASEAN Vision 2020, which called for an ASEAN Partnership in Dynamic Development aimed at forging closer economic integration within the region (Daquila, 2006; 41-62). The vision statement also resolved to create a stable, prosperous and highly competitive ASEAN economic region, in which there would be a free flow of goods, services, investments, capital, as well as equitable economic development and reduced poverty and socio-economic disparities. The Hanoi Plan of Action, adopted in 1998, serves as the first in a series of plans of action leading up to the realisation of the ASEAN vision.

Table 2: Chronology of Developments between ASEAN and India

Year	Development
1992	ASEAN invites India to be a Sectoral Dialogue partner
1995	ASEAN announce that India is a Full Dialogue partner (Bangkok)
1996	India becomes a member of ASEAN Regional Forum (ARF)
	India attends ARF and First meeting of Post-Ministerial Conference of ASEAN (Jakarta)
1997	Economic Co-operation Agreement signed in Bangkok between Bangladesh, India, Sri Lanka and Thailand Forum held entitled Bangladesh, India, Myanmar, Sri Lanka, Thailand Economic Co-operation (BIMST-EC)
2000	Agreement signed in Vientiane, Laos by Cambodia, India, Laos, Myanmar, Thailand and Vietnam to form Mekong Ganga Co-operation
2002	ASEAN invites India to be a Summit partner at the Phnom Penh, Cambodia summit
2003	India is signatory to three documents at the ASEAN Bali Summit in October (see Appendix 1)
2004	India is signatory to an additional two documents at the Vientiane Summit in November (see Appendix 1)
	First BIMST-EC summit held in Thailand. Nepal and Bhutan join BIMST-EC, which is re-named as Bay of Bengal Initiative for Multi-sectoral Technical and Economic Co-operation.
2005	India participated at the First East Asia Summit in Kuala Lumpur, Malaysia

India as a member of ASEAN+3 played an active role in the ASEAN Summit that was held in Bali, Indonesia, during the first week of October 2003. Its role stems from its 'Look East Policy' that was formulated and initiated by the Ministry of External Affairs (MEA) in 1991. India, in that year became a partner in ASEAN in late-1991 in the key sectors of investment, tourism and trade. India and ASEAN signed an agreement for peace, progress and prosperity in the region to foster closer economic and political ties in November 2004. The document provides a structure for a multi-directional approach to strengthening research and development in the areas of science and technology of agriculture, health and culture. Table 2 presents a Chronology of India's Acceptance into the ASEAN Framework.

ASEAN and India: Enhancing Cooperation

During the numerous ASEAN meetings with India's Prime Ministers and other members of the Indian Cabinet with their respective portfolios, over the years there have been productive discussions on regional and international political and economic issues. ASEAN leaders expressed satisfaction at the rapid development of ASEAN-India relations and cooperation within a short period of two years as an ASEAN dialogue partner (Ariff and Lim, 2006; 69-73). ASEAN Leaders warmly welcomed India's accession to the *Treaty of Amity and Cooperation* (TAC) in Southeast Asia, as it confirmed India's willingness to contribute to peace and stability in the region.

ASEAN members were pleased to witness the signing of the Framework Agreement on Comprehensive Economic Cooperation between the Association of South East Asian Nations and the Republic of India (see Appendix). The agreement would strengthen and enhance economic, trade and investment cooperation between the two sides. They affirmed that the agreement would facilitate the effective economic integration of the new ASEAN member states and bridge the development gaps among ASEAN members. In this regard, ASEAN leaders also welcomed various initiatives proposed by India in the areas of agriculture, biotechnology, human resources development and agro-processing, especially in the establishment of a joint working group on agriculture. ASEAN leaders are of the belief that India's experience in information and communication technology (ICT) could be shared and jointly developed by the ASEAN member countries, to obtain mutual beneficial goals. In particular, the ICT initiatives employed to address India's agricultural and industrial issues in rural regions could be used as models for the least developed member states of ASEAN (Joseph and Parayil, 2006; 225).

The potential of India-ASEAN cooperation is not just confined to the economic sphere, but includes human resource development, science and technology, health and pharmaceuticals, information and communication technology and agriculture (Prasad, 2006; 261-262). During the East Asia Summit, Indian Prime Minister Singh met the leaders of Australia, Indonesia, Japan, Laos PDR, the People's Republic of China, Singapore and Vietnam, and exchanged views on issues of mutual interest. In his discussions with the Chinese Premier, the two leaders reviewed the progress made in the two rounds of talks between their Special Representatives on the international boundary question and agreed that these would continue with a focus on substantive issues (*New Straits Times*, December 2005; 5).

Other Indo-ASEAN Relations

A new dimension in India's 'Look East' policy was the first Indian-ASEAN Car Rally that coincided with the Third India-ASEAN Summit held in Vientiane, Laos. Prime Minister Manmohan Singh witnessed the occasion and signaled the start of the rally at Guwahati, Assam, on 22 November 2004. It was a symbol of India's strengthening bonds with the ASEAN countries. The second leg of the rally re-commenced at Vientiane on 30 November 2004. All of the ASEAN leaders together with India's Prime Minister were at Vientiane for this event. The rally, which was organized in co-ordination with the Confederation of Indian Industries and similar apex organizations of various ASEAN countries, also witnessed interactions with the business leaders of these countries as an adjunct of the rally. It was a great event as it promoted the re-establishment and opening of a land route from India to the ASEAN countries that would promote connectivity thus enhancing opportunities for trade, investment, tourism and people-to-people links between India and ASEAN.

Bay of Bengal Initiative — BIMST-EC

Another positive step in India's partnership with the ASEAN countries was the initiation of a forum that was held in 1997 wherein Bangladesh, India, Myanmar, Sri Lanka, Thailand established an Economic Cooperation (BIMST-EC) grouping (Reddy, 2006; 250). The India-ASEAN Summit dialogue was an integral link to the economic and security interests, particularly for India's East and Northeast regions. The adoption of the document on '*India-ASEAN Partnership for Peace, Progress and Prosperity*' at the Indo-ASEAN Summit on 30 November 2004 was a symbol that India now forms the inner core of countries in ASEAN's political relationship with the rest of the world.

The ASEAN leaders and the then Indian Prime Minister, Atal Bihari, held talks in 2003 on the issue of terrorism and agreed to enhance cooperation in fighting terrorism. Both sides adopted the Joint Declaration for Co-operation to combat International Terrorism. The document is an agreement for peace, progress and prosperity in the region and is designed to foster closer economic and political ties. It incorporated a plan of action for even more intensive cooperation on political and security issues as well as in the economic, social and cultural fields. A number of other new dimensions, such as cooperation in remote sensing, space technology and information technology (IT) have been added to the region's millennia-old cultural, religious and civilisational links. The document set out ways for a multi-directional approach to the strengthening of political and economic cooperation between India and ASEAN and covered fields such as science and technology, health, agriculture and culture. In addition to the Laos-India Entrepreneurship Development Centre in Vientiane, three more such establishments were planned for establishment in the capitals of Cambodia, Myanmar and Vietnam.

The First BIMSTEC (Bay of Bengal Initiative for Multi-Sectoral Technical and Economic Cooperation) Summit meeting was held in Bangkok on 31 July 2004. It was attended by the President of Sri Lanka and the Prime Ministers of Bangladesh, Bhutan, India, Myanmar, Nepal and Thailand. The Summit adopted a declaration that placed special emphasis on cooperation in the sectors of trade and investment, transport and communication, tourism, energy, human resource development, agriculture, fisheries, science and technology and people-to-people contacts. The follow-up meetings of BIMSTEC Trade Negotiating Committee, BIMSTEC Task Force and the meeting of the chief executives of the railway systems of these countries have generated a positive environment for greater economic cooperation among the BIMSTEC countries.

India and the ARF: Regional Peace and Stability

It was in this general context of cooperation that India became a member of the ASEAN Regional Forum (ARF), a grouping that includes major powers such as the Australia, USA, Russia and China with high security stakes in East Asia. The Indian Government having subsequently engaged the other ARF members on the Pokhran nuclear weapon tests of 1998, to some commentators seemed to have fended off an imminent collapse of its 'Look-East Policy'.

The specifics of the latest agreements between India and some ASEAN states may, if implemented suitably, enable India to maintain its 'Look East Policy' course. The move towards a comprehensive Indo-Singaporean economic agreement acquired importance in the light of the city-state's ability to capitialise on India's economic reforms (Reddy, 2006; 249-265). A concerted move by India and Thailand to establish a transport corridor across Myanmar needs to be viewed in its own context as a cooperative venture. Any perception to see this proposed project as a possible sign of Sino-Indian rivalry for the strategic affections of key ASEAN states will only raise the security stakes. India's strategic interaction with South Korea is still very much a dialogue, except for the economic dimension. The success of India's 'Look-East Policy' may depend in part on China's strategic and trade perceptions of the regional seas.

While welcoming India's 'Look East' foreign policy initiatives, China had expressed hope that India's increasing engagement with Southeast Asian states would lead to enhanced regional peace and stability. "We have taken note of the relevant reports. We welcome India and relevant countries engaging in friendly cooperative relations," Chinese Foreign Ministry spokesman Zhu Bangzao, said. "We hope that this relationship is beneficial to regional peace and stability", Zhu said while commenting on the 2002 visit to Vietnam and Indonesia by Prime Minister Atal Bihari Vajpayee.

At the same time, Chinese officials, experts and the media were closely watching India's attempts to reach out to key states in Southeast Asia and to forging defence pacts in an area widely considered a stronghold of Beijing. The Chinese official media has also been paying attention to India's 'Look East' diplomacy and Vajpayee's visit to Hanoi in particular received good coverage. The state-run *Xinhua* news agency noted that Vajpayee's visit to Indonesia and Vietnam "... will bring into sharper focus India's 'Look East' policy aimed at further consolidating relations with the Southeast Asian states". The visit also assumed significance as it was the first after India brought in a powerful cultural dimension to its ties with Southeast Asian states through the six-member Mekong-Ganga project in 2000 that involves Bangladesh, Cambodia, India, Laos, Thailand and Vietnam (Reddy, 2006; 258).

Contribution of the Indian Navy towards Regional Security

On 16 April 2006, Defence Minister, Pranab Mukherjee, commented that the transfer of the Indian Naval ship *Tillanchang* to the Government of the Maldives was to ensure an atmosphere of peace, stability and tranquility in the region so that both countries could attend to socio-economic development free from external interference (*The Hindu*, 2006). The Maldives is strategically located in relation to the crucial sea lanes that crisscross the Indian Ocean basin. Referring to the observations of the former Prime Minister, Indira Gandhi, during her visit in 1975 that

India did not subscribe to the concept of big and small states, India would always use its strength to promote peace and help neighbours and friendly countries.

The transfer of the ship was part of the cooperation between the two states in the fight against terrorism, piracy and smuggling under the broad framework of the 1982 United Nations Convention on the Law of the Sea. Relations between the two countries were not uni-dimensional but encompassed economic, cultural and educational fields. The request for the ship to perform multiple tasks such as patrolling the exclusive economic zone and taking action against non-state actors, had come from the Maldives Government. The ship was decommissioned from the Indian Navy and transferred to Maldives in the presence of its President Maumoom Abdul Gayoom, Defence Minister Isamel Shafeeu and Foreign Minister Ahmad Shaheed in the presence of the Indian High Commissioner to Male, A.K. Pandey, senior Defence Ministry official Rita Menon and Chairman and Managing Director of Garden Reach Shipbuilders and Engineers (the builders of the ship), *Ganeshan*. The Indian Navy will assist Maldives in maintaining the ship in its lifetime.

The Union Cabinet gave its approval on 20 April 2006 for the signing and ratification of the Regional Cooperation Agreement on Combating Piracy and Armed Robbery (RCACPAR) against ships on the seas of South and Southeast Asia. It also approved the designation of the Coast Guard as the focal point for the purpose of this agreement, Defence Minister, Pranab Mukherjee, told reporters after the meeting of the Cabinet. The agreement, the first of its kind for combating piracy and armed robbery at sea in Asia, was signed by 16 states including India, Bangladesh, China, Brunei, Japan, Korea, Singapore, Thailand, Vietnam, Malaysia, Indonesia, Philippines, Laos and Sri Lanka. The pact would pave the way for the establishment of an information-sharing centre concerning piracy and armed robbery that would be located in Singapore. Signatories to the Agreement would also extend mutual legal assistance and extradition in respect of the offences covered under it. The agreement will strengthen cooperation amongst the contracting parties in the prevention and suppression of armed robbery and in tracing, identifying and prosecuting persons involved in such acts and would help in making the sea lanes in the region secure. Japan, Laos and Singapore have already ratified the agreement (*Channel News Asia*, April, 2006).

A request by the United States for the Indian Navy to show a physical presence in the northern waters of the Malacca Strait was seen as a natural and positive step towards the crystallisation of the Look East Policy. The move was also welcomed by the littoral states of the Malacca Strait. These arrangements are obviously founded on the excellent reaction and support given by the Indian navy in the case of the m.v. *Aluondra Rainbow,* when the ship was hijacked shortly after departing Kuala Tanjong, Indonesia, en route to Miike, Japan (Prasad, 2006; 279). Fifteen pirates, allegedly Indonesian nationals, set the ship's 17-member crew adrift on a raft, on 28 October 1999, in the Andaman Sea, in the vicinity of northern Sumatra (Sumatera) Island. On 8 November, the raft and crew were spotted by fishers off the coast of Phuket Island, Thailand. The pirates were charged with setting the crew adrift, trying to scuttle the ship, attempting to set it on fire and committing armed robbery.

The International Maritime Bureau's involvement, which was coordinated by the Piracy Reporting Centre in Kuala Lumpur, in the eventual apprehension of the *Aloundra Rainbow*, began during the hijacking phase when it assisted the Indian Navy and Coast Guard track down the ship on 13 November 1999, off the south coast of India. The ship had been renamed *Mega Rama*. The Indian Coastguard was requested to investigate, and once the ship's identity was confirmed, it was challenged. A high-sea chase – hot pursuit – ensued before the ship was eventually boarded and taken to Mumbai where the pirate crew was arrested (Forbes and Sakhuja, 2004; 10-11).

On 25 February 2003, an Indian court charged the 14 pirates on eleven counts under Indian Penal Code for hijacking the Japanese-owned ship, m.v. *Aluondra Rainbow* and handed down sentences of seven-years 'rigorous imprisonment' (read, *hard labour*) to each of the pirates; a fifteenth member of the team died whilst in custody. The Court's (Indian) decision set a precedent that hopefully would assist to deter similar crimes of piracy. The court action taken by India was supported by the provisions of Article 105 of the 1982 United Nations Law of the Sea Convention. The pirates were released in 2005 due to a legal technicality whereby the exact geographical location of the apprehension whilst in hot pursuit was not recorded.

The Australia-India Connection

India's 'Look East Policy' has a wider horizon south of the Equator in that Australia is also encompassed in this vision of trade and cultural exchanges and regional cooperation. India and Australia have worked together constructively on key international issues that include the Asia-

Pacific Partnership on Clean Development and Climate and the East Asia Summit. Bonds of friendship were renewed and strengthened in early 2006 when Australia's Prime Minister, John Howard, visited India to advance Australia's foreign and trade policies. During that four-day visit in March, the Prime Minister signed a number of agreements in various fields that included education, trade, science and air services (*Media Release*, PM's Office, 4 March 2006).

Australia is a sparsely populated (estimated 20 million inhabitants in 2006) country of about 7.7 million square kilometers. It has one of the most stable economic, political and social environments in the Asia-Pacific region which has led to increased inward investment in the last decade. A recent diversification in Australia's export structure coupled with its 'Look West' (or was it intended as 'Look Northwest'?) policy means that, although Australia continues in its role as a commodity exporter, it now also relies on service industries and sophisticated manufacturing industries. Australia has one of the world's most open and innovative economies, and the Australian Government is committed to maintaining this direction. Strong growth over the past decade has been accompanied by low inflation and interest rates, and a solid productivity performance (Agrawala, 2002; 249-260). Collectively, ASEAN offers many opportunities for both Australia and India. Australia and India have common democratic traditions, a shared history and language, similar legal systems, sporting traditions and financial and Governmental structures. Commercial trade between the two countries is considered healthy and there is rapid growth in investment by Australian companies operating in India. Australia is now the third preferred destination by Indians and India is the second largest source of skilled migrants. In 2005, the two-way trade between Australia and India amounted to about $A 9.4 billion.

The Australian Government continues to take important steps to further improve Australia's international competitiveness. It has given a more active role in business and has undertaken a major reform of Australia's labour market and has reduced the regulatory burden on business. Already, Australia's general tariff rate is only five per cent. International trade now accounts for 40 per cent of Australia's GDP. Services amount to nearly a quarter of total Australian exports. A significant and growing proportion of Australia's exports are manufactured goods. Although 'farming' and 'quarrying' have stereotyped its economy, the change has necessitated an engagement with Asia. Nearly sixty per cent of Australia's exports and over half of its total foreign direct investment are directed to countries in the Asia-Pacific region. Australia is a better place for these changes and is now more competitive and confident.

India, likewise, has liberalised it trading policies with the world. Its economic transformation since 1991 has been remarkable. Economic growth, exports and foreign capital inflows have all risen dramatically. It has resumed its place as one of the world's leading agricultural and industrialized nation and is now recognised as an economically dynamic state. Such facts can only be achieved by releasing the energies of the private sector, and by joining fully with the world economy. Economic reform is an ongoing process and it requires the Government's commitment to ambitious development and growth goals. India's policy of increased engagement with East Asia is another positive development. Its influence in East Asia and the broader Asia-Pacific region will grow markedly in the future. For this reason alone, the Australian Government was supportive of India joining the ASEAN Regional Forum and welcomed India's attainment of dialogue partnership status with ASEAN. The Australian Government has cooperated with India in working through the multilateral system to achieve progress in the World Trade Organisation (WTO) (Hoda, 2006; 94-104; Sally, 2006; 122-130). Australia is committed to pursuing freer international trade and achieving the potential of the WTO and has encouraged India to adopt a similar stance on this issue. Because of the economic changes that have occurred in both Australia and India, there is now greater potential to strengthen the partnership, building on long-established and valued ties (Kaul, 2002; 220-226). Naturally, commercial links lead the way. For example, bilateral trade has nearly doubled in the past few years and is set to double again. Investment has also accelerated and Australia is now one of India's top ten investors. India is in the process of becoming one of Australia's most important regional and bilateral partners (Bala, 2002; 220-226).

Australia is committed to promoting the full potential of the Australia-India relationship. In order to sustain its rapid economic development, India requires world class technologies in areas like telecommunications, electric power generation, infrastructure and resource development, and environmental management. India will also need to strengthen its capacities in services like insurance, banking, education and the full range of professional services. Australia is a leading-edge competitor in all of these areas. Already, Australia supplies much of India's coking coal needs for its steel industry and Australian wool is found in Indian textiles. Australian engineers are helping in highway and port developments whilst

Australian universities and colleges are helping to educate and train Indians.

Australian mining skills and technology are being demonstrated at the Pipawar coal mine and in many other mineral and civil engineering projects. Australia has a large foreign banking presence in India, and its environmental, telecommunications and medical technologies are now widely utilised in India. Australia's largest companies are increasingly involved in India. They include ANZ Banking, BHP-Billiton, Rio-Tinto, Telstra and News Corporation, which are all operating successfully in India, while a host of small-to medium-sized Australian companies have now made their way into Indian markets.

On the other side of the equation, Indian companies are finding new opportunities to invest and trade in Australia. One example highlights the direction and potential of Indian commercial activity in Australia: Indian-made motor vehicles, like the Suzuki Alto and the Maruti Jeep, are making a real impression in Australian markets. The momentum of the Australia-India partnership is growing but there is still a great deal of unfulfilled potential. It is here that both Governments have an important role to play.

The Australian Cabinet approved a Memorandum of Understanding (MOU) between the Central Board for Excise and Customs of India and the Australian Custom Service for cooperation and mutual assistance in customs matters. The MOU would help in the availability of reliable, quick and cost-effective information and intelligence for the prevention and investigation of custom offences and apprehension of offenders. It also provides for the exchange of information for the simplification and harmonisation of customs procedures. (*The Hindu, 2006)* On 6 March 2006, another MOU was signed for bio-technology cooperation and for the establishment of a strategic research fund for exchange scholarships worth about $A 25 million. (PM Office, Media Release, 2006) At the Madras Institute of Technology, on 8 March 2006, another MOU was signed which relates to cooperation in areas of technology, more specifically, information technology.

India's Future Prospects with ASEAN and Australia

To fulfill the potential of the relationship, Australia and India must update and broaden the perceptions that each has of the other. The Australian Government is updating its image in India and project itself to modern India. The 'New Horizons' initiative highlights Australia's diversity and advanced economy. It aims to make Indians aware that Australia's prosperity rests in large part with the energy and skills of a multicultural society drawn from many countries.

Around 40 per cent of Australia's new migrants come from Asia. Among those migrants has been a strong contingent of people born in India. The contribution of Australia's Indian-born community to Australia's economic and social life and their vital role in fostering Australia-India relations has been very significant. New Horizons also aim to expose Australians to India's tremendous cultural vitality and its impressive scientific and technological achievements. These objectives are being realised through a range of business, science, technology, education, cultural and sporting events in six major Indian cities – Bangalore, Chandigarh, Chennai, Kolkata, Mumbai and New Delhi.

Australia's longstanding policy of only selling uranium to countries that are signatories (ratifiers) to the nuclear *Non-Proliferation Treaty* (NPT) is perhaps a bone of contention with India. In late-February 2006, the United States President, George W. Bush, and the Prime Minister of India, Manmohan Singh, signed an agreement towards positive development of the latter's nuclear programme. The terms of the agreement placed the Australian Government in an awkward situation especially as Australia possesses large reserves of uranium which could be sold at relatively high prices in 2006 and Australia is willing to sell the mineral but insists that the Government must be satisfied about the safeguards.

Within Southeast Asia and the Indian sub-continent, road and rail links could be improved so as to accelerate investment and trade and technology transfer (Reddy, 2006; 259). A proposal that regional cooperation in the area of energy security, sustainability of energy and the management of energy demand at national levels with due consideration to the local and regional environments has been put forward by Kumar (2006; 302). This mode of cooperation could be extended to the construction of transnational Asian gas and oil pipelines and more importantly joint patrolling of the sea lanes of the northeast basin of the Indian Ocean (Forbes and Sakhuja, 2004).

Conclusion

India, through the foresight of its leaders, has made a conscious effort to increase economic cooperation with ASEAN and Australia. The Look East Policy has crystallised into a highly focused foreign policy especially in directing attention to those states that are over its eastern horizon. It is to be commended. For many decades, India has been encompassed in a rim of insecurity, particularly because of terrestrial border alignment issues with China and Pakistan to the north; maritime boundary issues with Bangladesh and Pakistan; riverine and water rights issues with its neighbours; rebellion in its north-eastern State of Assam; internal problems in Sri Lanka to the south; and China's growing interest and development of its diplomatic and trade policies with its neighbours, both near and far.

India is one of the most dynamic and fastest growing economies of the world. It constitutes not only a vast and growing market, but also a competitive source of technologies and knowledge-based services. Countries across the globe are beginning to see India as an indispensable economic partner and are seeking mutually rewarding economic and commercial links with the emerging economy. The growing recognition of India as a dependable partner is reflected in its emergence as a compulsory destination in the itineraries of the world leaders and reflects the high standing and credibility that the Government and its leadership enjoy.

There is confidence that the New Horizons will be the beginning of a new era in relations between Australia and India. The concept is not a culmination, but the start of new links and projects between Australia and India. It is an important initiative that will make a lasting contribution to the development of mutual contact and understanding between the business sectors of both countries. India's contribution to this endeavour cannot be underestimated, for it is the contacts that are made and the contracts that the two states sign that will significantly define future relations between Australia and India. Australia has much to offer India and it is always willing to work in partnership with India in its enormous and vital task of development. The foundations of the Australia-India relationship are strong, and the potential for fruitful collaboration is immense. Both countries along with ASEAN are there for a long-term partnership, not short-term gain, and the synergies which are being created are becoming very clear. The cooperation between ASEAN and India has progressed steadily on three streams: economic, political and security cooperation, which is seemingly a renewal of a bygone era of freedom of the seas and trade in the Indian Ocean Region.

REFERENCES

Agrawala, Reena (2002) 'Australia and globalization: Economic Integration with India' in Gopal, D., ed., *Australia in the Emerging Global Order*, Delhi, Shipra Publications, pp. 249-256.

Ariff, Mohammed and Lim, C.C. (2006) 'ASEAN and India FTA: Issues and Prospects'.

Kumar, Nagesh; Sen, Rahul and Asher, Mukul (2006) (Eds.) *India-ASEAN Economic Relations Meeting the Challenges of Globalization*, Singapore, Institute of Southeast Asian Studies and New Delhi: Research and Information System for Developing Countries, pp. 69-92

Athukorala, Prema-Chandra (2006) 'Foreign Direct Investment in ASEAN and India: Trends and Prospects' in Kumar, Nagesh; Sen, Rahul and Asher, Mukul (2006) (Eds.) *India-ASEAN Economic Relations Meeting the Challenges of Globalization*, Singapore, Institute of Southeast Asian Studies and New Delhi: Research and Information System for Developing Countries, pp. 145-182

Bala, Madhu (2002) 'India-Australia Trade and Investment Relations in the 1990s', in Gopal, D. (Ed.) *Australia in the Emerging Global Order*, Delhi, Shipra Publications, pp. 235-248

Chaudhuri, K.N. (1990) *Asia before Europe: Economy and Civilisation of the Indian Ocean from the Rise of Islam to 1750*, Cambridge, Cambridge University Press, pp. 470

Chia Lin Sien (2003) *Southeast Asia Transformed: A Geography of Change*, Singapore, Singapore University Press, pp. 452

Curzon, Lord G.N. (1906) *Lord Curzon in India* Being a selection from His Speeches as Viceroy and Governor-General of India, 1898-1905, London: Macmillan and Co., Ltd. pp. 597

Davare, Sudhir (2006) *India and Southeast Asia Towards Security Convergence*, Singapore, Singapore University Press, pp. 252

Fisher, C.A. (1964) *South-East Asia A Social, Economic and Political Geography*, London, Methuen and Co. Ltd., pp. 831

Forbes, V.L. (1995) *The Maritime Boundaries of the Indian Ocean Region*, Singapore, Singapore University Press, pp. 267

Forbes V.L. and Sakhuja, Vijay (2004) 'Challenging Acts of Marine Trans-boundary Transgressions in the Indian Ocean region, *MIMA Issue Paper*, Kuala Lumpur. Maritime Institute of Malaysia, pp. 23.

Gopal, Darvesh (Ed.) *Australia in the Emerging Global Order*, Delhi, Shipra Publications, pp. 369

Gaopal, Darvesh and Rumley, Dennis (2004) *India and Australia Issues and Opportunities*, Delhi. Authorspress, pp. 412

Hall, D.G.E. (1981) *A History of Southeast Asia*, 4th Edition, London. MacMillan Press, pp. 1070

Hindu, The (2004) 'Editorial: UPA Government to adhere to six basic principles of governance' 28 May

Hoda, Anwarul (2006) 'India in the WTO: Issues, Challenges and prospects of Co-operation with ASEAN', in Kumar, Nagesh; Sen, Rahul and Asher, Mukul (2006) (Eds.) *India-ASEAN Economic Relations Meeting the Challenges of Globalization*, Singapore: Institute of Southeast Asian Studies and New Delhi, Research and Information System for Developing Countries, pp. 93-120.

Joseph, K.J. and Parayil, Govindan 92006) 'India-ASEAN Co-operation and Communication Technologies (ICTs): Issues and prospects', in Kumar, Nagesh; Sen, Rahul and Asher, Mukul (2006) (Eds.) *India-ASEAN Economic Relations Meeting the Challenges of Globalization*, Singapore, Institute of Southeast Asian Studies and New Delhi: Research and Information System for Developing Countries, pp. 219-248.

Kaul, M.M. (2002) 'Australia-India Relations: A Critical Survey', in Gopal, D. (Ed.) *Australia in the Emerging Global Order*, Delhi: Shipra Publications, pp. 220-235

Kumar, Nagesh (2006) 'Long-term Vision of India-ASEAN partnership: Towards an ASEAN Economic Community' in Kumar, Nagesh; Sen, Rahul and Asher, Mukul (2006) (Eds.) *India-ASEAN Economic Relations Meeting the Challenges of Globalization*, Singapore: Institute of Southeast Asian Studies and New Delhi: Research and Information System for Developing Countries, pp. 291-313

Kumar, Nagesh; Sen, Rahul and Asher, Mukul (2006) (Eds.) *India-ASEAN Economic Relations Meeting the Challenges of Globalization*, Singapore: Institute of Southeast Asian Studies and New Delhi: Research and Information System for Developing Countries, pp. 313

Kumar, Nagesh; Sen, Rahul and Asher, Mukul (2006) 'India-ASEAN Partnership in an Era of Globalisation: An Overview', in *India-ASEAN Economic Relations Meeting the Challenges of Globalization*, Singapore: Institute of Southeast Asian Studies and New Delhi: Research and Information System for Developing Countries, pp. 1-14

McPherson, Kenneth (1993) The Indian Ocean A History of People and the Sea, Delhi: Oxford university Press, pp. 318.

Nageswaran, V.A. and Krithivasan, Sivakumar (2006) 'Capital Market Reforms in India and ASEAN: Avenues for Co-operation', in Kumar, Nagesh; Sen, Rahul and Asher, Mukul (2006) (Eds.) *India-ASEAN Economic Relations Meeting the Challenges of Globalization*, Singapore: Institute of Southeast Asian Studies and New Delhi: Research and Information System for Developing Countries, pp. 183-218.

Osborne, Milton (1990) *Southeast Asia* An Illustrated Introductory History, 5th Edition, Sydney: Allen and Unwin, pp. 263

Parikh, K.S. (2006) 'Indian Economy: a Shinning Star or a passing Comet?' in Kumar, Nagesh; Sen, Rahul and Asher, Mukul (2006) (Eds.) *India-ASEAN Economic Relations Meeting the Challenges of Globalization*, Singapore: Institute of Southeast Asian Studies and New Delhi: Research and Information System for Developing Countries, pp. 15-40

Prasad, M.V.S.V. (2006) 'Political and Security Cooperation between India and ASEAN: Implications for Economic Co-operation', in Kumar, Nagesh; Sen, Rahul and Asher, Mukul (2006) (Eds.) *India-ASEAN Economic Relations Meeting the Challenges of Globalization*, Singapore: Institute of Southeast

Asian Studies and New Delhi: Research and Information System for Developing Countries, pp. 267-290

Reddy, K. Raja (2006) 'Sub-regional Economic Co-operation between India and ASEAN', in Kumar, Nagesh; Sen, Rahul and Asher, Mukul (2006) (Eds.) *India-ASEAN Economic Relations Meeting the Challenges of Globalization*, Singapore: Institute of Southeast Asian Studies and New Delhi: Research and Information System for Developing Countries, pp. 249-266

Sally, Razeen (2006) 'ASEAN in the WTO: Prospects of Cooperation with India' in Kumar, Nagesh; Sen, Rahul and Asher, Mukul (2006) (Eds.) *India-ASEAN Economic Relations Meeting the Challenges of Globalization*, Singapore: Institute of Southeast Asian Studies and New Delhi: Research and Information System for Developing Countries, pp. 121-144

Savage, V R., Kong Lily and Neville, Warwick (1998) *The Naga Awakens* Growth and Change in Southeast Asia, Singapore: Times Academic Press, pp. 351

Savage, V.R. and Tan-Mullins, May (2005) *The Naga Challenged* Southeast Asia in the Winds of Change, Singapore: Marshall Cavendish Academic, pp. 489.

Schwartzberg, J.E. (Ed)(1978) *A Historical Atlas of Southeast Asia*, Chicago: University of Chicago Press, 375 pp.

Suarez, Thomas (1999) *Early Mapping of Southeast Asia,* Singapore: Periplus, pp. 280

Web Page References

Department of Commerce, India Web address:
http://commerce.nic.in/india_trade/region_analysis_mar2004.htm <accessed 23-11-05>

Cabinet nod for agreement to combat ship piracy
http://www.hinduonnet.com/thehindu/thscrip/print.pl?file= 2006010706451200.htm&date=2006/01/07/&prd=th&

http://www.thehindu.com/2006/04/17/stories/2006041706371200.htm <accessed at various dates prior and during period of research>

Office of the Prime Minister of Australia Web page: http://www.pm.gov.au

Indo-Asian News Service: http://www.24x7updates.com

Channel News Asia, 20 April 2006 'China and India should use economic leverage to persuade Myanmar: ASEAN Chief http://www.channelnewsasia.com/afp_asiapacific

The *Economic Times of India* "World Bank clears loan of Rs. 2,817 cr". http://economictimes.indiatimes.com/articleshow/1512878.cms

APPENDIX

FRAMEWORK AGREEMENT ON COMPREHENSIVE ECONOMIC COOPERATION BETWEEN THE REPUBLIC OF INDIA AND THE ASSOCIATION OF SOUTH EAST ASIAN NATIONS

Article One

Objectives

The objectives of this Agreement are to: (a) strengthen and enhance economic, trade and investment co-operation between the Parties; (b) progressively liberalise and promote trade in goods and services as well as create a transparent, liberal and facilitative investment regime; (c) explore new areas and develop appropriate measures for closer economic co-operation between the Parties; and (d) facilitate the more effective economic integration of the new ASEAN Member States and bridge the development gap among the Parties.

Signed by India's Prime Minister on 8 October 2003 at Bali, Indonesia

INSTRUMENT OF ACCESS TO THE TREATY OF AMITY AND CO-OPERATION IN SOUTHEAST ASIA

"...now, therefore, the republic of India, having considered the aforesaid treaty as amended by Protocols, hereby accedes to the same and undertakes faithfully to perform and carry out all the stipulations therein contained."

Signed by India's Minister of External Affairs on 8 October 2003 at Bali, Indonesia

ASEAN-INDIA JOINT DECLARATION FOR CO-OPERATION TO COMBAT INTERNATIONAL TERRORISM

Objectives

1. The participants re-affirm the importance of having a framework for co-operation to prevent, disrupt and combat international terrorism through the exchange and flow of information, intelligence and capacity-building.
2. The participants emphasise that the purpose of this co-operation is to enhance the efficacy of those efforts to combat terrorism.

Signed: Head of State, Republic of India on 8 October 2003 at Bali, Indonesia

ASEAN-INDIA PARTNERSHIP FOR PEACE, PROGRESS AND SHARED ROSPERITY

Signed in Vientiane, Laos on 30 November 2004

PLAN OF ACTION TO IMPLEMENT THE ASEAN-INDIA PARTNERSHIP FOR PEACE, PROGRESS AND SHARED PROSPERITY

Signed in Vientiane, Laos on 30 November 2004

9

Australia's Regional Security Challenges

A Geopolitical Perspective

DENNIS RUMLEY

The changing nature of globalisation processes and their differential regional security impacts have yet to be matched by a 'new' Australian regional security paradigm. Rather, Australia is still principally associated with the application of an 'old' security paradigm which emphasises threats which emanate from regional states even though those states are 'neighbours' and among its closest trading partners. Not only are Australia's regional economic ties incongruent with the structure of its defence expenditure, but globalisation has thrown up new security challenges which have yet to be fully incorporated into the policy framework. Of course, Australia is not unique in this regard, since the Asia-Pacific region is in a process of transition from its former Cold War status to a status which remains to be designed by regional states. In short, 21st century regional geopolitical realities require the construction of a 'new' security paradigm designed to meet the current regional security challenges.

It is neither immediately apparent what kind of regional order is emerging in the Asia-Pacific nor whether there is regional agreement among alternative orders (Harris, 1997). On the one hand, the ongoing 'open' economic process of "new regionalism" has served to enhance regional stability and minimise potential intra-regional conflict. On the other hand, a host of geopolitical challenges such as ideological conflict, political development and environmental insecurity, for example, are often working in an opposite direction. However, it has been concluded that, for the region as a whole, the balance of stabilising factors outweighs any potentially destabilising forces such as territorial disputes, religious fundamentalism and nationalism (Alagappa, 1997). The aim of the present chapter is to present an overview and evaluation from a geopolitical standpoint of some of Australia's main regional security challenges in order to identify any potential threat to regional stability and thus to Australian security interests broadly defined. In order to achieve this aim, the Chapter is divided into four main sections. The first section deals with some of the tensions associated with a closer regional orientation which Australian policy-makers face and which are perceived by regional states and peoples. The second section reiterates a geopolitical model to describe Australia's regional relations. The third section discusses how the cooperative security front to Australia's north and the aid front to Australia's east appear to be have been transformed into an arc of instability in the 21st century. The final section deals with Australia's role in recent attempts to create a "new regionalism" as a geo-political counterweight to NAFTA and the EU.

The Tension in Australia's Regional Orientation

It can be argued that Australia's geopolitical tension arises out of a set of conflicts which are generated as a result of differing ideological orientations towards any or all of three contested models which describe the essence of Australia's external relations – a cultural/colonial model, a security/old War model and an economic/post-Cold War model (Rumley, 2006).

The Cultural/Colonial Model

In essence, the colonial model for Australia's external relations argues that Australia is, in fact, a far-flung outpost of Western Europe, and that, since its population structure is primarily European, and that Europe is the largest source of foreign investment ($340.7 million or 34.8% of the total in 2003), Europe, and especially the UK, should remain the principal target for Australian external (especially socio-cultural) linkages. This model is thus associated with the question of Australian national identity, which has been slowly changing as Australia has been increasingly linked into the Asia-Pacific region. However, it is also related to the changing nature of traditional security and to the emergence of regionalism in Europe itself.

Of course, Australia is no different from most other states in the Asia-Pacific region in that it is an example of a multicultural, post-colonial state engaged in the process of nation-building. Australia still possesses a quasi-colonial political map that exhibits a clear 'royal' structure with its colonial boundaries, English royalist names and economic and political power located in the southeastern corner, as in the "mother country"

(Rumley, 1999; 151). It is also a federal state in which its principal national symbols – the head of state, the flag and the national anthem-are contested. These characteristics create considerable pressures on the conduct of Australia's external relations since they generate some uncertainty over Australia's orientation on the part of regional states and peoples. The regionally-perceived lack of a truly 'independent' Australia, which was reinforced by the Republic referendum result of 6 November 1999, continues to constrain the enthusiasm of some Asia-Pacific states regarding Australia's true regional intentions. The referendum question, which asked Australian voters if they wished to establish a Republic and if the President should be appointed by the Federal Parliament, received a 54.9 per cent "no" vote nationally. Despite there being majority public support for a Republic, the provision in the referendum question for the President to be appointed by Parliament ensured its defeat. Interestingly, there were some significant variations in the level of support for the referendum question by State and Territory. Perhaps not surprisingly, the largest "no" vote was recorded in *Queens*land (62.6%). However, what is surprising, perhaps, is that the only majority vote in favour of the question was in the Australian Capital Territory (63.3%).

As a result of a combination of these factors, among others, Australia is thus often regionally perceived as being a surrogate for European, primarily British, interests. Furthermore, its regional 'orientation' has been sometimes seen as a superficial and "practical" means of enhancing its trade position. Material goals deriving from a desire for trade enhancement thus invariably collide with other non-material principles. From this viewpoint, notions of an Australian long-term regional commitment are often perceived to be ambiguous both by regional governments and by the regional peoples.

The Security/Cold War Model

The Cold War model primarily incorporates traditional security thinking, and, to a lesser extent, cultural and economic considerations. It suggests that the United States ought to remain the pre-eminent Australian security linkage, that this linkage ought to be strengthened (Baker and Paal, 2000) and that West Pacific security regionalism ought to be accorded a lower priority. One variant of this model argues that Australia should discard its regionalism linkages with West Pacific states and engage in a new regional grouping along with the United States, Canada and New Zealand (Huntington, 1996).

Conventional explanations of Australia's military security prior to the end of the Cold War period have relied heavily on a dependency thesis-that is, an Australian security dependency relationship with a powerful non-regional state was seen to be necessary based on the assumption that, in the event of a hostile geopolitical environment, Australia did not possess the capacity to defend itself (Bell, 1993). In return, Australia would commit itself militarily to non-regional wars. From the time of European colonisation to the end of the Cold War period, Australia has in turn been dependent for its military security upon the world's greatest economic power.

From an Australian societal viewpoint, there exist a number of contested views over the nature of mutual images and relationships between the United States and Australia (Rolfe, 1997). On one hand, there is a warm and robust relationship which is built around past security ties, similar cultural and political institutions, a genuine admiration for the US liberal tradition and a strong economic relationship. Indeed, many elements of Australian life used the United States as a model, although, despite the fears of some, Americanisation has not necessarily threatened Australian national identity (Bell and Bell, 1998). Furthermore, the current US-Australian alliance has been characterised as the most intimate relationship in Asia (*sic*) (Blackwill, 2000; 118). Among other things, from the early 1960s, the relationship was strengthened by the operation in Australia of a number of joint facilities, including Northwest Cape in Western Australia (1963) and Pine Gap in Alice Springs (1966). However, it is likely that only the latter will remain a central element of cooperative intelligence into the twenty-first century (Department of Defence, 2000; 98-9).

On the other hand, there is considerable Australian concern over the unchanging reality of the asymmetrical nature of these linkages, and, when coupled with an Australian traditional dislike of authority and sense of independence, in part contributes to a sense of unease among many over US security dominance. In addition, there is a kind of innate Australian distrust of dominant states that are perceived to pursue their own interests at the expense of other states. Associated with this, there is still some residual concern among the Australian Left about possible past US interference in Australia's internal affairs (Whitlam, 1985, 29-53; Pilger, 1989; 139-178; Johnson, 2000; 163). This residual concern is often associated with a view about regional security in the Asia-Pacific –that is, in the final analysis, regional security can only be guaranteed regionally.

The Economic/Post-Cold War Model

One of Australia's responses to globalisation and to the end of the Cold War was to engage in the construction of its own brand of economic regionalism. As a part of this process of so-called "new regionalism", economic cooperation with Asia-Pacific states was taken by policy-makers to be an Australian priority (Bonnor, 1994). However, during this process, which became more concrete during the 1980s, Australia had to face a number of interrelated economic dilemmas, out of which derive three broad interrelated dimensions of contestation. First, is what might be referred to as the *trade dilemma*, associated with Australia being a trade-dependent maritime state. This is tied up with a number of other factors-the notion of market access and free trade and an associated appropriate regional structure; second, Australia's past and present role and perception of APEC; third, the respective long-term goals of APEC; fourth, the relationship between Asia-Pacific sub-regionalisms; and, finally, the use of Asia-Pacific regionalism as a counterweight to Europe and the USA and as a response to their own regionalisms. A second dimension of contestation relates to the *geographical nature of regionalism*; first, whether it takes an economic versus a cultural regionalism perspective; second, whether it is a Western compared with a non-Western regionalism; third, what should be the size and scope of the region both from an Australian and a non-Australian perspective? A third, and perhaps more important, dimension of contestation, is the degree to which the post-Cold War economic orientation to Asia is matched by cultural and security relationships.

The Trilateral Geopolitical Tension

Among other things, such issues touch at the heart of Australian identity and raise questions of an imagined identity. Broinowski (2003; 219) aptly describes the tensions which are raised as a result between an imagined European and an imagined Asian identity. However, the crosscutting cleavages arising from Australia's basic trilateral geopolitical tension are potentially among the most problematical for Australian policy-makers (Figure 1).

From a global and a regional perspective, Australia is seen to follow the United States militarily and politically; economically, Australia connects with Asia; culturally, Australia identifies with Europe. The question of an imagined Australian identity for the 21st century is something that has divided the two main political groupings. The more so-called "progressive" opposition Australian labour Party (ALP) is seen by some to favour stronger security, economic and cultural ties with Asia at the expense of the United States and the UK. On the other hand, the current governing conservative coalition is seen as moving closer to the United States and the UK at the expense of Asia. This ideological dichotomy is perceived both within and outside of Australia.

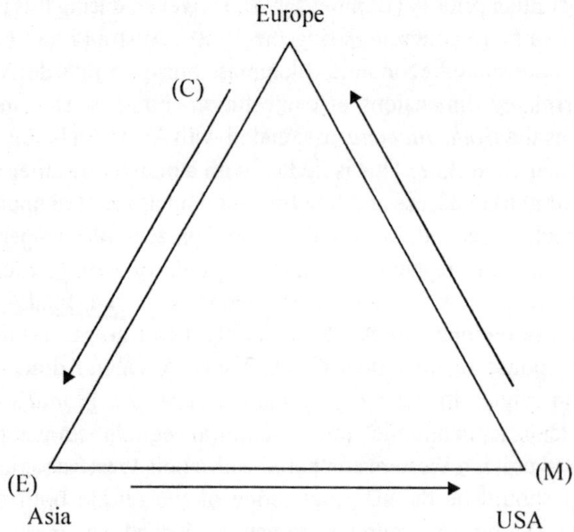

Fig. 1: Australia's Trilateral Geopolitical Tension

Dilemmas, Conflicts and Perceptions

Such an ideological dichotomy appears to be especially important from an Asian perspective and as having an impact upon bilateral relationships. For example, in Japan, the influential newspaper, the 'Asahi Shimbun', noted in the early 1990s that Australia was "rejecting Europe and entering Asia". In 1996, however, following the election of the present Australian government, the same paper reported that Australia was "rejecting Asia and entering the United States" (Broinowski, 2003; 227).

In a 1996 survey, Quantum Market Research found that slightly more Australians favoured turning the national orientation towards Asia as opposed to the West – 32 per cent compared to 31 per cent. However, by 2002, Quantum's survey showed a different perception of Australia's view of itself and found that only 17 per cent of respondents favoured an Asian orientation, while 38 per cent said that Australia should aim to favour the West. The decline in those favouring Asia is especially marked immediately following both the 1996 and the 2001 Federal elections.

Clearly, Australia has played a leading role in the construction of new regionalism in the Asia-Pacific, especially in terms of the creation of APEC. However, one of Australia's principal dilemmas has been the danger that the combination of a possible collapse or sidelining of APEC and the emergence of East Asian regionalism will lead to regional economic isolation. Indeed, a few years ago, the Australian Foreign Minister seemingly acknowledged this prospect by drawing a distinction between what he saw as "cultural regionalism" (regionalism built on common ties of history, of mutual cultural identity-that is, ASEAN + 3) from which Australia might be excluded, and "practical regionalism" (where regionalism achieves practical goals-that is, APEC) within which Australia would continue to operate (Downer, 2000).

An influential international relations scholar has used cultural diversity as an argument against the development of Australia's West Pacific regionalism (Huntington, 1996). It seems that the Asia-Pacific region is replete with Asian civilisational core states-for example, China, India, Japan and Russia-as well as a number of representatives from Western civilization (Huntington, 1996, 135). In short, the Asia-Pacific is a vast multi-civilisational region, and thus, from a cultural perspective, according to the Huntington hypothesis, the potential for ongoing conflict and a lack of community of interest is thus quite considerable. Such potential civilisational conflicts might become especially focussed along several international political boundaries (Rumley; 1999, 28). Following Huntington, all attempts at cultural-geographical relocation have failed, and, from this cultural deterministic ahistorical perspective, regionalism in the Asia-Pacific as a whole is destined to fail. In short, it seems that Asian and Western values cannot be reconciled.

Given its undoubted cultural incompatibility with West Pacific states, Huntington's prescription for 'torn' Australia is for Australian leaders to propose a new form of regionalism by expanding NAFTA into a North American-South Pacific (NASP) arrangement incorporating the United States, Canada, Australia and New Zealand. Such a regional grouping, according to Huntington, would reconcile culture and economics and provide a solid and enduring identity for Australia that will not come from "futile efforts" to make Australia Asian (Huntington, 1996; 154).

Clearly, Australia's social and cultural linkages with Asian states have lagged well behind economic ties. Furthermore, it does seem that Australia possesses something of a regional image problem that arises partly out of false perceptions, but also as a result of perceived contradictory signals and mixed intentions which have done little to eradicate old barriers, suspicions and stereotypes (Broinowski, 2003).

The politicisation of ethnicity and the rise (and fall) of Hansonism in Australia have been especially damaging to Australia's regional image, especially as a result of the government's apparent unwillingness to strongly condemn it. However, the ongoing treatment of asylum seekers and the way in which the *Dark Victory* in the 2001 Federal election was managed dismayed many of Australia's regional friends (Marr and Wilkinson, 2003).

The awful events of 9/11/01 and 12/10/02 have changed the nature of Australia's security orientation. In addition, over the past decade, Australia's Region Of Primary Strategic Interest (ROPSI) has become something of an arc of instability (Rumley, Forbes and Griffin; 2006). Rather than talking of the prospect of being a 'deputy sheriff' and of undertaking 'regional pre-emption', one critically important mechanism for dealing with the new security environment is to actively construct regional security cooperation. This is predicated upon the view noted earlier that, in the final analysis, regional security can only be guaranteed regionally.

A Geopolitical Model of Australia's Regional Relations

It has been argued that Australia's regional relations can be described in terms of a 'directional front model' that is both temporal and also represents the degree of importance which is attached to each front (Rumley, 1999). Thus, the first front to Australia's north has been referred to as a "cooperative security front"; the second front to Australia's East has been characterized as an "aid front"; the third front to Australia's South has been dubbed an "environmental security front"; and, the fourth front to Australia's West has been referred to as a "trade front". Since Indian independence, the development of the western front towards the Indian Ocean has been accorded a relatively low priority, especially when compared with Australia's new economic core in Northeast Asia (Rumley, 2004). The Indian Ocean front clearly offers considerable scope for the development of a new cooperative security regime concerned principally with non-traditional security threats. This issue is explored further in the final Chapter of this book.

The current cooperative security front to the north and the aid front to the east together contains Australia's nearest neighbours and thus they have been the most important fronts from the viewpoint of maintaining stability and ensuring good regional relations. ODA is seen by the

Australian government as one of the key objectives in promoting regional stability and cooperation (Australian Government, 2006). The outcome of the 'logic' of traditional security thinking assumed that any military threat from these two fronts was highly unlikely implied that non-traditional security approaches – diplomacy, aid, educational exchanges, cooperative regimes and so on – would be the most useful to meet these goals. However, much of the current Australian, and indeed regional, security debate continues to illustrate the lingering preeminence of the realist paradigm – that is, that security threats emanate from other states and are perceived primarily in military terms. Although this paradigm has dominated Australian security thinking and policy since Federation, there have been some important paradigm shifts, especially after the Second World War (Lee, 1999). Each shift in the nature of the strategic environment has been accompanied by a shift in security thinking and defence policy. Thus, the Cold War realist policy of "forward defence" was gradually replaced by a post-Cold War realist "defence of Australia" strategy. Furthermore, this latter "old defence policy" (Monk, 2003) is being replaced in the twenty-first century with a post-Cold War post-realist regional strategy which emphasises "cooperative intervention". However, to some regional commentators, this latter strategy sits uneasily with political rhetoric which espouses a doctrine of pre-emption.

It is noteworthy that the shift from a post-Cold War realist to a post-Cold War post-realist posture has also been associated with a shift in the scale of policy application – that is, away from a state-based scale and towards a more regionally-oriented strategy. For example, one statement of Australian foreign policy refers to a broader conception of security set in the context of *regional* stability: "Australia's national security and its economic interests are inextricably linked to the security and stability of the Asia-Pacific region" (DFAT White Paper, 1997; 1). Thus, any threat to regional stability, such as an economic crisis, social conflict, military confrontation or environmental degradation, also potentially threatens Australian security. Seen in the context of this broader regional conception and definition of security, it can be argued that the process and policy of Australia's reorientation towards the Asia-Pacific region is driven principally by the need to fulfill a more self-reliant and independent requirement for economic, social, military and environmental security.

To some degree, however, it has been said that historically Australia has been subject to something of a 'regional security paradox'. On the one hand, Australia has traditionally possessed a relatively high level of insecurity and perceived vulnerability, and even a sense of being alone and regionally isolated. At the same time, however, in spite of a number of regional geopolitical challenges, Australia has been located in a relatively benign geopolitical environment (Rumley, 1999; 166).

Prior to the 1970s, these locally-derived regional perceptions, informed to some degree by the British colonial view of the spatial structure of the state, became fused into what has been referred to as the "gravity theory" of Australian security – that is, what was up there (the North) must sooner or later come down! (Evans and Grant, 1995, 110). To a considerable degree, these regional perceptions were reinforced during the second world war and during the Cold War period and thus served to strengthen the efficacy of the realist security concept.

However, throughout the Australian security debate in the 1980s and 1990s, there emerged a concept of security which was more geographically-based and which was much broader in scope than the traditional military concept. In particular, this has been associated with factors of distance and proximity, with Australia's perceived regional sphere of influence and has incorporated non-military considerations such as environmental security. One of the most explicit considerations of Australian regional geopolitical priorities was the identification of what was considered to be Australia's "region of primary strategic interest" (ROPSI) noted earlier, which comprised two broad zones stretching from the Cocos Islands in the west, eastwards in an arc around to New Zealand and to the South Pacific islands, and from the archipelago and island chain in the north to the Southern Ocean (Dibb, 1986). In short, Australia's ROPSI incorporated Southeast Asia, the South Pacific and the eastern edge of the Indian Ocean. Some critics have suggested that, since this vast region comprises about ten per cent of the earth's surface, that, from a practical policy perspective, the implementation of non-military strategies is most likely to guarantee Australia's security (Rumley, 1992).

Nonetheless, arising out of this geopolitical analysis, it was suggested that Australia should concentrate its defence priorities along three strategic fronts – first, the north and northern approaches; second, the South Pacific; and, third, the Indian Ocean. This was to have a direct policy impact because, by the mid-1990s, an air and sea "ring of defence" was in place to secure all three fronts and comprised a series of airfields and naval facilities.

For the twenty-first century, of the joint US-Australia facilities, only Pine Gap is expected to remain as a key element in the cooperative intelligence programme. However, both Cockburn Sound as well as the Fremantle porting facilities are expected to continue to be used, and, if required, Australia may well be amenable to the location of future US bases on its territory consequent upon relocations from elsewhere in the Asia-Pacific region. Certainly, due to a number of key changes in the nature of the regional geopolitical environment, ANZUS in its original form has become much less important as a "cornerstone" of traditional Australian security policy (Fry, 1991). Indeed, in a practical policy sense, ANZUS currently no longer exists due to New Zealand's withdrawal. However, under the current conservative Howard administration, security ties with the United States have become much stronger in the post-Cold War period, a situation which has been a cause for concern among some Asian neighbours (Woolcott, 2003; 298-303).

Australia's Arc of Instability

In the mid-1980s, the Dibb Report declared that Australia was "one of the most secure countries in the world" due to the nature and structure of its geopolitical environment. Not only was Australia distant from the main global centres of military conflict, it was also surrounded by large expanses of water which made it difficult to attack, and, furthermore, regional states possessed only limited capability to project military power (Dibb, 1986). However, in the post-Cold War period, and especially since 9/11 and 12/10, it has become clear that the nature of security threats can no longer be viewed solely through the lens of traditional realist frameworks and that the geopolitical character and structure of Australia's cooperative security front had changed. However, not only had there been a fundamental shift in the geopolitical character of the cooperative security front but that also it was clear that this change represented another shift in the type and scale of security threat – that is, increasingly away from the state to intra-state and non-state threats. In particular, the impacts of 'non-conventional' threats, such as terrorism, transnational crime, drug trafficking, people smuggling and money laundering (Dupont, 2001) in combination with a unique array of regional circumstances, have resulted in a series of intra-regional conflicts – for example, in Bougainville, East Timor, Fiji and Indonesia-and the associated emergence of an "arc of instability" to Australia's north and east (Rumley, Forbes and Griffin, 2006). Furthermore, as noted by the most recent Government White Paper on Australian foreign policy, instability is likely to be characteristic of Australia's immediate region for the foreseeable future (Commonwealth of Australia, 2003; 92).

Characterisation of the Regional Concept

Many geo-politicians and policy-makers have a penchant for regional geometrical characterisation, especially in the form of crescents, circles, triangles and arcs. There also exists a long geo-political tradition of identifying global regions of power (for example, the "Heartland" – Mackinder, 1919), regions of geo-political commonality (for example, "geo-strategic regions" – Cohen, 1964) as well as regions of instability (for example, "The Eurasian Balkans" – Brzezinski, 1997). From an American global perspective, the region stretching from the Middle East to Northeast Asia, for example, has been referred to as a "broad arc of instability" (US Department of Defence, 2001, 4). It has also been characterised as an "arc of terror" since it is seen to comprise many unstable states with few strong Western allies which possess an assemblage of either chemical and/or nuclear weapons (Bracken, 2000; 2).

In the Australian regional case, over the past several decades, its current "arc of instability" has been geopolitically characterized in various ways. For example, during the Cold War period, some geopolitical analysts referred to the region to Australia's immediate North as a "shatterbelt"- that is, a region characterized by considerable internal fragmentation, which, to a degree, was exacerbated by external great power competition (Cohen, 1964). Others represented the region as a "cultural shatterbelt" as a result of a complex process of interaction among local ethnic groups, early culture impacts, primary religions, European influence and Indian and Chinese settlement (Spencer and Thomas, 1971). Such representations tended to reinforce the "gravity theory" conception for Australian security noted earlier. Second, in the late Cold War period, the region to Australia's North was characterized as the Region of Primary Strategic Interest (Dibb, 1986). Third, in the post-Cold War period, as noted earlier, the geo-politics of Australia's regional relations have been represented as consisting of four broad 'fronts' (Rumley, 1999). Regional security to the North was to be guaranteed regionally via a series of agreements among states and regional stability to the East was to be enhanced through appropriate Australian development assistance. Indeed, during the post-Cold War period, the highest per capita aid allocations have consistently been given by Australia to states in this region, which is the only one in the world to have been regarded as being a part of Australia's traditional sphere of influence (Rumley, 1999; 188). As has been pointed out, this was formerly expressed in terms of an "Australasian Monroe Doctrine", which emerged during the colonial period, in the latter part of the nineteenth century, and which regarded the South Pacific Islands as an Anglo-Saxon preserve in which "other 'powers' should not trespass" (Fry, 1991; 12).

In the 21st century, however, many observers now commonly use the term "arc of instability" to characterise the region to Australia's immediate North and East (for example, Hughes, 2003; 25) and it is a term which now appears in official Australian government reports (for example, Commonwealth of Australia, 2003c; 105; Commonwealth of Australia, 2004a; 45). It is also a term which has been popularised by the media, especially following the close involvement of Australia in INTERFET in 1999. As a result, Australia's immediate region has been portrayed as being beset by separatist movements, dysfunctional governance and actual or potential failed states (Barker, 2002). Furthermore, concerns over such a potentially threatening regional environment were reinforced by the Bali terrorist bombings of 12 October 2002 and lent weight to a view that Australia's defence planning should concentrate on its proximate region (Ayson, 2002).

However, it can be argued that Australia's immediate region is not homogeneously unstable, that the term "arc" is not a healthy metaphor and that it is an artificial construct. Furthermore, it can be suggested that the arc of instability concept is an over-generalisation, an oversimplification and even an exaggeration and that the term 'vulnerability' might be preferred to 'instability'. Indeed, the geographical extent and limits of the region are often vaguely defined with some suggesting that it extends into the Philippines and even into southern Thailand. This contested nature of the "arc of instability" appellation has prompted one influential commentator to refer to the region as an "alleged 'arc of crisis'" and to argue that this characterization is being used as a mechanism for increasing military spending or as a rationale for an outdated regional strategic orientation (Dupont, 2003). On the other hand, given the multidimensionality of the term security, then "the region's underlying problems which are overwhelmingly economic, social and environmental" (Dupont, 2003, 60) will inevitably be associated with national and regional instability. Such a situation, in turn, requires a multidimensional security policy response.

Causes of Regional Instability

The causes of the twenty-first century geopolitical characterisation of the region, as an arc of instability, are multiple, complex and interdependent. In summary, regional instability is as a result of a combination of economic problems and limited resources, social tensions, rapid population growth and poor governance (Commonwealth of Australia, 2003a; 92). However, as has been argued, this region has also become more of a threat to Australian security as a result of the increasing globalization of non-state threats. The attacks of 9/11 and 12/10, for example, indicate the global reach of terrorism and demonstrate that the region "is no longer immune" to such events (Commonwealth of Australia, 2003b, 18). In short, a fundamental assumption of the Dibb Report regarding Australia's security on account of distance is no longer relevant. Thus, as has been argued, Southeast Asia is no longer the "strategic shield" it was expected to be for Australia when it possessed strong economic growth and was politically stable (Dibb, 1999). Indeed, other analysts have gone further to suggest that Southeast Asia may well have become the "second front" in the "war against terror" (Gresham, 2002; Commonwealth of Australia, 2004b).

A second cause of regional instability is linked to the regional history of colonialism in which the European powers arbitrarily divided territory without due regard to local, social, economic and political structures. The decolonisation process in this region is not yet complete and is made more complex by the resurgence of ethnic identity and the requirement for much greater local political participation, even freedom and justice, on the part of colonised peoples. Of the sixteen Non-Self-Governing Territories identified by the United Nations, five are located in the Pacific – American Samoa (USA), Guam (USA), New Caledonia (France), Pitcairn (UK) and Tokelau (New Zealand). The current status of these territories not only is a cause for international concern, but is also potentially a factor contributing to regional instability. On the other hand, territories which have been incorporated into a larger state (as was the case with West Papua) inevitably will agitate for greater local control as the host state itself moves towards greater democratization. In short, regional political development is itself likely to be associated with an increase in territorial instability (Rumley, 1999; 31).

A third cause of conflict in part arises from the second; that is, given decolonisation and freedom, can the resultant political jurisdiction remain socially, economically and politically viable? Many of these jurisdictions have small populations, are ethnically diverse, have few resources and rely heavily on a limited number of export commodities such as agriculture, fishing, tourism and mining. Furthermore, all of these commodities are highly susceptible to fluctuations in world markets. Consequently, economic security questions are a regional cause for concern (Commonwealth of Australia, 2003; 13). As has been argued, failed states can fall prey to lawlessness and to terrorist activities (Rotberg, 2002). Furthermore, problems of viability in a highly competitive globalised environment can result in political jurisdictions becoming hostage to a range of illegal and controversial social, economic and environmental practices that invariably negatively impact upon the quality of governance. The end result can thus turn out to be a state which is the antithesis of the one anticipated at decolonisation.

A fourth associated cause of instability is that many of the regional states and territories are economically unstable and have experienced low or even negative economic growth rates in recent years (Commonwealth of Australia, 2003c, 24; Australian Government, 2004; 92). As a result, most are heavily dependent upon a relatively small number of donor states for development assistance. In 2000, for example, the United States was the largest regional donor to the Federated States of Micronesia and the Marshall Islands; Japan was the largest donor to Fiji, Indonesia, Kiribati, Pulau, Samoa and Tuvalu; Australia was the largest donor to Nauru, Papua New Guinea, the Solomon Islands, Tonga and Vanuatu; New Zealand was the largest donor to the Cook Islands, Niue and Tokelau; and, France was the largest donor to New Caledonia (Development Assistance Committee). Perhaps it is no surprise that, as Pacific states, official development assistance from Australia and New Zealand is the most regionally-targetted of all of donor states reflecting a mixture of security, paternalistic responsibility and humanitarian motives. Aid dependency, of course, is potentially problematical when it comprises a high proportion of a recipient state's budget (historically the case for Papua New Guinea) and where a very large proportion of ODA derives from a single donor state (for example, in the cases of Indonesia, Nauru, New Caledonia, Niue, Papua New Guinea and Tokelau). For Australian ODA, the degree of regional aid dependency varies from 41.5 per cent and 37.1 per cent for Nauru and Fiji respectively to 19 per cent for Vanuatu (Australian Government, 2004; 91). Furthermore, questions have been raised about the efficacy of development assistance programmes, especially in terms of their relation to positive human development outcomes (Hughes, 2003).

Aid motives, whether they are humanitarian, strategic, or some combination, too often in the past have been determined by donor states and have been subject to change. Indeed, regional competition among potential donor states has included other countries such as the former USSR, China and Taiwan. However, the dynamics of recipient state aid are equally evident, regionally. Thus, for a time, France became Fiji's largest aid donor after aid from Australia and New Zealand was suspended following the 1987 coup (Bates, 1990; 123). This appears to illustrate, in the case of much regional Australian ODA, for example, that there has been a considerable tendency for it to be overtly "crisis driven" (Commonwealth of Australia, 2003c; 105).

A further source of regional conflict has been ethnic tension, caused often, but not always, as a result of the territorial division of colonial control, and expressed usually between indigenous communities and/or between indigenous communities and more recent immigrant groups. Conflicts are triggered invariably by disputes over resources and/or the felt need on the part of some groups for greater economic and political participation, especially when the non-indigenous groups have a controlling interest or possess a disproportionate degree of economic and political power. Regional secessionist movements (for example, in West Papua), independence movements (for example, in New Caledonia), and actual and potential disputes over land and sea resources generally possess a strong ethnic dimension.

Religious fundamentalism is also officially seen as a contributory cause of the arc of instability. It has been argued that various types of religious fundamentalism are often both a response to globalisation, which engenders a mismatch between ideological needs and available opportunities to satisfy those needs, as well an instant remedy to rapid change which is imposed from the outside (Misztal and Shupe, 1992). In Southeast Asia, for example, it has been suggested that "extremists within Southeast Asia target not only Westerners, but also seek to destabilise the region's secular governments" (Commonwealth of Australia, 2003a; 40). From this perspective, religious fundamentalism not only functions as an internal threat to the host state, but is also a direct threat to the Australian regional interests.

The emergence of all of these issues requires a new security policy orientation in the 21st century and one which is based on regional cooperation and non-military strategies in order to deal with the causes rather than the effects of such security challenges.

Regionalism – Prospects for the 21st Century

It is possible that in the 21st century a "new regionalism", which has a geo-political basis, may be in the process of replacing a "new regionalism", which has an economic basis, since the Asia-Pacific region is still in a process of transition to a new post-Cold War order (Rumley, 2005). On the one hand, Asia-Pacific states are in the process of reacting to Western visions of a new world order which is resulting in new regional tensions (Rumley, 2003). On the other hand, Cold War security structures are still essentially in-tact and post-Cold War Asia-Pacific regional arrangements are internally conflictual and are relatively weak, apart from those at the sub-regional level. It has been suggested that, at the sub-regional scale, "transnational ethnic social capital" is an additional factor facilitating inter-state cooperation (Chen, 2000). At the region-wide Asia-Pacific scale, on the other hand, in order to construct a Western Pacific Community (WPC) or an East Asian Community (EAC), there is a need not only to democratise security and facilitate regional identity, but also to create a grouping that would confront intra-regional tensions and thus enhance long-term regional stability.

The Western Pacific and Western Security Domination

In the current geo-strategic environment of the Asia-Pacific region, the management of actual and potential regional conflicts effectively remains in the hands of a series of Western military alliances, especially the US-Japan security alliance, ANZUS and the Five Powers Defence Agreement (FPDA), all of which are guaranteed by extra-regional powers (Rumley, 2003). Indeed, as one commentator has put it, the basic structure of the Cold War still remains in the Asia-Pacific region, since the general relaxation of tensions evident from the late 1980s more closely resembles that of the 1970s European détente – that is, a recognition of a Cold War status quo – rather than the actual end of the Cold War (Hara, 1999).

As has been noted: "The region lacks any restraining cooperative structure of regional security" (Brzezinski, 2004; 107). The only region-wide security forum, the fledgling ASEAN Regional Forum (ARF), although not confined solely to Western Pacific states, has led to an increasing commitment to confidence-building measures (Catley, 2001; 150). While conceived as a mechanism for maintaining continued US regional security involvement, it is also seen by China as an instrument to facilitate Asia-Pacific multipolarity and thus act as a counter to US hegemony (Emmers, 2001). However, as has been pointed out, there is a need for the ARF to move from being just a consultative forum to one which begins to address difficult regional issues, if it is to remain relevant (Garofano, 1999; Naidu, 2000). With the current global security configuration, consequent upon the new internationalist agenda and the spread of nuclear weapons, Western states need to sufficiently recognise Asia-Pacific regional interests and to more effectively accommodate these in new regional and global economic and security structures.

The Construction of an East Asian Community

While the concept of a Western Pacific regionalism was basic to early ideas of APEC, its reemergence is especially linked to Asian concerns over Western geopolitical and economic domination consequent upon the end of the Cold War. The growth in regional economic interdependence, however, which remained relatively low until the mid 1980s, has been achieved without the benefit of any regional institutional framework (Masood, 2001, 7). The nomenclature of the new process, however, rejects the terms "West" and "Pacific" and substitutes them with "East" and "Asia" in order to foster a new independent sense of identity. The Malaysian proposal in 1990 for an East Asian Economic Grouping (EAEG), which was designed to be solely Asian, was an important forerunner in this regard. However, the 1997 Asian financial crisis was a significant additional trigger; since some ASEAN states in the region felt that they were left at the mercy of Western interests. Indeed, the first ASEAN + 3 meeting was called, at Malaysia's suggestion; in Kuala Lumpur in 1997. The meeting in Kuala Lumpur in December 2005 thus represented the 9th ASEAN + 3 Summit. The ASEAN + 3 grouping, which was initially aimed at exploring common interests and identity, at the same time institutes a collective Asian economic and geopolitical voice for the 10 ASEAN states plus the 3 Northeast Asian states of China, Japan and South Korea (Dalrymple, 2003; 146-7). This would result in the creation of the world's "third major economic zone" (Kimura, 2004).

Like all regional groupings, there exist a variety of perspectives among, as well as within, the thirteen members of the new grouping (as well as the excluded states) on the goals and long-term objectives of ASEAN + 3. From the 'outside', some commentators have argued that East Asian regionalism will necessarily weaken the prospects of trans-Pacific cooperation (Elek, 2003; 264). This prospect will thus inevitably generate opposition and pressure from the United States on regional allies. From the 'inside', while Singapore has promoted a distinctive set of Asian values, Malaysia has strongly supported an Asian community which aims to combine both a resistance to the dominance of Western values and the creation of a mechanism to facilitate regional economic growth (Katzenstein, 2000; 356). Some commentators have argued that Japan has not been an active supporter of the new grouping and that "the challenge for the Japanese government is to counter this drive for regionalism" (Masood 2001; 9). Other commentators, however, believe that Japan possesses an "obligation to the region as an advanced country" to support ASEAN + 3 (Kimura, 2004, 9).

China appears to strongly support the ASEAN + 3 concept for reasons based on maximising its own economic development and the facilitation of regional integration (Dalrymple, 2003; 146-7; De Santis, 2005). Furthermore, China sees regionalism as a "hedge against the onset of globalisation", as a means to consolidate its own power and influence and as a mechanism to try to resolve the so-called "Chinese dilemma". From this latter perspective, an important underlying rationale is that, as a result of receiving benefits from Chinese economic development through regionalism, East Asian states would view China more favourably and with less apprehension (Takahara, 2002). While Japan seems to favour a "loose East Asian regionalism", China sees itself as its central player and thus might object to an enhanced Japanese role (Masood, 2001; 17). On the other hand, one Japanese commentator has noted that there is a growing recognition in China that the key to East Asian regionalism is the improvement of relations with Japan (Takahara, 2002, 39).

'Excluded' states, such as Australia, face a difficult dilemma regarding ASEAN + 3. In short, it is possible that the new East Asian economic regionalism of the 21st century could exclude all Western states. Such excluded states would then have to rely on bilateral economic arrangements with those which are included, and, to some degree, this prospect is in the process of being pre-empted both by Western (for example, Australia) and some Asian (for example, Singapore) states.

The East Asian Summit

The inaugural East Asian Summit (EAS), which was held in Kuala Lumpur in December 2005, marked a major shift in the enlargement of East Asian regionalism. One of the several reasons for this was that the meeting comprised the group of ASEAN states plus the three Northeast Asian states plus 3 'outside' states (India, New Zealand and Australia).

At the 10th ASEAN Summit in Laos in 2004, India was officially inducted into the East Asian regional cooperation process. ASEAN is currently negotiating a Free Trade Agreement (FTA) with India and this should be in place by 1 January 2007. From an Indian viewpoint, its inclusion in the EAS demonstrates some further concrete success of its 'Look East' policy. China has already been in negotiations with ASEAN regarding a FTA and its normalisation of relations with India also helped the latter's case.

Like India, the Australasian states have been 'outsiders' to the East Asian community process. In addition, of course, unlike India, both New Zealand and Australia are 'non-Asian' states. Furthermore, Australia's 'outsider' position was not only a product of the trilateral geopolitical tension noted earlier in this Chapter. It was also a result of its apparent reluctance to sign the ASEAN Treaty of Amity and Cooperation (TAC). While the New Zealand Prime Minister, Helen Clark, did not appear to have similar reservations about signing the TAC and thus becoming a part of the EAS process, Australia's hesitation in part reflected something of its perceived regional role. Consent was given by the ASEAN states for New Zealand to be a part of the TAC in July 2005. Outside of Australia and within the region, rightly or wrongly, Australian reluctance to sign the TAC rekindled concern over its possible preemption policy as well as diplomatic indignation over "puerile comments about it being America's deputy sheriff in the region" (Alexander Downer quoted in the Japan Times, 11 December 2005). From an Australian government perspective, however, being a part of the TAC agreement would have prohibited Australian participation in the East Timor intervention in 1999. The regional perception was that there was some reluctance to give away this type of regional intervention prospect. In the event, in addition to receiving strong regional support for its participation in EAS, Australia signed the TAC on 10 December 2005 and thus belatedly became a part of the community process.

Some Remaining Issues for EAS

To some extent, the problems confronted by APEC are likely to be replicated in the new East Asian regional community process and they are essentially of three type-questions over membership, concerns over EAS goals and internal divisions and rivalries among member states.

There is always likely to be some residual opposition to the inclusion of the two non-Asian states. While ASEAN + 3 was the brainchild of the former Malaysian Prime Minister Mahatir, his view was and still is that the EAS should be comprised solely of Asian states. In addition, some member states already seem to want to expand the EAS to include other states, especially the United States (*New Straits Times*, 2004). In any event, while the United States continues to prefer bilateralism over regionalism it will likely gain entry through the 'back door', via a series of bilateral trade deals.

In terms of EAS goals, some member states favour the view that the new 16 state grouping could/should become the world's largest free trade area of nearly three billion people. Others see the EAS as a good forum to discuss strategic issues such as security and poverty eradication. Yet others see the overall goal of EAS as one of 'community building' from within and the development of strategies which are not determined externally. As one regional newspaper put it:

We are hopeful that local players will be the primary determinants of this region's destiny, without being subject to the American national interests (*Jakarta Post* 2005).

Nonetheless, internal divisions and rivalries will need to be overcome in order for this to be successful. Clearly, the new EAS grouping contains considerable internal cultural, economic and political differences (similar to APEC, but smaller). The incidence of internal territorial disputes, conflicts over democracy and human rights and rivalries over 'leadership' will all need to be confronted. Indeed, even chairing the EAS by a non-ASEAN state is likely to become a contentious issue. Furthermore, there is always internal concern that the EAS will become dominated by the world's two largest states.

On the one hand, the construction of a new regionalism in East Asia has intrinsic appeal to regional peoples and states in order to democratise security and to provide a geopolitical counterweight to the EU and NAFTA. On the other hand, a number of longstanding regional tensions remain which have the potential to forestall such a process (Ravenhill, 2002). Cebu's hosting of the second EAS Summit in 2006 not only confirms ASEAN's leadership role, but also indicates a long-term ASEAN determination to facilitate its success. It is likely that at that meeting the group's agenda, scope and goals will be more clearly articulated and more substantively fleshed out.

Conclusion

This chapter has taken an explicitly geo-political orientation towards a consideration of Australia's regional security challenges. It has been argued that Australia possesses a trilateral geo-political tension in terms of its external relations and that it is imperative that Australian policy makers remain sufficiently cognizant of the regional sensitivities involved in attempts to try and balance and effectively manage competing interests. Furthermore, it has been suggested that Australia's regional relations can be described in terms of a geopolitical model that comprises four fronts of differing geopolitical importance. In order to maximise regional stability it is essential that the Indian Ocean front receives a much higher priority during the 21st century than it has to date, and that non-traditional security issues, especially human security and the management of the Ocean itself, are given greater attention. Both Australia and India can take the lead in confronting these matters. The emergence of an arc of instability to

Australia's North and East also requires the implementation of a range of non-traditional security strategies (Rumley, Forbes and Griffin, 2006; 305-317). From the perspective of India-Australia relations, the new regionalism potentially affords an ongoing opportunity for both states to engage in the multilateral solution of regional problems. Despite any pessimistic concerns over the possible success of EAS, in addition to helping to facilitate regional economic growth and interdependence, the new new East Asian regionalism should primarily be viewed as a vehicle to enable internal tensions to be confronted and mediated in order to facilitate long-term regional stability.

REFERENCES

Alagappa, M. (1997), 'Systemic change, security and governance in the Asia-Pacific', in Chan Heng Chee, ed., *The New Asia-Pacific Order*, Singapore, ISEAS, pp. 29-89.

Australian Government (2004), *Pacific Programme Profiles 2003-04*, Canberra, AusAID.

Australian Government (2006), *Australian Aid: Promoting Growth and Stability*, Canberra, AusAID.

Ayson, R. (2002), 'Spotlight on security planning', *Australian Financial Review*, 15 October, page 71.

Baker, R.W., ed. (1994), *The ANZUS States and Their Region: Regional Policies of Australia, New Zealand, and the United States*, Westport, Praeger.

Baker, J. and Paal, D.H. (2000), 'The US-Australia Alliance', in Blackwill and Dibb, *op. cit.*, pp. 87-109.

Barker, G. (2002), 'The arc of instability', *Australian Financial Review*, 1 August, page 61.

Bates, S. (1990), *The South Pacific Island Countries and France*, Canberra, ANU.

Bell, C. (1993), *Dependent Ally: A Study in Australian Foreign Policy*, St Leonards, Allen and Unwin.

Bell, P. and Bell, R., eds. (1998), *Americanization and Australia*, Sydney, University of NSW Press.

Blackwill, R.D. (2000), 'An action agenda to strengthen America's alliances in the Asia-Pacific region', in Blackwill and Dibb, *op. cit.*, pp. 111-134.

Blackwill, R.D. and Dibb, P., eds. (2000), *America's Asian Alliances*, Cambridge, Mass., MIT Press.

Bonnor, J. (1994), 'Regional economic cooperation in the Asia-Pacific: an Australian priority', in Baker, *op. cit.*, pp. 139-152.

Bracken, P. (2000), *Fire in the East: The Rise of Asian Military Power and the Second Nuclear Age*, New York, Perennial.

Broinowski, A. (2003), *About Face: Asian Perceptions of Australia*, Sydney, Scribe.

Brzezinski, Z. (1997), *The Grand Chessboard: American Primacy and its Geostrategic Imperatives*, New York, Basic Books.

Brzezinski, Z. (2004), *The Choice: Global Domination or Global Leadership*, New York, Basic Books.

Catley, B. (2001), 'The Bush administration and changing geopolitics in the Asia-Pacific region', *Contemporary Southeast Asia*, Vol. 23, pp. 149-167.

Chen, X. (2000), 'Both glue and lubricant: transnational ethnic social capital as a source of Asia-Pacific subregionalism', *Policy Sciences*, Vol. 33 (3), pp. 269-287.

Cohen, S.B. (1964), *Geography and Politics in a Divided World*, London, Methuen.

Commonwealth of Australia (2000), *Defence 2000: Our Future Defence Force*, Canberra, DOD.

Commonwealth of Australia (2003a), *Advancing the National Interest: Australia's Foreign and Trade Policy White Paper*, Canberra, DFAT.

Commonwealth of Australia (2003b), *Australia's National Security: A Defence Update 2003*, Canberra, DOD.

Commonwealth of Australia (2003c), *Australia's Relations with Papua New Guinea and the Island States of the South-West Pacific*, Canberra, Senate Foreign Affairs, Defence and Trade Committee.

Commonwealth of Australia (2004a), *Australia's Maritime Strategy*, Canberra, Joint Standing Committee on Foreign Affairs, Defence and Trade.

Commonwealth of Australia (2004b), *Transnational Terrorism: The Threat to Australia*, The Australian Government, Canberra.

Dalrymple, R. (2003), *Continental Drift: Australia's Search for a Regional Identity*, Aldershot, Ashgate.

De Castro, R. 'US grand strategy in post-Cold War Asia-Pacific', *Contemporary Southeast Asia*, Vol. 16, pp. 342-353.

Department of Defence (1993), *Strategic Review*, Canberra, Defence Centre.

Department of Defence (1994), *Defending Australia*, Canberra, AGPS.

DFAT White Paper (1997), *In the National Interest: Australia's Foreign and Trade Policy*, Canberra.

De Santis, H. (2005), 'The dragon and the tigers: China and Asian regionalism', *World Policy Journal*, Vol. 22 (2), pp. 23-36.

Development Assistance Committee (DAC) web site.

Dibb, P. (1986), *Review of Australia's Defence Capabilities*, Canberra, AGPS.

Dibb, P. (1999), 'Crunch time for defence', *Australian Financial Review*, 16 September, page 18.

Downer, A. (2000), 'China: Asia Leaders' Forum', opening speech, Beijing, 23 April.

Dupont, A. (2001), *East Asia Imperilled: Transnational Challenges to Security*, Cambridge, Cambridge University Press.

Dupont, A. (2003), 'Transformation or stagnation? Rethinking Australia's defence', *Australian Journal of International Affairs*, Vol. 57 (1), pp. 55-76.

Elek, A. (2003), 'Review of *APEC and the construction of Pacific Rim regionalism*', *Economic Record*, Vol. 79 (245), pp. 262-4.

Emmers, R. (2001), 'The influence of the balance of power factor within the ASEAN Regional Forum', *Contemporary Southeast Asia*, Vol. 23, pp. 275-291.

Evans, G. and Grant, B. (1995), *Australia's Foreign Relations*, Melbourne, Melbourne University Press, second edition.

Fry, G., ed. (1991), *Australia's Regional Security*, North Sydney, Allen and Unwin.

Garofano, J. (1999), 'Flexibility or irrelevance: ways forward for the ARF', *Contemporary Southeast Asia*, Vol. 21, pp. 74-94.

Gresham, J. (2002), 'Is Southeast Asia the Second Front?', *Foreign Affairs*, Vol. 81 (4), pp. 60-74.

Hara, K. (1999), 'Rethinking the "Cold War" in the Asia-Pacific', *Pacific Review*, Vol. 12, pp. 515-536.

Harris, S. (1997), 'US-Japan relations in the new Asia-Pacific order', in Chan Heng Chee, *op. cit.*, pp. 157-185.

Hughes, H. (2003), 'Aid has failed the Pacific', *Issue Analysis*, No. 33, The Centre for Independent Studies, Sydney.

Huntington, S. (1996), *The Clash of Civilizations and the Remaking of the World Order*, New York, Simon and Schuster.

Jakarta Post (2005), quoted in the *Weekend Australian*, 19 November, p. 32.

Japan Times (2005), 11 December, in 'Asia-Pacific Briefs'.

Johnson, C. (2000), *Blowback: The Costs and Consequences of American Empire*, New York, Metropolitan Books.

Katzenstein, P.J. (2000), 'Regionalism and Asia', *New Political Economy*, Vol. 5 (3), pp. 353-368.

Kimura, F. (2004), 'FTAs: the foundation of an East Asian Community', *Asia-Pacific Perspectives*, Vol. 2 (7), pp. 8-9.

Lee, D. (1999), 'Australia's defence policy: a historical overview', in Malik, J.M., ed., *Australia's Security in the 21st Century*, St Leonards, Allen and Unwin, pp. 8-31.

Mackinder, H. (1919), *Democratic Ideals and Reality: A Study in the Politics of Reconstruction*, London, Constable.

Marr, D. and Wilkinson, M. (2003), *Dark Victory*, Sydney, Allen and Unwin.

Masood, S.J., ed. (2001), *Japan and East Asian Regionalism*, London, Routledge.

Misztal, B. and Shupe, A., eds. (1992), *Religion and Politics in Comparative Perspective: Revival of Religious Fundamentalism in East and West*, Westport, Praeger.

Monk, P. (2003), 'A strategic changing of the guard', *Australian Financial Review*, 6 June, page 6.

Naidu, G.V.C. (2000), 'Multilateralism and regional security: can the ASEAN Regional Forum really make a difference?', *Asia Pacific Issues*, no. 45, East-West Center.

New Straits Times (2005), 7 December, p. 10.

Pilger, J. (1989), A Secret Country, London, Cape.

Ravenhill, J. (2001), *APEC and the Construction of Pacific Rim Regionalism*, Cambridge, CUP.

Rolfe, J. (1997), 'Australia and New Zealand: towards a more effective defence relationship', *Working Paper*, No. 286, SDSC, ANU.

Rotberg, R.I. (2002), 'Failed states in a world of terror', *Foreign Affairs*, Vol. 81 (4), pp. 127-140.

Rumley, D. (1992), 'The Australian state and its external relations', University of Tokyo, *Journal of the Department of Liberal Arts*, No. 24, pp. 1-25.

Rumley, D. (1999), *The Geopolitics of Australia's Regional Relations*, Dordrecht, Kluwer.

Rumley, D. (2003), 'The Asia-Pacific region and the new world order', *Ekistics*, Vol. 70 (422/423), pp. 321-326.

Rumley, D. (2004), 'Geopolitics of Australia-India trade', in D. Gopal and D. Rumley, eds., *India and Australia: Issues and Opportunities*, New Delhi, Authors Press, pp. 1-25.

Rumley, D. (2005), 'The geopolitics of 21st century Asia-Pacific regionalism', *The Otemon Journal of Australian Studies*, Vol. 31, pp. 3-25.

Rumley, D. (2006), 'Balancing Australia's Trilateral Geopolitical Tension: Dilemmas, Conflicts and Perceptions', in Santosh Sareen, ed., Proceedings of IASA International Conference in New Delhi.

Rumley, D., Forbes, V.L. and Griffin, C., eds. (2006), *Australia's Arc of Instability: The Political and Cultural Dynamics of Regional Security*, Dordrecht, Springer.

Spencer, J.E. and Thomas, W.L. (1971), *Asia, East by South: A Cultural Geography*, New York, Wiley, second edition.

Takahara, A. (2002), 'Beijing embraces regionalism', *Japan Echo*, Vol. 29 (1), pp. 38-9.

Toohey, B. (2005), 'Defence spending plan flawed', *The West Australian*, 10 October, page 19.

US Department of Defense (2001), *Quadrennial Defense Review Report*, 30 September.

Whitlam, G. (1985), *The Whitlam Government, 1972-1975*, New York, Viking.

Woolcott, R. (2003), *The Hot Seat: Reflections on Diplomacy from Stalin's Death to the Bali Bombings*, Sydney, HarperCollins.

10

East Asian Regionalism and Australia

H.S. PRABHAKAR

The purpose of this chapter is to analyse the processes of regionalism and regionalisation in East Asia by focusing on the positions of different countries in the region, the leading role being played by Japan and by providing an assessment of how Australia has attuned its position through foreign policy adjustment. In a way, this also explains Australia's relations with the major players in the region. East Asia is one of the world's most significant strategic zones – the intersection of global and regional powers – the US, China, Russia and Japan. The holding of the ASEAN+3 meeting in 1997 and the subsequent agreement to institutionalise it in subsequent meetings, along with the emergence since the early 1990s of other region-wide fora such as the ARF, all represent a significant step forward in the delicate process of East Asian regional integration in the post-Cold War period and Japan's important role within this process. These developments are made even more extraordinary in the context of the highly divergent nature of the East Asian regional political economy.

Given the indications of a reevaluation of Japan's standing within the region in the context of hostility and dislocation in the past, it is interesting to examine Japan's remarkable political economic integration into East Asia in the post-Cold War era. The extent to which Japan has regained a decisive position in creating the East Asian region, as well as its capabilities and the methods it has employed to regionally integrate become important in studying any Japanese course of action, even those associated with Australia.

Located at the northern and southern points of the Western Pacific, Japan and Australia have a shared sense of concern, responsibility and opportunity over their neighborhood. Australia and Japan want the United States to remain engaged in the region and allow China's integration as a constructive regional partner. Scholars often express a concern about the lack of integration between comparative politics and international relations, in particular as they relate to East Asia. Globalisation has impacted on the conduct of international relations and the process of domestic politics. Throughout the world, domestic and international actors receive stimuli to adjust their thought and approach in the conduct of domestic and international affairs. Globalisation leads to a proliferation of non-state actors as well as new issues. For example, old security issues take on new and altered realities. No policy-maker can ignore the impact of globalisation in determining the course of public policy. Of the many definitions available on globalisation, most relate to the idea of political economy based on an increase in global trade and the role of transnational corporations (Freedman, 2000).

The East Asian Political Economy

Many economists considered the East Asian economies in the 1950s and 1960s as 'basket cases'. Import substitution policies and the lack of natural resources prevented them from exploiting comparative advantage. Besides natural resources, most East Asian countries lacked a highly industrialised economy at that time. Nevertheless, since then, many governments have developed a strategy referred to as 'guided development', drawing the power of the state to propel economic advancement (see for example, Amsden, 1989; Johnson, 1995). Between the 1960s and the late 1990s, the 'developmental state' provided the initial catalyst for economic development. Though the impact of government on economic development varied from country to country, there were also common features in the development of the regional economy of East Asia. Besides Japan's strong economic presence in the region, the rise of China as a strong economic power, the quick recovery of the affected countries from financial crisis, and the expansion of ASEAN into ASEAN+3 will remain a cause of concern for any neighbour such as Australia. The following points comprise some of the main ingredients of the rapid economic growth of the region:

- Targeted government subsidies to potentially successful industries;
- Protection and nurturing of infant industries;
- Emphases on the creation of a banking system with high levels of national savings;
- Use of traditional values to maintain political quiescence, curtail social welfare spending and establish enterprise unions;
- The use of financial incentives and the manipulation of traditional symbols for maintaining the dominance of the ruling elite.

Many Asian economies performed well because they tapped into the global capitalist economy and benefited from an international division of labour that allowed labour-intensive production to shift away from the industrial states and towards those with low labour costs. Japan gradually rebuilt its economy after the war, with increased value-added production, and South Korea, Hong Kong, Taiwan and Singapore became industrial states. This process was facilitated by two major factors-one at the regional level and the other at the global scale. At global level, the Cold War coupled with the dramatic expansion of free trade among the non-Communist countries, promoted the economic development of Asian states.

Since the United States placed military security over economic security, it allowed the developmental state to thrive by ignoring violations of free trade principles and continued to resist communism and maintained solidarity within the Western camp. At the same time, many rounds of GATT opened up the American market more so than the Asian ones. Since fragile Asia had lacked strong military security, the Cold War situation provided Asian states with a chance to improve both economic and political security.

Secondly, Asian economies, on a regional scale, developed a high level of integration and division of labour as a subset of the international economy. In the 1980s, as the value of the Japanese Yen increased due to large trade surpluses, many firms attempted to cut production costs and transplant production to South Korea, China, Taiwan, Indonesia and Malaysia (Katzenstein and Takashi, 1997). As a result, a comprehensive Japanese network of production and finance developed in East and Southeast Asia (Hatch and Yamamura, 1996). Under the rubric of the Association of Southeast Asian Nations (ASEAN) and the Asia Pacific Economic Cooperation (APEC) group, Japan and the other East Asian countries worked to coordinate economic policies and foreign direct investment, primarily from Japan (Pempel, 1997). In particular, the Japanese, and to a lesser extent the South Korean government, began a concerted effort to provide foreign aid and fund capital projects throughout Asia. In addition, both governments began to encourage FDI into Southeast Asia as a key element of their foreign policy objectives.

The end of the Cold War altered the basic structures of the East Asian regional economy and produced profound alterations in state domestic politics and foreign policies (Crompton, 2000). Internationally, the end of the Cold War resulted in increased attention being paid to low profile politics of trade and democratisation by the US and other regional foreign policy leaders, such as Japan and China. Globalisation shaped the contours of democracy as East Asian countries experienced democratic transition and consolidation (Crompton, 2001). In particular, Japanese firms became active in seeking opportunities in a bid to lower labour costs by creating branch plants in Southeast Asia and China. Part of the foreign policy diversification included the increased importance of ASEAN and regional cooperation issues. In particular, peace keeping and environmental concerns became reflected in the foreign policies of Japan and South Korea. It is in this context that one can observe East Asian foreign policies becoming more independent of the United States and more integrated with each other than during the Cold War.

The strong Japanese economy of the 1980s led to a great deal of work on Japan's superior economic system (Johnson, 1995). Meanwhile, the value of the Yen continued to soar and Japan's trade surpluses grew, apparently immune from exchange rate mechanisms and leading to protectionist sentiments throughout the world. Japan became the world's largest creditor state. By 2000, however, the discussion of Japan's economic superiority had almost disappeared and the country and the entire region, with the exception of PRC, remained mired in an extended economic depression.

It is only now that some studies have attempted to concentrate on questions such as – what went wrong with Japan? Can Japan escape from the myriad of problems it currently experiences and lead Asia to 'Pacific Century'? Some explanations offered relate to the fact that Japan's problems have a socio-cultural rather than a socio-economic basis. Japan's unique cultural construction together with the global changes taking place have created conditions that inhibit the development of Japan's future leadership role in Asia and the world. Put another way, the very bases of Japanese society prevent it from becoming an effective economic, political and cultural force for the foreseeable future. The synergetic effects of Japan's cultural construction with its impact on domestic politics and economics coupled with the integrative nature of globalisation create conditions anti-thelical to Japan's future success. While at the same time, for cultural reasons Japan cannot significantly alter its basic orientation because such an abrupt or dramatic change would lead to the loss of its cultural identity (Crompton, 2002; 69). Thus, increasingly Japan came to be perceived by its neighbours as a part of a set of Asian problems rather than their solution.

Despite a Japanese threat to the US economic security in the 1980s and 1990s, and some alarm over *Pax Nipponica*, the weakness of Japan has became manifest in the past decade or so. The origins of primary problems that Japan currently experiences can be traced to culture and to the social construction of the Japanese State. The nature of the Japanese construction of the nation-state precludes its ability to excel in an increasingly globalised world. This is precisely what Japan is missing in becoming a global leader.

Japan's insular nature already accounts for its difficulty in dealing with the post-developmental state and the post-Cold War reality. Japan fails to benefit from many aspects of globalisation (Crompton, 2002; 80). At best, Japan is likely to continue to experience the marginal growth and ultimately it may become a regional player weaker than China and perhaps even than a united Korea.

Japan's Regional Economic Relations

Japan's economic relations with its Asian neighbours have so far been complementary, unlike its clear competition with the West. Japan has been seeking advantages through economic cooperation with neighbouring Asia to enhance its competitiveness versus the West and to maintain a structural advantage over East Asia (Ming Wan, 2001; 3). Most Asian countries expect that a perfectly cooperative Japan should spend as little on defence as possible, transfer official and private financial resources, open its market to Asian goods, serve as the lender of the last resort and avoid sanctions on its neighbours (Ming Wan, 2001). Even in economic matters Japan has not taken the lead on all issues. Japan has taken a lead in providing official and private lending and investments, although its influence also comes from its example as the first modernised non-Western state, its model of development and its impact on the incentive structures of East Asian states.

Japan has thrived and consolidated its hold on the region despite strong historical resentment among its Asian neighbours. It has been said that East Asia resembles a formation of 'flying geese', with Japan at the centre. What then emerged in Asia is due to the interaction among countries large and small and the underlying historical processes. In the mid-1990s, developing countries were carefully following Japanese policies since Japan was offering its approximately US$13 billion in an annual foreign aid budget to countries that attempted to replicate its model. The Japanese model-government-sanctioned cartels, price fixing, forced savings, import barriers, cheap loans to targeted industries and cross-share holding –

forged the world's pre-eminent exporter of manufactured goods in the post-war period. If nothing else, the East Asian economies had been effective at least in promoting their export industries.

Japan's economics-based non-confrontational approach to the region helped it come out on top. Its ability to exercise regional leadership in Asia is generally seen in its response to the issues affecting the region in the 1990s. Japan's economic leadership was tested when a severe financial crisis started in Thailand in mid-1997 which soon spread to other countries in the region. Compared to a weak American response, Japan actively reacted by pledging millions of dollars. However, when the crisis deepened and the Americans vetoed Japan's proposal to create a regional monetary arrangement, Japan retreated and allowed the IMF and the US to take the lead. For this precise act, Japan came under heavy criticism. Japan was seen as being unable to reform its own economy and open its market to goods from the region. By contributing about US$44 billion, Japan emerged from the Asian financial crisis as a stronger economic supporter/leader. Japan's selective leadership in Asia is explained by its bargaining position, its historical legacy and its norms and ideas. Japan's emphasis on both cooperation and competition is best captured in the distinct Japanese theory of 'flying geese'. Japan is the head goose, followed by other Asian states, according to their level of economic development. The lead goose assists its followers through investment capital, technology transfer and infrastructure development, consistent with market forces. In the end, every goose benefits from the arrangement, though the lead goose enjoys a structural advantage/competitive edge.

Japan's Economic Power

The dynamic in Japan's relations with East Asia is different from its relations with the United States. While the US has treated its security relationship with Japan as most important since 1952 (Mendl, 1995; 118), Asian countries basically seek a cooperative Japan in the economic field. Japanese government publications on ODA highlight Japan's substantial contributions to Asian economic growth. The Japanese business community has also helped the Japanese government to create a potentially exclusive production alliance in the region, as an extension of the Japanese domestic base (Hatch and Yamamura, 1996). East Asia was subsumed into the global rivalry between the Americans and the Japanese (Encarnation, 1992; 152). Some Asian countries sought Japanese leadership. Malaysia's 'Look East' policy announced in 1981, called for an emulation of the Japanese development model. Singapore also indicated strong interest in learning from Japan in the 1980s. As the largest donor to East Asian countries, Japan has facilitated the realisation of the development objectives of its East Asian neighbours. Even now, most Asian states seek to better their economies than compete with Japan, while leaving it to the US to take on Japan head on.

Japan's trade followed its investment in Asia. Between 1985 and 1996, Japan's trade with East Asia almost quadrupled. In the process, Japanese firms had little interest in transferring very advanced critical technologies and managerial skills to potential Asian competitors and often raised the technological sophistication only enough to export to third countries. Thus, Japanese multinationals did not bring in as many positive benefits as their American counterparts did in Asia. For example, Japanese expatriates dominated in management and technological positions. Although Japan became an increasingly important market for Asian goods in the 1980s, most Asian exports still went to North America. Consequently, Japan's FDI in Asia grew and its exports of capital goods and components to the region also increased.

Japan's active role during the Asian financial crisis prompted the media to view Japan as willing and able to come to the rescue of the region (The Economist, 1997). Actually, Japan proposed an Asian Monetary Fund (AMF); that would include $100 billion in contributions from Asian countries. Concerned that the AMF would undermine IMF influence or conditionality and threaten US economic leadership, US officials lobbied and killed the proposal. In addition to the US, China also opposed the Japanese plan, fearing that it would take over regional leadership at the cost of China. In the end, the IMF, ADB and World Bank together committed $59.7 billion whereas Japan contributed $43 billion to the Asian crisis by 1998. Nevertheless, Asia needed much more than merely financial assistance. With an economy accounting for two thirds of the total GDP of East Asia, Japan's economic revival is considered central to the revival of the whole region.

As Japan has become a global player, Asia's share of Japan's bilateral ODA disbursement has declined (from 75% in 1975 to 62.5 in 1998). Japan has used its financial assistance to further regional cooperation and to enhance its leadership. Until the Asian financial crisis, Japan had preferred multi-lateralism at the global level and had shown little inclination to exclude the US from any serious regional grouping. With the slow movement in the WTO and APEC to promote further trade liberalisation, the advancement of regional integration is taking shape through bilateral and regional free trade agreements Japan too is actively seeking. There are also serious discussions to link an eventual North East Asian free trade area with the ASEAN free trade area. East Asian regional economic integration may benefit Japan more than the US. Japan and the other East Asian countries are pursuing greater regional cooperation partly because they are resentful toward the IMF's perceived heavy-handedness during the Asian financial crisis. While East Asian regionalism may well become a building block for global free trade, it may also lead to discrimination against 'outsiders'. Japan's preference for East Asia hence forth will have important global ramifications in the long-term.

Due to its growing economic strength, Japan started talking about using economic statecraft to ensure its comprehensive security and mainly resorted to cooperative measures to encourage stability and modernisation in other Asian countries which would enhance their own security. Japan's negative use of its economic power has been insignificant compared to the extent of its economic cooperation with other Asian countries. Since Japan's foreign policy towards Asia has been heavily economically-based, it naturally prefers not to adopt measures that would hurt its economic and commercial interests.

Japan's Political and Security Role

Japan's political and security roles in East Asia have gradually expanded. Nonetheless, its political moves remain tentative and its security role is limited and is restrained by domestic politics, a security alliance with the United States and resistance from its Asian neighbours. Japan has been more successful in playing a political role in South East Asia than in North East Asia and more successful in playing a security role in North East Asia than in South East Asia due to a different power balance, historical memory, and domestic politics (Ming Wan, 2001; 39). Japan is contributing to Asia's security by 'holding off' the Soviet Union/Russia in North East Asia, but its military power cannot be used for anything else (Okazaki and Sato, 1991; 21). Since the end of the Cold War, Japan has been reassessing its foreign policy toward Asia. It has made some bold political and security moves in Southeast Asia on its own initiative, albeit with little success. Japan has been drawn into a tighter security arrangement with the United States as a partner and this clearly has great security implications for North East Asia.

The above details reveal the fact that economic cooperation is the dominant theme in Japan's relations with East Asia. Japan's economic power rose rapidly in the 1980s and has relatively declined since the early 1990s. In spite of an initial setback, during the 1997-98 financial crisis, Japan has emerged as a stronger economic leader based on its huge financial aid and efforts to promote regional economic cooperation. Rise or decline, Japan's economic dominance in the region is overwhelming. Its relative power explains its willingness and capacity to impact on developments in the region. Despite economic stagnation and recession during much of the 1990s, Japan still remains the world's second largest economy and much more powerful economically than the rest of the region combined. Thus, Japan maintains a significant structural power and advantage in East Asia. Nevertheless, it has not acted assertively as a regional hegemon based on its economic and technological capabilities.

The Japanese 'economic miracle' was achieved with a minimum of social and political disharmony, while Japan sat quietly and safely within the US alliance system. This only ended in the early 1970s following Nixon and the oil 'shocks'. Japan bounced back from these shocks apparently with the same breathtaking ease with which it had overcome its defeat and destruction in the second world war. The Japanese government began to rethink its security relationship with the US, East Asia and beyond, and subsequently developed a 'comprehensive' security policy. The bureaucracy began to rethink its existing approach to economic growth and development. Business began to automate and further subcontract stages of the production process and moved offshore to the US, Europe and East Asia where costs were lower. By March 1991, Japanese corporations had employed 4,52,000 in North America, 2,11,000 in Europe and 6,66,000 in Asia (Itoh, 1994, 46). The development and impact of these changes on Japan and East Asia is important. Japan's contemporary role in all East Asian production, financial, security and knowledge structures also explains the evolution of the contemporary Japanese state-society complex and how it is changing.

Japan's Post-War Emergence

The Occupation of Japan was far from successful in achieving its stated objective of democratisation and demilitarisation, despite the purge of war-time leaders and a variety of initiatives including constitutional revision, liberalisation of the economy, land and labour reform and reform of the civil service and the educational system. Economic power remained highly concentrated in the hands of big business and Japan retained its military capability. The 'low posture' policy, combining the single-minded pursuit of economic growth and subservience within the US alliance structure succeeded beyond expectation, allowing Japan to take its place today as the second largest economy in the world. Commensurate with these achievements came membership in all of the relevant major economic and political organisations, such as GATT/WTO (1955), OECD(1964), World Bank(1952), IMF(1952), UN(1956), IAEA(1957), and so on. Membership does not infer influence, and until the 1980s, Japan refrained from attempts at playing a major role in policy-making, preferring instead to follow very closely the US line on almost all issues.

Industrial relations are breaking down under the pressure brought to bear by the US and other competitors in East Asia and elsewhere and have forced structural adjustments onto the Japanese economy, and also by its rejection at home in the face of severe pollution and other social costs. The political system/settlement is breaking down because of the rejection by the populace of the corruption endemic in political life and the associated perceived inability of politicians to solve real economic problems. It is breaking down also because politicians are apparently in the process of ending Japan's post-war rejection of militarism and militarisation (Kelly, 2002, 63).

To some extent, any move-political or military-by Japan is also being checked by China. Observing the rapid economic rise of China since the 1980s, some writers even say it is China rather than Japan that will be the dominant force in the region in the future. Japan also needs China's support and influence to become a political major power. Japan is burdened by "its past misdeeds and *ad hoc* attempts to resolve them" (Funabashi, 1998; 29). The strength of the Japanese domestic economy and its status, as the second largest world economy and the largest creditor state, has enabled it to deploy maximum financial and technological resources in various global institutions and in Asian economies as well.

Since 1978, when the Peace and Friendship Treaty was signed, Japan's China policy has been overshadowed by the mutual agreement struck at that time, stating that Japan, as an expression of its repentance for past aggression in China, would strive to help China to modernise, while China, in exchange, would relinquish war reparations (Taylor, 1996). Japan's China policy has been stable and continuous despite all the changes in China and the US. Its key principle is to have China as a friendly neighbour, despite occasional difficulties, compared with the lack of affordability of having a China that is utterly unstable, miserably poverty stricken, clearly hostile and outwardly-threatening (Inoguchi, 2002; 17-18). Sino-Japanese relations are in transition under the post-Cold War circumstances. China and Japan may be able to establish a positive sum relationship. Japan has been engaging China so that the key principle would not be jeopardized.

Japan's policy towards the authoritarian regimes of the Republic of Korea was characterised by looking at the Korean government's anti-Japanese policy on the one hand, and the infusion of Japanese financial, technological and other kinds of assistance and guidance, on the other. Japan's Korea policy has been changing steadily, particularly since Kim Dae Jung became President in 1998. Japan's Korea policy struggles under inherent difficulties. Japan does not have normal diplomatic relations with North Korea. Though Japan and North Korea have had a lot of economic, technological, financial and other linkages of various kinds, they do not have inter-governmental interaction. Japan's Korea policy has been based on the premise that Japan needs a Korea that serves the purpose of minimising the negative effects of the politics on the continent by acting as a buffer. South Korea acknowledges Japan's economic status. However, collective identity, formed through the historical memory of colonial domination and subjugation, still remains a major hindrance in South Korea accepting Japan's ascension to the regional leadership. It will continue to be quite wary of Japan's assertive regional security policy. The key to sustaining cooperative relationship between South Korea and Japan will depend largely on their ability to identify common interests and their pursuit in a mutually beneficial way.

East Asia and Australia

East Asia matters to Australia because the region is one of the major drivers of the global economy. Now the developments in the economies of Japan, Korea, China, including Hong Kong and Taiwan, profoundly affect the development in the old developed world. The dynamics is not new, of course. The competition between Tsarist Russia, Meiji Japan and Imperialist China, in the late nineteenth and early twentieth centuries, was intense. Throughout the twentieth century, strategic competition has boiled over with dire consequences for the countries in the region. Thus, the dynamic, in the Northern part of East Asia results from two main forces – economic strength and strategic interests-and then the challenge is to maximise the potential of these forces to reinforce each other rather than generating periodic systemic tensions and move towards a more harmonious, cooperative and prosperous direction.

Australia's engagement with the East Asian region has its own rich and long past. In the financial year ending June 2000, 40 per cent of Australia's exports, amounting to about $70 billion went to this region. Of all the economies of the area, it is only the DPRK that fails to figure in the first ten countries for Australian merchandise exports in 2000: Japan ranks first, ROK third, China fifth, Taiwan seventh and Hong Kong ninth. Any threat to the security of the region will have an immediate and deleterious impact on the national interests of Australia. Therefore, now Australia has a high level of economic, political and military discussions with Japan, China and Korea. The US engagement has guaranteed stability on the Korean peninsula, and has lessened the possibility of violent conflict between China and Taiwan. Furthermore, without the US-Japan Security Treaty, the region may have seen a destabilising strategic competition between China and Japan.

Australia supports a leadership role for Japan in the region and welcomes Japan's interests in promoting closer regional economic integration. Alongside Japan, the largest donor in the region, Australia has targeted the strengthening of economic, legal and governmental institutions, including markets. Realising the importance of Japan's role within the US-Japan Security Treaty, and Japan's generous contribution to the International Force in the East Timor Trust Fund that enabled the developing countries to participate in its operation, Australia supports Japan's bid for permanent membership of the UN Security Council. During his visit to Australia, the Japanese Prime Minister Junichiro Koizumi announced on 1 May 2002 that he would "advance Japan-Australia cooperation in global challenges such as measures against terrorism, the environment/Kyoto Protocol, and the WTO".

China is in many ways the region's fulcrum. China weathered the Asian economic crisis in surprisingly good shape, and is now benefiting from the recovery around the region. China's WTO accession and accommodating position in the South China Sea have had positive economic and strategic implications for the wider region. Though South Korea has failed to extract, even through negotiations, an agreement from North Korea to abandon its nuclear weapons programme during the marathon talks of January 2003, yet both sides pledged to resolve the issue peacefully. The joint statement issued after the talks mentioned that both sides would work together to avoid a nuclear crisis escalating into a military conflict. Recognising these developments, Australia continues to encourage the DPRK government to persist with its more open approach and expects continued prosperity and peace in the region.

Japanese Economic Growth and East Asian Regionalism

The 1980s and early 1990s were a period of unprecedented growth in East Asia and saw the emergence of regional institutional structures designed to secure East Asian development in a political arrangement encompassing the shared objectives and priorities of the plurality of societies within the Asia-Pacific region. Through APEC, Japan helped to define a strategy for trade and economic diplomacy-liberalisation and reform organised around the principles of open regionalism-peculiarly suited to the development objectives and diversity of the Asia-Pacific region. Through regional cooperation building, Japan could regain some high ground simply by virtue of its financial strength. Still, leadership and authority in these and in other international affairs comes from better strength, for example, in policy behaviour and articulation of policy strategy (Drysdale, 2002; 76-7).

Japan's success in Southeast Asia is also attributed partly to the role of ASEAN as a regional organisation and its growing importance. The Asian economic crisis could have been better resolved if the Japanese economy were to recover. Should Japan go beyond the economic context, the result is not likely to be positive. The South East Asian region does not see itself sufficiently troubled by aggressive external powers (Sheah, 2002; 99). ASEAN countries have their own military resources as well. The ability to recover from the economic crisis is the major challenge for the region to preserve peace and stability. Japan could see a continuation of its economic leadership as a much more important exercise than ever before.

Japan was the leading edge of East Asian industrialisation, and in the post-war period, has emerged to join the same league as the industrial economies of North America and Europe. The new role that Japan has assumed since 1980s has been defined in a pluralistic structure of economic power, encompassing the effective representation of broader Asia-Pacific and global interests (Funabashi, 1995). The East Asian region has suffered seriously from international investor confidence. During the recent financial crisis, the region witnessed a collapse in the asset market in Thailand, Indonesia, Malaysia and Philippines and significant capital outflows. Few countries in the region have remained immune from major currency depreciation. The IMF intervention subsequently in Thailand, Malaysia and Indonesia saw the implementation of policies aimed at stabilising currencies and introducing further economic reform. The prospects of an export-led recovery in individual countries of the region were complicated by the region's reliance on intra-East Asian trade which makes up about 50 per cent of total East Asian trade, and the extent to which these countries compete with one another in other export markets. Fortunately, there had not been any major repercussions for the security of the region following the economic crisis.

According to a World Bank half-yearly report, on East Asia and the Pacific, the sharp rise in world oil prices will sap income in a majority of East Asian countries. The external environment for the region is both weaker and more uncertain, and sustaining adequate rates of economic and social development will depend more than ever on each country's policies and institutions. East Asian exports to China have offset the loss of similar exports to Japan in 2001-2002. The pace of poverty reduction in East Asia, during recent decades, has been unparalleled in history. For example, in China, the number fell from 361 million in 1990 to 195 million in 2000. The emergence of China as a major economic power is one of the most striking features in the region. China's size in territory and population terms has always given it a prominent place, though the real reason is its own economic development since 1978. With a GDP of around $1,000 billion and concomitant with China's rise, has come a trend for some scholars to assert a so-called 'China threat'. In economic terms, China's impressive performance has been a positive development for itself, the region and the world.

Since a stable and peaceful regional and international environment provides the necessary climate for continued growth in trade and economic activity, Australia is therefore encouraged by and supportive of China's growing engagement with the East Asian region. China is already a participant in regional security dialogues and exchanges – ASEAN, ARF and APEC. These are some of the essential building blocks for the promotion of regionalism, regional stability and regional security. Furthermore, China's constructive involvement in the region was highlighted during the economic crisis when it chose not to devalue its currency.

Australia-Japan Cooperation

Australia and Japan share a history of cooperation in the East Asian regional context. They have worked together for years to advance closer cooperation and trade liberalisation in the Asia-Pacific region. They have played major roles in developing APEC and in the expansion of the agenda to address the key trade issues facing the region. They share a strong commitment to 'open regionalism', whereby APEC's trade liberalisation does not disadvantage non-APEC members. This is the driving force behind their close cooperation at multilateral forums.

While Japanese officials indicated Australia and New Zealand would eventually be included in ASEAN+3 to make it ASEAN+5, as they did in 2005, sometimes one notices that spread of developments is likely to spark concerns that Australia risks being sidelined from the new East Asian regionalism. For instance, "Australia is isolating itself from East Asia because of its intimate ties with the US is the message in the regional media". The Malaysian P.M., Mahathir, has remarked that, "Australia has gone too far in identifying with the US by not criticising any of its acts, and for this Australia would always be regarded as an outsider in its own region" (Mahatir, 2002). Nonetheless, Australia remains committed to its own judgement that continuing rise of East Asia and globalisation as two most profound influences on Australia's foreign and trade policy over the next ten years (Garnaut, 1989). Australia is committed to making a contribution to East Asian regional development.

In assessing the strength of the Japanese challenge in East Asia, nevertheless, there are clear indications that the Japanese state-society complex is reaching out beyond Japanese shores in such a way that it is visibly shaping the regional order in East Asia. The development of the East Asian production structure over the past forty or so years has been profoundly affected by the region's relationship with Japan who has quietly supplanted the US as the dominant external factor in growth. No doubt that Japan accounts for about 70 per cent of East Asian output and is a determining factor in enhancing the region's status and profile. However, the recent long-lasting domestic economic recession has limited its ability to absorb exports from the region. Japan's imports from Indonesia, Thailand, South Korea and China fell about 25 per cent, 9 per cent, 6 per cent and 3 per cent respectively since 1998. Further weakening of the Yen could reduce imports from the region, including from Australia. Japanese FDI, throughout the region, has been scaled back. The only good news for Japan is its economic strength and status, low-inflation economy, powerful work ethic, a strong manufacturing sector and remarkable export performance. Nevertheless, one certain option-less way for Japan to rise from the domestic economic crisis is ongoing structural reforms. According to several studies and forecasts, the continued reforms would allow 2-3 per cent growth beyond 2004-05.

The basic asset Australia has is an economy with strong fundamentals and a firm foundation – stable currency, annual average growth rate of 3.8 per cent since 1996, low inflation of 2.3 per cent, and low interest rates among OECD countries. Australia is, and will remain, Japan's most important and dependent supplier of energy, raw materials and food. Australia exported to Japan about $15 billion worth of goods while importing $10 billion worth in 2001-2002. Conversely, access to Japan's growing import market will remain critical for the Australian economy.

Therefore, Australia welcomes Japan's recent initiatives on import promotion and economic deregulation.

In Australian East Asia policy, Japan is the key element (Cheeseman and Bruce, 1996). Australian security interests display avoiding destabilising rivalry between the major regional powers, preventing the emergence of a regional hegemony, maintaining stability in Southeast Asia, helping neighbours in strengthening their security and preventing the proliferation of nuclear weapons (Trood, 1994). In the 1990s, many countries have closely linked their security and economic interests and had a greater coordination of defence, foreign and trade policies. Australia also similarly safeguards its national security, in a broader sense, by promoting economic cooperation, development assistance, cooperation in science and education, cultural exchange and people-to-people contacts with countries in the region (Somjee and Somjee, 1995).

Since Japan is, in material economic terms, obviously a major power, it has come to dominate the region's economic activities and also it is welcomed by the region. The ripple effect of rapidly growing Japanese FDI is changing the economic face of the Asia-Pacific region. This, in a way, also reflects the myriad contradictions inherent within Japanese foreign policy and within Japan's overall relationship with the region. Japan's consolidation of its relations with countries in the region has been well underway. Japan's East Asian policy is not going to become a hegemony-seeking exercise; rather, it is likely to become part of the regional politics in which Japan's presence has long been somewhat subdued.

Conclusion

Both China and Japan plan to start talks with the ASEAN group on concluding a free trade agreement with Southeast Asian countries over the next ten years. China, which is seen as being already a step ahead of Japan concerning FTA talks with ASEAN, has proposed a feasibility study on reaching a trilateral free trade agreement with Japan and South Korea. With China, continuing to advance its global economic position as a producer of various goods and an embracer of market with high potential, Japan is planning to reconstruct its FTA strategy, including with ASEAN, if it is to compete successfully with China. Japan has supported APEC over the EAEC, and avoided uncomfortable conflict between its interests with the US and those with East Asia. Japan remains the effective economic power in East Asia due to extensive influence of its MNCs region-wide, while the APEC framework keeps the US engaged in the region. North

Korea remains the main black spot on Japan's record of upgrading its ties with North East Asia. Japan has instrumentalised this remarkable revival in its political fortune in the region by the use of economic power, caution, and quiet diplomacy.

The development of close and mutually beneficial links between Japan and Australia, in the latter half of the twentieth century, was inevitable. In light of the significant restructuring taking place in the Japanese economy, Australian exporters are positioning themselves better to take advantage of opportunities in Japan. There is also more than ample scope for wider cooperation on a bilateral, regional and global basis.

REFERENCES

Amin Samir (1997), *Capitalism in the Age of Globalisation: The Management of Contemporary Society*, London: Zed Books.

Amsden, A. (1989), *Asia's Next Giant: South Korea and Late Industrialisation*, Oxford University Press: New York.

Ann Cappling (2001), *Australia and the Global Trade System*, Cambridge University Press: Cambridge.

Arase David (1995), *Buying Power: The Political Economy of Japan's Foreign Aid*, Boulder: Lynne Rienner.

Bernard Mitchell and John Ravenhill (1995), 'Beyond Product Cycle and Flying Geese: Regionalism, Hierarchy, and the Industrialisation of East Asia', *World Politics*, 47: 2, pp. 171-209.

Bridges Brian (1993), *Japan and Korea into the 1990s: From Antagonism to Adjustment*, London: Edward Elgar Publishers.

Calder K. (1996), *Pacific Defense: Arms, Energy and America's Future in Asia*, New York: William Morrow & Co.

Cheeseman, G. and Robert Bruce, eds. (1996), *Discourses for Danger and Dread: Australian Defense and Security Rethinking after the Cold War*, St. Leonards: Allen Unwin/ANU.

Crompton R. (2000), *East Asian Democratisation: Impact of Globalisation, Culture and Economy*, Praeger: Westport.

Crompton R. (2001), 'Reconstructing Political Legitimacy in Asia: Globalisation and Political Development', *International Journal of World Peace*, vol. 17, pp. 19-39.

Crompton Jr. Robert W. (2002), 'Political Culture as a Source of Japanese Immobilism in the New World Order', in Robert W. Crompton, *Transforming East Asian Domestic and International Politics*, Ashgate: Aldershot.

Cronin Patrik M. (1996), 'The US-Japan Alliance Redifined', *Strategic Forum* (Institute for National Strategic Studies, National Defense University, 75: 5.

Curtis G., ed. (1993), *Japan's Foreign Policy After the Cold War: Coping With Change*, Armonk, New York: ME Sharpe.

Czempiel Ernst-Otto (1993), 'US-Japan Relations in a Post-Cold War Context', *Japan Review of International Affairs*, 6: 3, Fall.

D. Brouwer Gordon (1999), *Financial Integration in East Asia*, Cambridge University Press: Cambridge.

Dobson W. (1992), *Japan in East Asia: Trading and Investment Strategies*, Institute for Southeast Asian Studies: Singapore.

Drysdale Peter (1988), *International Economic Pluralism: Economic Policy in East Asia and the Pacific*, Allen & Unwin: Sydney.

Drysdale Peter (1990), 'Japan and the Idea of Open Regionalism', *Journal of Social Science*, University of Tokyo, 51, pp. 5-6.

Drysdale, P. (2002), 'Beyond East Asia's Economic Crisis: Development paradise Lost?', in Takashi Inoguchi, ed., *op. cit.*

Economist (1997), 'Japan to the Rescue, October 11, pp. 89-90.

Encarnation D. (1992), *Rivals Beyond Trade: American Versus Japan in Global Competition*, Cornell University Press: Ithaca.

Fallows James, ed. (1994), *Looking at the Sun: The Rise of New East Asian Economic and Political System,* Pantheon: New York.

Freedman, Thomas (2000), *The Lexus and Olive Tree*, Farrar Straus and Giroux: New York.

Fukushima Akiko (1999), *Japan's Foreign Policy*, Palgrave: London.

Funabashi Yoichi (1995), *Asia Pacific Fusion: Japan's Role in APEC*, Institute of International Economics: Washington DC.

Funabashi, Y. (1998), 'Tokyo's Depression Diplomacy', *Foreign Affairs*, 77, no. 6, November/December.

Garnaut, Ross (1989), *Australia and the Northeast Asian Ascendancy*, Australian Government Publishing Service: Canberra.

Garnaut Ross (1997), *Open Regionalism and Trade Liberalisation*, Institute of Southeast Studies: Singapore.

Garnaut Ross and Drysdale Peter, eds. (1994), *Asia Pacific Regionalism: Readings in International Economic Relations*, Harper Educational: Sydney.

Harada Chikahito (1998), *Russia and North East Asia*, International Institute of Strategic Studies: London.

Hatch W. and K. Yamamura (1996), *Asia in Japan's Embrace: Building a Regional Production Alliance*, Cambridge University Press.

Paul Hirst and Grahame Thompson (1996), *Globalisation in Question*, Polity Press: Cambridge.

Ikenberry G. John (1998), 'Choosing Partners in Asia', *Australian Journal of International Affairs*, 52: 3, November, pp. 229-32.

Inoguchi Takashi (1996), *Japan's Foreign Policy in an Era of Global Change*, St. Martin's Press: New York.

Inoguchi Takashi, ed. (2002), *Japan's Asian Policy: Revival and Response*, Palgrave Macmillan: New York.

Itoh (1994), 'Is the Japanese Economy in Crisis?', *Review of International Political Economy*, I.

Johnson Chalmers (1995), *Japan: Who Governs?* W.W. Norton: New York.

Katzenstein Peter ed. (1998), *Asian Regionalism*, Cornell University Press: Ithaca.

Katzenstein, P. and S. Shiraishi, eds. (1997), *Network Power: Japan and Asia*, Cornell University Press: Ithaca.

Kelly, D. (2002), *Japan and the Reconstruction of East Asia*, Palgrave: New York.

Kojima Kiyoshi (1996), *Trade, Investment and Pacific Economic Integration*, Bushindo: Tokyo.

Lam Peng Er (1997), 'Japan's search for a Political Role in Southeast Asia', *Southeast Asian Affairs*, Singapore.

Mahatir, M. (2002), 'Australia Closing itself out of Asia', *Sydney Morning Herald*, 24 November.

Mendl Wolf (1995), *Japan's Asia Policy: Regional Security and Global Interests*, Routledge: London.

Ming Wan (2001), 'Unique Leader in East Asia', *The Japanese Economy*, Vol. 26, no. 6, November-December.

Moon Chung-in and Paark Han-kyu (1999), 'Globalisation and Regionalism in Japan's Foreign Policy', in G. Curtis, ed., *Japan's Foreign Policy in an Emerging New Order*, St. Martin's Press: New York.

Okazaki Hisahiko and Seizaburo Sato (1991), 'Redefining the Role of Japanese Military Power', *Japan Echo*, 18, no. 1.

Pempel T.J. (1997), 'Transpacific Torii: Japan and the Emerging Asian Regionalism', in P. Katzenstein and S. Shiraishi, eds., *Network Power: Japan and Asia*, Cornell University Press: Ithaca.

Pempel T.J. (1996), 'Gulliver in Lilliput: Japan and Asian Economic Regionalism', *World Policy Journal* 13: 4, Winter, pp. 13-26.

John Ravenhill, J. (2000), 'APEC Adrift: Implications for Economic Regionalism in Asia and the Pacific', *Pacific Review*, 13 (2), May, pp. 319-333.

Rix Allen (1993), 'Japan and the Region: Leadership from Behind', in R. Higgott, R. Leaver and J. Revenhill, eds., *Pacific Economic Relations in the 1990s: Conflict or Cooperation?* Allen & Unwin: Sydney.

Sheah, D. C-M. (2002), 'ASEAN and Japan's Southeast Asian Regionalism', in Inoguchi, *op. cit.*

Somjee, A. and G. Somjee (1995), *Development Success in Asia Pacific*, St. Martin Press: New York.

Taylor, R. (1996), *Greater China and Japan: Prospects for an Economic Partnership in East Asia*, Routledge: London.

Trood, R. (1994), 'Perspectives on Australian Foreign Policy-1997', *Australian Journal of International Affairs*.

Wang Jisi (1995), 'Building a Constructive Relationship, in Mortor I. Abramovitz, Funabashi Yoichi and Wang Jisi, eds., *China-Japan-US: Managing the*

Trilateral Relationship, Japan Center for International Exchange: New York.

World Bank (1993), *The East Asian Economic Miracle: Economic Growth and Public Policy*, Oxford University Press: New York.

Yamazawa Ippei (1998), 'Asian Economic Crisis and Japan', *The Developing Economies*, 36: 3, Tokyo, September.

11

Combating Terrorism: Australia's Approach

ANTHONY BERGIN

Australians are and will continue to be vulnerable to potential terrorist attacks in South East Asia, as well as in Australia itself. The reasons for *Al Qaeda* and *Jemaah Islamiah* targeting Australia are many, with most analysts arguing that Australia's profile as a terrorist target has increased in recent years. A fundamental reason is that Australia is perceived to be a predominantly Western, Christian country and a longstanding ally of the United States. Australia's direct military engagement in East Timor in 1999 resulted in a specific threat warning against Australia by Al Qaeda's leaders. Australia's military participation in the Afghanistan war and participation in the invasion of Iraq as one of only three members of a US-led coalition has also raised Australia's profile (Walters, 2004b).

The threat posed by terrorism is now well understood. We are living and working in a security environment that has changed significantly in recent years. The threat we face is very real. The tragic events of September 11, the Bali bombings, the Madrid bombings, the intentional targeting of children by terrorists in Beslan, and the bombing at the Australian Embassy in Jakarta on 9 September 2004 all demonstrate the dangers we confront. Terrorism is not a static threat. Groups like *Al Qaeda* and *Jemaah Islamiah* (JI) are proving to be tough and resourceful. While many of the original leaders of Al Qaeda have been arrested or killed, younger ones have replaced them. Groups like Jemaah Islamiah have adopted the Al Qaeda model and this was reflected tragically in the Bali bombing. The effective deployment of suicide bombing by both groups has forced the re-writing of assumptions on operational responses to potential terrorist actions.

Terrorism is an asymmetric form of warfare. The Bali bombings in which 202 were killed led to the estimated loss of more than $1 billion in tourism revenue for the country. The bombing itself cost under $35,000. While terrorism is not new, what is relatively new is that in the war against terrorism we are now engaged in a global war. Terrorist networks wish to take their fight against global targets. Their fight has been facilitated by globalisation itself and the revolutions in information and communications technologies and the speed of international financial flows.

The war against terrorism is a war against militant Islamism and in that sense it is a political and military struggle for the hearts and minds of the world's Muslim population. It is in many ways a struggle between moderate Muslims and the more extremist elements within Islam who regard moderate Muslim governments as corrupt. The extremists see Western governments as supporting these so-called corrupt regimes or target Western countries in their own right as representing forces that are themselves evil and that must be destroyed.

In Southeast Asia, the Bali bombings of October 2002 have been followed by the Marriott Hotel bombing of August 2003 and the bomb detonated outside the Australian Embassy in September 2004 that resulted in nine Indonesian fatalities and around 150 people injured. The Al Qaeda network, including the Al Qaeda terrorist franchise in Southeast Asia of which JI is a major part, represents a major continuing threat to regional states and to Australia (ICG Brussels Report, 2003). While there is a debate within JI over whether it should focus on more populist activities to foment Muslim-Christian unrest, rather than terrorism, that alienates the broader Indonesian Muslim community, most experts predict that JI will continue to be involved in violent action (ICG Brussels Report, 2004). JI's main goals are the establishment of a fundamentalist Islamic government in Indonesia, followed by the formation of a unified Islamic state in the Southeast Asian region, stretching from southern Thailand, through the Malay peninsula across the Indonesian archipelago and into the southern Philippines (Chulov, 2004; Powell and Lyall, 2004; Walters, 2004a). JI has probably something in the order of 25,000-30,000 supporters in Indonesia. It continues to recruit through its Islamic boarding schools. The regional nature of the terrorist threat mandates that any effective, long-term strategy for dealing with the terrorism must be based on a coordinated regional counter-terrorism strategy.

Australia's Approach – Layered Defence

If some remained unconvinced, we certainly know after the bombing at Australia's Jakarta Embassy, that Australia, and Australians overseas, are a target (although the main enemies are still the US, then Israel, and, to a lesser extent, the UK). This is the first time terrorists have specifically attacked Australians. There have been previous Al Qaeda and JI target lists that have included Australian diplomatic missions in Southeast Asia, but they were never acted on. One hundred and forty Australians have been killed overseas in terrorist incidents, 88 in Bali and 10 on 9/11. Over 50,000 Australians are based in Southeast Asia and 400 Australian companies have a presence in Indonesia.

Australian authorities expect that Al Qaeda and its affiliates are continuing to probe for weaknesses and opportunities to set up cells within Australia, although there is no evidence to date that Australia is host to such cells or groups that could launch a mass casualty attack. (Australia currently has a Muslim population of around 2,80,000 but there is no significant radical faction that has emerged at this stage.)

While Australia has a very effective system of border and immigration control, the terrorist threat presents a range of complex challenges, not only for Australian plans to prevent attacks but also for the community and the Australian business sector in minimising and responding to the effects of an attack. Terrorist action is by nature unpredictable and its most recent evolution challenges states to develop structures, procedures and attitudes to deal with greatly escalated threats to national security.

Government response requires planning and organisation of not only the defence force, police forces and intelligence and security services, but also transport, health, emergency services, agriculture and border agencies. It affects the owners and operators of business, particularly critical infrastructure. All three levels of Australia's government-Federal, State and Local-are involved. Ensuring Australia's preventive strategies, preparedness and response plans are optimal is a key challenge, for, on the basis of previous terror campaigns, the fight against terrorism is likely to last at least another two decades. At the Australian government level alone there are over 30 separate Commonwealth departments and agencies contributing to safeguarding Australia from terrorism. In each of the State and Territory jurisdictions, there are up to ten agencies involved. In addition, there are over 700 local government authorities in Australia and hundreds of government-owned enterprises and businesses that have some responsibility for critical infrastructure. While many government agencies are not required to focus on terrorism as a core role, it is touching virtually every Australian government agency in some way.

The Howard government, that was re-elected in 2004 for a fourth (three-year) term of office, claims it has spent over $3 billion dollars since September 11 2001 on measures to boost counter-terrorism capabilities and to improve Australia's domestic security responses (Also see Annex). In 2004-05, the Commonwealth State and Territory governments spent $649 million on homeland security measures. This figure includes spending in areas of international security related to counter terrorism, intelligence, law enforcement, emergency services, public awareness, transport and border security as well as infrastructure protection.

In the age of terrorism there is a need for a clear articulation of a comprehensive Australian national strategy on counter-terrorism. The Australian Foreign Minister, Alexander Downer, issued a government White Paper on terrorism in July 2004, *Transnational Terrorism: The Threat to Australia.* The paper emphasises that the strategy is to deliver concrete results against the terrorists through effective operational-level cooperation; to help other countries develop and strengthen their capabilities to fight terrorism; and to build political will among governments to combat terrorism over the longer term. Overall, this appears to be a sound approach. Nowhere in the Australian terrorism White Paper, however, is there a clear articulation of our how this overall international strategy links with Australia's domestic counter-terrorism strategy. The terrorist threat clearly cannot be defined by national borders as terrorism is truly a transnational phenomenon.

Joining the dots of various Australian actions since 9/11, (Also see Annex), it seems that the overall Australian approach to combat terrorism is a layered defence approach-preventing and defending against terrorist attacks through geographic layers starting overseas and leading to mainland Australia. First, the strategy comprises broad-based offensive action, (including, if necessary, pre-emption), winning friends, de-legitimising terror as an instrument of policy and a close coordination of diplomatic, police, military and intelligence assets to find, track and defeat terrorists overseas. The strategy is aimed at keeping foreign terrorists out of Australia and to prevent them from gaining access to weapons of mass destruction. Australia's approach to combating terrorism has been to establish cooperative activities with regional states with the objective of sharing information about terrorist activities, coordinating operational activities and generating the political will and technical capacity in the region to fight terrorism. Australia has, for example, concluded bilateral agreements on counter terrorism with a number of regional states and supported the establishment of a Jakarta Centre for Law Enforcement to provide counter-terrorism training.

In September 2004 the Howard government announced that there would be two counter-terrorism teams which were to be located in the region and a number of capacity-building projects. Much greater emphasis has been put on intelligence efforts since 2001. A recent report into Australia's intelligence services pointed out that Australia should have known, by the end of 2001, much more about JI, its development of terrorist capabilities and its intentions towards Western targets (Flood Report, 2004; 177). More limited steps have been undertaken by Australia to assist regional countries in winning the battle of ideas through development and educational programme and by building linkages with Muslim religious leaders in the region. Much of this activity has been co-ordinated by Australia's Ambassador for Counter-Terrorism.

The second layer in Australia's strategy is border security to keep out dangerous individuals and goods. The third layer is better coordination arrangements among federal and state agencies and the fourth layer is improved cooperation across business and the public sector to protect critical infrastructure. The final element is the improvement of consequence management to limit the damage and recover from any terrorist attacks that may occur.

While the overall approach is sensible, although there are some missing elements in the Australian Terrorism White Paper. In fully subscribing to the 'terrorists hate Australia for what we are, not what we do' school of thought about terrorism, the White Paper has no analysis of whether any changes to Western policies toward the Islamic world would contribute to victory. There is no analysis of the important position, for example, of Saudi Arabia. Muslim communities in many parts of the world have come under extremist Saudi influence. The Saudis have been heavily involved in financing the radical Islamic groups. Nor is the central role of Pakistan highlighted by the White Paper as a key incubator for terrorist recruits.

The White Paper does not outline the clear advantages of bilateralism in shaping national strategy, although Australia has now concluded nine agreements with regional countries on counter-terrorism. In general, the bilateral strategy is sensible when it comes to counter-terrorism – the larger the gathering to address terrorism the less effective it is. The White Paper is surprisingly complimentary about the UN's role on terrorism. In reality, the UN is a very small player in dealing with terrorism-it lacks the police, intelligence and military assets to play an active role to suppress terrorist groups or to pre-empt specific terrorist strikes.

The White Paper argues that the campaign against Muslim extremists involves a 'contest of ideas'. True enough, but the White Paper does not discuss the role of Australian public diplomacy in the Islamic world and how Australia might engage moderate Muslims in the war of ideas. How Australia might play a role in suppressing theological schools that become indoctrination centres is not analysed. The potential role of public diplomacy and, in particular, Radio Australia, where budget cuts have forced it to limit its broadcasts into Indonesia and downgrade coverage in other parts of Asia, is not considered in the White Paper.

Business does not rate a mention in the White Paper strategy. As much of the revenue of Australian companies comes from international markets, business is well placed to undertake a very useful role in public diplomacy programs. In 2004, Australian business invested $152 billion abroad, providing economic opportunities in developing countries and building human capital that might undermine support for terrorism.

The White Paper warns Australians not to become complacent in the face of a threat that may last a generation. That is sensible. Australians may see long periods when terrorist dangers represent potential rather than imminent danger. Given that few Australians have experienced or are likely to experience a terrorist attack, continuous reinforcement will be needed to convince significant numbers of Australians to take common sense precautions in anticipation of terrorist attacks over threat periods that may span many years (also see below).

Selected Issues in Australia's Homeland Security Strategy

Countering terrorism requires exceptionally broad policy responses on the home-front as well as at the regional level. Here six issues will be touched which are of current interest to Australia's political decision-makers attempting to protect Australians against terrorism.

The Role of Business

Around forty Chief Executives of Australia's largest companies met in Canberra in mid-2004 with the Prime Minister and all key Ministers involved in the effort to protect Australia from terrorism. As 90 per cent of critical infrastructure in Australia is privately owned, any strategy to protect Australia's vital assets will depend on a greater sharing of information between the public and private sectors. The business of industry is business, and not counter-terrorism. However, much of the key information that the Australian government needs to detect and prevent terrorist attacks now lies with the corporate sector.

Information sharing is, however, not without risks. The government often does not want to release classified information that would compromise existing intelligence. As more information is shared the likelihood of terrorists accessing the information increases. Business has concerns about the extent to which any information on vulnerabilities will be kept confidential and whether trade secrets may be passed to a regulator. Australian industry wants to be reassured that in agreeing to work with the public sector to assist in developing security measures they will not risk litigation costs should these measures in the end fail to deter terror attacks. With the heightened concern about infrastructure vulnerability there is increased sensitivity about giving the public locational and other information related to critical facilities.

The interconnected nature of Australia's critical infrastructure means that all levels of government and the private sector must communicate more frankly and frequently to eliminate vulnerabilities and create effective response plans. Business in Australia needs to be involved in planning terrorism exercises and cooperative research. The most significant vulnerability confronting business in Australia is that, currently, it cannot depend on receiving timely advice of changes to intelligence. Without such intelligence it is not possible to manage security and react appropriately to changes in threat levels. The recent Australian Business-Ministerial Forum on Terrorism will be a useful first step if it strengthens the efforts of Chief Executives and company boards to improve their efforts to integrate security considerations into corporate governance arrangements and if it assists in redefining the intelligence community to include the business community.

Public Education

Since 11 September, Australians have heard a lot about potential terrorist threats, but very little on what they can do to enhance their security. Few Australians would know, for example, how to respond to an attack by terrorists involving biological agents-yet how they respond in the first hours of such an attack could mean life or death, and a small number of casualties or more catastrophic effects. For a country like Australia, that has been unusually immune from terrorist threats, public education is a critical element of any effective homeland security strategy.

In 2003, Australia introduced a brief public education counter-terrorism campaign – the slogan was 'Be Alert and not Alarmed'-with a booklet to each household and a fridge magnet with a key telephone number to a new national security 'hotline'. The campaign was met with much cynicism with many suggesting that the Prime Minister wanted Australians to wake up to a fridge magnet reminding them that this was another day of terror. Just before the October 11 2004 election another round of newspaper and TV ads began informing the public that they should report anything suspicious that might assist in preventing terrorist attacks. The current security environment does mandate that we inform the public of possible threats and what they should do about them. Emergency preparedness can save lives – potentially a lot of lives. Alerting the country about terrorist risks is an act of prudence. Just as we ought to have plans on the shelf to deal with fire and flood, we need security plans. And we should review them regularly.

Many of the measures to prevent and mitigate the consequences of a terrorist attack have broader national benefits. The tools used to save lives and property in the wake of a terrorist attack are largely similar to those used in the event of a major industrial or transport accident or a natural disaster. Many people prepare for disasters only after they have had some experience with that threat. And the perceived need to be prepared recedes as the event becomes more remote. As few Australians are likely to experience a terror attack, continuous education is important to convince us to take common sense precautions in anticipation of an attack over threat periods that may span many years. An official or agency needs to be resourced to be responsible for this public education function that will assist in reducing the risks that terrorists will take their fight here. Perhaps a distinguished Australian, outside of politics, should be given this vital role in public education.

A National Terrorist Alert System

No alert system can deliver perfect security or tell us exactly what we should look for. Intelligence is almost never that precise. In the new terror age we need to be vigilant all the time, regardless of the exact alert level in force. And we will rarely know if the alert system works. It is hard to know if a planned attack is aborted due to better security. In 2003, the Australian government added a fourth level of alert – extreme-to its alert system. Since the September 11 attacks, Australia has been on medium level alert under a three tier system, but in 2004 the government introduced four classifications: low, medium, high and extreme.

The Prime Minister stated that the change was to eliminate confusion, provide a sharper public focus and represented a more 'realistic' approach. The US system-five threat conditions, each identified by a description and a corresponding colour, was rejected. Instead, the PM noted that 'plain English words' are better to inform the public. He pointed out that the alert terms are those used in relation to the Australian bushfire warnings. The purpose of terror alerts is to deter attacks by making success less certain and to ensure an efficient response if deterrence fails. Raising the alert level has significant economic costs affecting areas like tourism. The key issue is whether the alert system tells people what to do when conditions change. Does it tell us if a threat is serious enough to divert time, money and people from normal activities? Not really; Australia's system is very much a 'one-size-fits-all' approach. It does not do much to inform state and local governments of specific threats. That means that those levels of government are likely to either do nothing or put in place wasteful measures if threat levels change. Of course, no national terrorism alert system can tell us precisely what to do. That will always come back to local authorities informing the public what to do in some detail, just as in the case of fire alerts.

Unfortunately, Australia's terror alert system does not assist those designing local guidelines with any framework to organise their responses. We need alerts to specific regions and for different types of business sectors. Adding an extra level of alert may, however, reassure the public because there are now two steps before an attack is imminent and normal business stops. A psychologist rather than a security analyst may have advised the government on the last change to Australia's national terrorist alert system.

Mass Transit Security

Long before the tragic events in Madrid, public transport systems were under attack by terrorists. Over the last decade there have been hundreds of incidents where terrorists have bombed, shot and gassed people on railways, trams and buses. Public transport presents an easy target. By its very nature the system is open. There is little security and, unlike at airports, passengers and luggage are not inspected. Unfortunately, terrorists aim to create maximum alarm. Attacking public transport and causing major destruction meets that objective.

The question is what best to do? At peak hour, public transport systems are highly vulnerable to conventional explosives. Since well before 9/11, security experts have been aware of the vulnerability of public transport, and, as a result of the attacks in Madrid, security on public transport is being accorded an even higher priority by the Australian National Counter Terrorism Committee. It is important that transport authorities in Australia continue to review their security assessments and meet on a regular basis with the intelligence community to canvass security issues.

The New South Wales transport authorities convened numerous exercises prior to the 2000 Olympics in Sydney. However, now all Australian transport authorities need to be in regular contact with the official counter-terrorism community on possible terrorist threats to transport systems. They need to participate in counter-terrorism exercises. Transport employees will need training to realise that preparing for terrorist incidents is different than for other transport emergencies, such as derailment, that do not have the unknown dangers of a terrorist attack. They will need to communicate with passengers to ensure that commuters are made aware of their surroundings and know to watch for anything suspicious. Transport authorities will need to have plans in place that will enable them to restore normal services if these were to be disrupted by terrorist attacks. Keeping the transport system moving will impact on restoring community confidence.

There is not likely to be a technology safety fix and the costs associated with adequate security patrols are likely to be prohibitive. The emphasis, therefore, needs to be on transport employees and the public being provided with guidance on how to deal with suspicious circumstances. The challenge will be to maintain vigilance without creating undue fear or vigilantism. While the patrons of public transport will continue to be a specific target of terrorism, we can do much to mitigate the damage through appropriate training and emergency responses. In many ways, it means a change in commuter culture. Instead of ignoring other public transport patrons. Australians are beginning to recognise that the new security threats mean that it might be time for them to engage with those around them on mass transit more than they perhaps have done in the past.

Who Pays?

Who pays for anti-terrorism measures is now shaping up as a key economic and political issue in Australia. Should it be federal, state or local governments, the private sector or the individual stakeholders? Airlines such as Qantas and Virgin Blue face more than $1 billion in extra security costs. The Tourism Task Force Managing Director described the government decision to make industry pay for new airline baggage screening costs as the government is "outsourcing its national security responsibility". Virgin's Chief Executive argued that "security is the government's responsibility" and is not an aviation issue. He questioned whether the government would now start looking at taxes for nightclubs, shopping malls and football games.

Generally speaking, the principle the Australian government has adopted is that the users, providers and owners of the property or service pay for the costs of security. This is a sound approach. Once governments start subsidising anti-terrorist measures money will be wasted. Some firms will take unnecessary and expensive security measures. There will be intense lobbying to gain government anti-terror funding support. Companies which would have undertaken appropriate security steps, anyway, may benefit. The public should not be subsidising private sector protective measures. Costs should be borne by the users of the service in order to reduce overall costs. This will provide an incentive for companies to innovate in their anti-terrorism protection.

Some industry leaders argue that industry can take care of its own security, as it has a powerful incentive to make sure it is safe. Government has no real role here. Leave it to market forces. However, that approach will not offer adequate protection for all of the Australian community. We cannot afford terrorists to gain access to high explosives. The public should expect that government will set minimum standards and regulations in areas such as codes for skyscrapers and food safety, where there may be terrorist threats. Certain threats, such as biological attacks, require a response with specialist equipment, which would be difficult to achieve without direct government intervention.

Similarly, there is almost no traditional terrorism risk insurance available for commercial properties and infrastructure in Australia. Lack of adequate information to price the risks associated with terrorism has resulted in a market failure. The government has now intervened. An Australian ?e-insurance Pool Corporation has been established to provide re-insurance cover for losses arising from a declared terrorist incident. The Australian Treasurer has stated that the re-insurance scheme would wind down once appropriate commercial cover is available. This is sensible. As a general rule, the government should fund only those anti-terrorist activities that are not supplied, or are inadequately supplied, in the market.

Who is Responsible?

The Government has decided, and the States have agreed, that the Cabinet will be the commanding body for counter-terrorism. In practice, the National Security Committee of Cabinet (NSCC) would be central both in making policy decisions and in counter-terrorist operations. In some circumstances, decisions usually falling only to the PM may be required during a counter-terrorist operation. Yet within the NSCC no one Minister is responsible for homeland security; after changes in October 2003 the PM speaks for policy development and the Attorney-General for operational aspects of counter-terrorism. However, neither can be across both fields all of the time. The PM is more than occupied, while the Attorney-General is credited with some 29 portfolio responsibilities, only five of which are directly relevant to counter-terrorism.

The establishment of a National Security Division in 2003, in the Prime Minister's Department, should improve the advice on counter-terrorism going to the National Security Committee of Cabinet and the Secretaries Committee of National Security (the top group of Australian public servants with security responsibilities). It should improve coordination between federal and the state instrumentalities. The real test of the National Security Division, however, will be whether it can develop new policy ideas in the face of the terrorist threat, looking out at what needs to be done to reduce our vulnerabilities over the medium to longer-term. One of the greatest threats to homeland security is the way in which democratic societies tire of the disciplines of on-going terrorist alerts and slacken their vigilance, providing terrorists with options to renew their activities.

The Labour Party opposition wants a Department of Homeland Security on the US model. The government argues that, for many reasons, including cost and effectiveness, it is not the best option for Australia. This is a sound response. Australia does not have anything like the 18,000 different law enforcement bodies that exist in the United States or the bureaucratic turf wars such as those that exist between the FBI and CIA. However, does the National Security Division initiative go far enough? Without effective organisational structures to address issues of coordination there is a danger of creating a situation where everybody's problem is nobody's responsibility. The problem with the 'whole-of-government' approach in Australia is that it often creates a hole, with no one official or agency in charge. And herein lies the risk inherent in the current Australian arrangements. The Prime Minister cannot be across the policy aspects of counter-terrorism all of the time, while the Attorney General is in effect a part-time Counter-Terrorism Minister.

In a coordinated system, it is necessary for someone with appropriate authority to oversee the entire jigsaw and to have the time to drive the pieces into the right place. The government should therefore seriously consider appointing a Minister Assisting the PM for counter-terrorism. A senior figure with Cabinet rank should be given the job. A better option, however, would be to have a full-time dedicated Minister at Cabinet level to provide a single focal point for assessing and developing the wide range of elements that comprise homeland security, from intelligence to health. A dedicated Minister would not require a new bureaucracy. The title, Special Minister of State, has been used before in Australia to designate a Minister with a special role outside the normal departmental system. Senior staff would report to a Minister with executive authority, rather than relying on the irregular pattern of Cabinet meetings. Essential matters, therefore, would be pursued with greater speed. A dedicated Minister for Counter-Terrorism would ensure improved public accountability, without the need for a large staff.

Concluding Remarks

The terrorist threat is one that faces all states. It is unlike any other threat that we have faced before and is entirely dissimilar to the conventional warfare that is comprised of mainly military targets, standing armies and clear rules of engagement. The terrorist threat today is unpredictable; it can be directed at us anywhere at anytime. The terrorists choose their targets without moral limits. They do not try to avoid civilian deaths, but rather try to maximise them. They do not abide by any laws of armed conflict. They use whatever means are available to them to achieve their political and ideological objectives.

Australia has taken a strong lead in developing a regional approach to combating terrorism, although there is still a fair way to go in the substantive exchange of information between regional governments and better coordination among the range of new counter-terrorism centres in Malaysia, Thailand, Indonesia and a proposed new training centre in Australia. There is a further need for Australia to work with regional states to audit counter-terrorism capabilities and to analyse where the capability gaps exist and how they can be met in each country. There is more work to be done by Australia in addressing its neighbours, the economic and social factors, that contribute to winning recruits to extremism, and improving education in secular and mainstream religious schools. On the home front, Australia will need to continue to critically examine and review its counter-terrorism arrangements in the context of the threats Australia faces; also whether existing measures are necessary or outmoded.

The Indonesian police has performed well in combating JI, securing 33 convictions associated with the Bali bombing. The extremist Islamic cleric and accused JI leader Abu Bakar Bashir has been prosecuted on terrorism charges. However, JI possesses three training camps in the southern Philippines carrying on operations so that it is able to replenish its ranks. JI also has links with the new and increasingly violent insurgency in southern Thailand (ICG, 2003; ICG, 2004).

There is no quick fix in the 'war on terrorism'. The threat is likely to get worse, it can be predicted that Australia will continue to emphasise enhanced cooperation with regional countries, especially Indonesia (possibly including a formal Australian-Indonesian Security Treaty also see *The Australian*, 2004; Behm, 2004). Greater efforts are required in intelligence, police and military cooperation with Southeast Asian states, whilst, at the same time, strengthening efforts in domestic counter-terrorism preparedness and response.

REFERENCES

Australian Department of Foreign Affairs website, www.dfat.gov.au

Australian Government (2004), National Security Policy released in the election campaign in October 2004 and available at www.liberal.org.au

Behm, A. (2004), 'Look at Indonesia as an ally', *The Australian*, 19 October.

Chulov, M. (2004), 'Region's Terrorists in secret alliance', *The Australian*, 21 September.

Department of Premier and the Cabinet (2004), *Protecting Australians Against Terrorism*, Canberra, June, available at www.pmc.gov.au

Flood Report (2004), Inquiry into Australian Intelligence Agencies, July.

ICG Brussels Report (2003), *Jemaah Islamiah in South East Asia: Damaged but still Dangerous*, August.

ICG Brussels Report (2004), *Southern Philippines Backgrounder: Terrorism and the Peace Process*, July.

Powell, S. and K. Lyall (2004), 'Lessons in Militant Ivy league' *The Australian* 18-19 September.

The Australian (2004), 'Downer to seek treaty with Jakarta', 18 October.

Walters, P. (2004a), 'Lethal lethargy', *The Australian*, 11-12 September.

Walters, P. (2004b), 'Canberra refuses requests for troops to protect UN staff in Iraq' *The Australian*, 18 October.

ANNEXURE

AUSTRALIAN COUNTER-TERRORISM MEASURES SINCE 9/11

(Information here is drawn from *Protecting Australians Against Terrorism*, Department of Prime Minister and Cabinet, Canberra, June 2004, available at www.pmc.gov.au and the government's National Security policy released in the election campaign in October 2004 and available at www.liberal.org.au)

Since 9/11 Australia has committed over $3.2 billion in additional funding to strengthen security and law enforcement agencies.

Resources for Intelligence: They are now funded at an unprecedented level, receiving over $870 million since 2001. The budget of the Australian Security Intelligence Organisation (ASIO) has more than doubled since September 2001 with its number of personnel employed now higher than at any previous time.

Resources for Law Enforcement: The Australian Federal Police (AFP) has had its budget increased by 270 per cent over the last eight years. The AFP's off-shore counter terrorism capability now includes rapid deployment teams as well as teams already co-located in the region.

Legislative Framework: Law enforcement and intelligence agencies have greater powers to detain and question those suspected to be involved in terrorist activities. Laws have been tightened to prevent suspects being granted bail when they represent an ongoing threat to the community. Convicted terrorists now face stiffer penalties.

National Co-ordination: Australia has established a national counter-terrorism committee that brings Federal, State and Territory governments together to share information and implement effective counter-terrorist strategies. The responsibilities of each level of Government are set out under a National Counter Terrorism Plan launched in June 2003. There are more frequent counter-terrorism exercises.

Regional Coordination: Australia has now concluded bilateral agreements on counter-terrorism cooperation with nine of its neighbours and funded a number of counter-terrorism capacity building projects in the region, Australia co-hosted, with Indonesia, a Ministerial meeting on Counter-Terrorism, hosted the first Regional Special Forces Counter-Terrorism conference and is working with the countries making up the Five Power Defence Arrangement to conduct maritime interdiction exercises in the Malacca Straits.

Public Information: With the establishment in December 2002 of a national security hotline it has received over 35,000 calls. It is a means by which the public can provide information to authorities that may assist them disrupt potential terrorist activity.

Critical Infrastructure: Australia has moved to secure sites and systems within key sectors of the economy including energy, banking, information technology, transport, food and water supplies.

Border Protection: Australia over the last three years has implemented a wide range of measures that allow the Immigration, Customs and Quarantine authorities to better monitor the movement of people and cargo to and from Australia.

Transport Security: Air marshals, increased passenger and baggage screening, and government mandated security plans for regional and commercial airports and shipping and port authorities have been introduced.

Science and Technology: Australia has established a special Science, Engineering and Technology Unit for counter terrorism within the Department of Prime Minister and

Cabinet which has the specific task of coordinating research and development relating to the fight against terrorism.

Response Capabilities: The Australian Defence Force has created new teams of personnel dedicated to responding to domestic security threats. These units can respond to a wide range of incidents, including those of a chemical, biological and radiological nature.

Recent Commitments: The Howard government was re-elected on October 11 and has recently stated that it would undertake wide range of new counter-terrorism measures

Local Government and Emergency Services: The Government will establish a new Local Government Security Partnership Programme. The key components are: developing a national strategic plan, establishing a local grants programme to fund practical security measures and security awareness, training and creating a dedicated Office of Local Government Emergency Management. Capital city Mayors will be briefed by intelligence agencies on security issues relevant to them.

Counter-terrorism Exercises: There will be additional National Counter-Terrorism exercises, involving cooperation between Territory, State and Federal authorities. These multi-jurisdictional exercises will cover at least six major counter-terrorist scenarios including, but not limited to, an airline hijacking, a bio-attack, an attack on the food chain, an attack on a ferry, an attack on an offshore oil rig and an attack on the national electricity grid.

International Cooperation and Law Enforcement: A major upgrade of the Australian Institute of Policing at Manly, NSW. This Institute will become a key training facility where senior police officers from neighbouring countries will be brought together with senior officers from Australian Federal, State and Territory police forces. A $76.4 million commitment to strengthen the AFP's regional counter-terrorism capability which will include: the establishment of two new counter-terrorism Regional Engagement teams to be co-located in the region; the establishment of two counter-terrorism criminal intelligence teams and two counter-terrorism surveillance teams to operate both within Australia and in the region. Each of these AFP teams will work closely with counterpart agencies in the region to disrupt the terrorist networks. $9 million will be given to counter terrorism capacity building projects in the region. These include support for the establishment of full time Bomb Data Centres in Jakarta, Singapore and Malaysia and short-term postings for selected Australian Bomb Data Centre members to Indonesia, Singapore, Malaysia and the Philippines.

Legislative Framework: Australia will sign and implement the twelfth and final United Nations Counter-Terrorism instruments, the Convention on the Marking of Plastic Explosives.

Intelligence: Australia will establish a Centre for Counter-Terrorism Intelligence Cooperation and Joint Training for Australia, South East Asia and the Pacific, enhance ASIO's linguistic capability in Arabic and South East Asian languages and strengthen ASIO's capacity to undertake background security checks on persons seeking to lawfully enter Australia. The budget of the Office of National Assessments (ONA) will expand from $13.1 million to $25 million. Staff levels at ONA will effectively double from 74 to 145. Australia will establish a Business Liaison Unit within ASIO to strengthen coordination and information flows between business and the intelligence community.

Transport Security: Australia will seek to build the Air Marshal programme with Singapore and the United States by extending their operation to a range of new flight routes, including to Malaysia, Indonesia, Thailand, Philippines and Canada.

Science and Technology: Australia will establish a special collaborative research and development programme between the Defence Science and Technology Organisation, the Commonwealth Scientific and Industrial Research Organisation and the Australian Nuclear Science and Technology Organisation to further their work on counter-terrorism related projects. Projects will focus on chemical and biological protection, intelligence support tools, explosive detection, biometrics and counter-measures for civilian aircraft from shoulder fired missiles.

12

Australia as a Factor in India-ASEAN Relations

GANGANATH JHA

There is a convergence of political, economic and social interests between India and Australia in connection with the Association of South-East Asian Nations (ASEAN). It is obligatory and complementary for both to maintain close neighbourly relations with South-East Asian states. Their long-term security, and economic and political interests are interrelated. Both India and Australia were British colonies in the historical past but there was a sharp divergence in their perception and policies during the Cold War years. However, they have remained associated with the Commonwealth and some other regional forums. Both of them have faith in a democratic system of government and they tend to identify themselves as an integral part of the Asia-Pacific region. However, Australia's projection, as being a part of South-East Asia has been more pronounced ever since its association with the South-East Asia Treaty Organisation (SEATO). Its linkages with the ASEAN region have proved to be more successful than those of India in the post-1954 era.

The principal purpose of this Chapter is to argue in favour of stronger policy cooperation and dialogue among India, Australia and the ASEAN states. A greater degree of dialogue and mutual trust will inevitably lead to a greater level of understanding of regional state motives, ideals and values. As a result, such a strategy will not only enable misperceptions and policy contradictions to be overcome and thus ensure consistent policy settings, but it will also facilitate a much more effective approach in resolving many of the regional security problems associated with increasing globalisation.

India's Relations with ASEAN

India was faced with certain constraints in the beginning while dealing with ASEAN. For example, Indian leaders believed South-East Asia to be their cultural extension and thereby treated the region as an integral part but this was disliked by South-Eastern Asian leaders. It was indeed counterproductive, whenever Indian leaders and intellectuals tried to locate, Indian culture and civilisation in the ASEAN region. Although Indian intellectuals and diplomats started to change their perception decades ago, but it was not fast enough to cope with the challenges. India, as being identified with the Soviet bloc and Communist Vietnam, was viewed more as a threat than a prospective partner for ASEAN. It was only after the end of the Vietnam War, and the dissolution of the Soviet Union, that we witnessed substantial changes in the perception of ASEAN towards India.

It was in 1992 that India became a sectoral partner of ASEAN and it was in 1996 that it became a full dialogue partner and subsequently a member of the ARF. On the other hand, Australia became an observer of ASEAN immediately after its formation in 1967 and remained closely associated with its deliberations. Australia has been a senior partner of ASEAN and has played a constructive role in peace-making and peace-keeping. Its contribution, in conflict resolution in Cambodia and East Timor, for example, has been globally recognized. The geo-political realities of the region suggest that India has to learn a lot from Australia's experience while dealing with ASEAN. Australia, China and India are the three large states on the three sides of ASEAN and their understanding and common strategies can transform the socio-economic contours of the regional inhabitants.

Australia and India, the advocates of democracy and human rights, can contribute to building a regional consensus against terrorism and ethnic disputes. Australia constructed the Lao-Thai Friendship bridge over the Mekong and thus directly linked China and ASEAN with roadways. This phenomenon inspired Japan to construct another bridge over the Mekong, to facilitate trade and investment. Now attention is being given to linking ASEAN with South Asia directly through rail and road. The Tamu-Moreh road is insufficient to fulfil regional requirements. A network of railways and highways is needed to promote trade, investment and tourism and in that endeavour the contribution of India, China and Australia may prove to be crucial.

Australia has emerged as an important partner of India especially in the post-Cold War era. India attaches importance to "Australia in line with its Look East policy" and Australia reciprocates the feeling through its evolving "Look West Policy". Indian and Australian interests complement each other in the ASEAN region and India attaches importance to this because the two are collectively associated with the ASEAN dialogue partnership, the ASEAN Regional Forum and the Indian Ocean Rim-Association ?or Regional Cooperation (IOR-ARC). India and Australia have been closely associated with regional peace negotiations and they have jointly contributed to peace-keeping in Cambodia. Australia has claimed to be an integral part of the ASEAN region and has considered the latter as an area of its forward defence. Its substantial contribution to the South East Asia Treaty Organisation, (SEATO), the Five-Power Defence Pact (FPDP) and anti-Communist movements was appreciated by ASEAN leaders (Gopal, 2002). On the other hand, India stood far behind in these calculations. Although India has considered the ASEAN region under the cultural and geographical domain of the sub-continent and has spoken of cultural, linguistic and religious similarities, and has made mention of Southeast Asian references in various Indian literature and folklore, it did not have much impact on transforming ASEAN attitudes. It was only when India and Australia worked together for the restoration of peace in Cambodia, then this proved to be a positive turning point. ASEAN began to attach importance to India after the signing of the Cambodian peace pact in 1991. India became a "sectoral dialogue partner" of ASEAN in 1992 which was upgraded to full dialogue partnership status in 1996. Hence, India also became a partner in the ASEAN Regional Forum in the same year. The summit meeting of ASEAN in Brunei in 2001 decided to hold a summit level meeting between ASEAN and India, which was held in 2002 to provide a new dimension and dynamism to the growing relationship (Ministry of External Affairs, 2002; 13).

In fact, since India, China and Australia are the three big countries on the three sides of ASEAN, they have great potential to contribute to the security and prosperity of the ASEAN region. India and Australia are democratic regimes and their perspectives about democracy and human rights are similar. If there is peace, stability and development in the ASEAN region, it is bound to suit the interests of the countries in the region, and, at the same time, if there is chaos and anarchy, it will harm the interests of regional prosperity and the integrative spirit. Both India and Australia will have to forget the legacy of the Cold War years and evolve a new mindset and common strategies with ASEAN to promote common regional interests.

India-Australia Relations

Australia and India were colonised by Great Britain for centuries and the two evolved democratic traditions, laws and judicial systems in the post-independence era. Australia opened its High Commission in New Delhi in 1944, much before India's independence and both became partners in the Commonwealth (Australian Information Service, 1986; 1). Senior officials from India's Ministry of External Affairs (MEA) and the Australian Department of Foreign Affairs (DFAT) have been meeting regularly in talks alternating between New Delhi and Canberra at which major international, regional and bilateral issues affecting the two countries have been reviewed. Both countries have established a Joint Ministerial Commission, Joint Business Council, and Joint Working Group on Energy and Minerals to promote trade and investment relations. Australian exports to India have been increasing rapidly in recent years and India is considered to be one of Australia's more important export markets. On the other hand, Australia is the eighth largest investor in India and shows a keen interest in promoting joint venture projects.

India-Australia relations received new momentum with the visit to Australia of Jaswant Singh, Minister of External Affairs, in June 2001, when the India-Australia Foreign Ministerial Framework dialogue was launched. During this dialogue, many areas of mutual interest were identified. The highlight was the announcement, to create a security dialogue, which was later held in New Delhi on 30 August 2001. This was preceded by Track II diplomacy in the form of the India-Australia Security Round Table in New Delhi between the Australian Defence Studies Centre and the Centre for the Study of National Security, Jawaharlal Nehru University (Ministry of External Affairs, 2002; 13). These deliberations are bound to complement the endeavours of the ARF whose primary goal is to promote confidence building and preventive diplomacy.

Needless to say, the Australia-India partnership is growing slowly. Trade and investment opportunities are expanding. The Australian Department of Foreign Affairs and Trade produced a comprehensive study, entitled, *India's Economy at the Midnight Hour: Australia's India Strategy*, (1994) which examined business opportunities at length. It pointed to the substantial growth in trade ever since 1992 wherein exports grew by 24 per cent and imports grew by 28 per cent over the 1991 figures. India's trade linkages with Australia, in the beginning, were limited. India used to export camels and gunny bags and imported horses and coal in the colonial period but subsequently Indian garments, jewellery, footwear and spices have also attracted the attention of the Australian market (Department of Foreign Affairs and Trade, 1994; 19). In 1993, India was Australia's 15th largest export market. Australian exports to India were worth A$920 million while imports from India were worth A$407. Major

Australian exports were cooking coals, wool, specialised machinery, and non-ferrous metals and ores. India exported textiles, clothing and footwear products. It also exported pearls, gems, fruits, nuts and chemicals (Department of Foreign Affairs and Trade, 1994; 130-131).

On the other hand, investment relations also started growing in the 1990s. From A$16 million in 1989, it grew to A$21 million in 1991 in wholesale business activities, and in the manufacturing and financial sectors (Department of Foreign Affairs and Trade, 1994; 134-135). This figure increased to A$41 million in 1992 in different collaborative areas. Although Australian investments in India were small, in view of total Australian investments abroad (A$36 billion), it was encouraging that a beginning was made. The largest Australian corporate presence in India is the ANZ Bank, resulting from its acquisition of the Grindlays International Banking network in 1984. ANZ Grindlays has 56 branches. Other areas where Australia has made investments are financial services, cellular phones, concrete products, railway parts and radio communications. Notable Australian companies which have recently established joint ventures or consultancy agreements with Indian counterparts are Telstra with the Modi Group for cellular telephones, Lexmark International for computer printers, Command Petroleum Holdings NL of Australia with Videocon Marubeni to develop the offshore oil field of Ravva and the Southern Pacific Hotels corporation to develop five-star hotels in India. India is also trying to reciprocate Australian investments. The two most significant investments are by Oberoi International Hotels which jointly manages the Windsor Hotel in Melbourne and the Tata Group, which operates a computing services unit in Australia.

It is clear that there is vast scope for expanding trade and investment relations between India and Australia (Rumley, 2004). The export opportunities for Australia in India include various areas of manufacturing, wholesale and retail trade, construction, electricity, gas, transport and communications. India could benefit from Australian collaboration in environmental, mining and agricultural technologies and telecommunications and education services (Department of Foreign Affairs and Trade; 2001).

India, Australia and ASEAN

A range of other types of relations and policies can also develop in the desired direction in cooperation with ASEAN. The ASEAN Vision 2020, adopted in 1997, which was aimed at accelerating the process of economic integration in the region, proposed to create a stable, prosperous and highly competitive ASEAN economic region allowing for a free flow of goods, services, investment and capital, in addition to equitable development and a reduction in poverty and socio-economic disparities. These endeavours would get a substantial support if the volume of trade and investments from India with its eastern neighbours were promoted. The Hanoi Plan of Action (1998), the first action plan of the ASEAN Vision, proposed the development of a trans-ASEAN transportation network, consisting of a major interstate highway and railway network, principal ports and sea lanes for maritime traffic, inland waterway transport and major civil aviation links. It also focussed on interoperability and interconnectivity of the national telecommunications equipment and services, and on building trans-ASEAN energy networks consisting of the ASEAN power grid and the trans-ASEAN gas pipeline (Sharma and Mehta, 2000; 9).

It was in line with the ASEAN vision that two projects-BIMST-EC and the Ganga-Mekong-were mooted. Thailand had taken a keen interest in the emergence of BIMST-EC but it was a coincidence that thereafter Thailand became embroiled in the economic crisis. There was a great shortage of foreign currency in 1997-98 when several banks and development projects were closed. The crisis gradually spread far and wide and thus work on several projects in different parts of ASEAN was discontinued. This had an adverse impact on the work on the Ganga-Mekong Project, which has immense potential to link ASEAN business with India. This project is not yet proving vibrant and recent developments under the BIMST-EC and the Mekong-Ganga cooperation framework have little output to cheer about. The partners of these groupings have a feeling that further cooperation among the member countries is needed in a more focussed manner in order to achieve their goals and objectives. They have resolved that India, Myanmar and Thailand should work closely together on the development of infrastructure and transport linkages among the three countries in order to enhance trade, investment and tourism flows (Ministry of External Affairs, 2002; 21). It is indeed a reality that if the goals of Ganga-Mekong projects are achieved, it would complement globalisation and free trade. As a result, Australia, Japan, Korea and China would have a direct access to enter India and other South Asian markets and it would facilitate trade between East Asia and West Asia. Australian expertise and technologies are superior and its presence in the region would further strengthen regionalism with its involvement in key projects in South Asia.

Peacekeeping

Australia has made a substantial contribution to establishing peace in Asia. It participated in the UN peacekeeping in Korea in 1949-50, for example. It sent contingents of armed forces to participate in the Vietnam war in 1967-68 under the aegis of SEATO. It supported Malaysia and Singapore against communist subversion under the FPDP in 1957-58 and assumed an important role in conflict resolution in Cambodia during 1987-91. While playing its role in Asian affairs, Australia thought as an Asian and acted as an Asian. Whenever it brought ASEAN into its confidence on major issues, its credentials in terms of Asian identity were not questioned. However, on occasions when Australia ignored ASEAN opinion, it became the subject of criticism. On some issues, like decolonisation, nuclear non-proliferation, and the fight against terrorism, the Australian position has been criticised. Its position is often perceived as adopting a double standard on those issues and its actions are projected as the product of a European mindset. It is quite well known that the Kanaks in New Caledonia have been fighting for independence ever since 1981 (Rumley, 2006). There has been lot of bloodshed and assassination in that territory in the past two decades. There has been a demographic transformation and abuses of human rights have been reported. The current movement for independence in Bougainville is a grave threat for the security of Papua New Guinea since the violence and bloodshed have been endemic on that part of the island as well. Both New Caledonia and Bougainville are situated in the Australia's "arc of instability" and naturally Australia was expected to assume a role in the conflict resolution (Rumley, Forbes and Griffin, 2006). There has also been racial conflict in Fiji, where the indigenous Fijians were trying to establish their racial and political dominance. All of these areas did not appear to be in Australia's focus, but the independence struggle in East Timor attracted its attention from the very beginning, however. Australia offered shelter to the East Timorese support groups and fugitives and aided and abetted their political activities. It constantly remained in touch with East Timorese and Indonesian leaders and influenced the Indonesian, President B.J. Habibie, to hold a referendum. When Habibie announced the referendum, there were reactions and disturbances in East Timor. It was reported that the Indonesian armed forces were aiding local Timorese militias to attack outspoken supporters of East Timor independence. Australia expressed its concern and came forward to support the referendum process. In August 1999, Australia provided a police force to protect the referendum and sought UN intervention when East Timorese overwhelmingly voted for independence and provoked pro-Jakarta militias to indulge in large-scale destruction of life and property. Australia committed to hold the referendum and also contributed the commander of the peace keeping force. Australia sent the largest single contingent (4,500 personnel) to the international force for East Timor and it subsequently dispatched about 2,000 personnel to help the UN Transitional Administration in East Timor (UNTAET) (Mequeen, 2002; 105). In the entire referendum operation US$20 million was spent of which US$14 million was contributed by Australia. The share of the Australian contribution in peace making and peace keeping in East Timor was far bigger than it had been for peace keeping in Cambodia, but the outcome of the two operations was quite different for Australia. The ASEAN leaders expressed their appreciation and gratitude to Australia for whatever it did to resolve the conflict in Cambodia. However, their response to the Australian role in East Timor was often critical and negative. Indonesia was most unhappy with Australia for its operations in East Timor. Malaysia also was not happy and it was found that the overall response of the ASEAN leaders was one of distrust. Their perceptual problems cropped up because Australia did not coordinate its East Timor activities with the ASEAN countries. As a partner in ASEAN, ARF, APEC and ASEM, Australia should have understood the opinion and sensitivities of the ASEAN countries before assuming an active major role in East Timor. It is a fact that Australia lost much goodwill in the ASEAN region and it would require a great effort and wisdom to bring about the situation in relations that prevailed before 1999.

The Non-Proliferation Treaty

The Non-Proliferation Treaty (NPT) is another area in which Australian perception and policies attract criticism. Australia claims to be a strong supporter of the NPT and was an active sponsor of the Rarotonga Treaty in 1985. However, when the Treaty was signed, it was not Australia but New Zealand which banned the movement of nuclear ships in its waters and stopped ANZUS operations at Christchurch. Australia continued to assist its ANZUS partners and allowed the movement of nuclear ships. It has been unable to articulate and voice regional opinion against nuclear experimentation and nuclear dumping in the South Pacific region. However, when India conducted its nuclear experimentation in 1998, Australian reactions were strong and vociferous. On 14 May 1990, the Australian Foreign Minister, Alexander Downer, described Pokharan II as an "outrageous act" while imposing sanctions on all bilateral, political and defence exchanges and on all humanitarian aid against India (Australian High Commission, 1988). The Indian response to the Australian reaction was limited. On 28 May 1998, India suspended all bilateral military cooperation by disallowing Australian naval ships from visiting Indian ports and territorial waters and by cancelling all overflight facilities to Australian military aircrafts (Government of India, 1988). Thus, there were strains in the bilateral relationship. It is strange that a country which assiduously cultivates Asian identity should criticise another Asian partner for scientific and technological achievements. In this case also, Australia did not try to understand ASEAN opinion at the outset. It retraced its steps and reactions towards Indian nuclear experiments as soon as the ASEAN perception became clear to it.

Terrorism

It is clear that Australia is keen to participate in fight against terrorism. Its leaders have given statements to that effect at international forums. It abhors the horrendous crimes of September 11, 2001 committed by the Al Qaeda network in the United States. Although the Taliban and Al Qaida were apparently liquidated in Afghanistan these organisations have generated international links. They have groomed Jemmah Islamia in South-East Asia for the resurgence of Islamic extremism. The operations of Al Qaida supporters are to spread the gospels of the Prophet Mohamad and to establish Shariat laws for governance. They are trying to terrorise the people to accept the superiority of Islam over other religions. They have been indulging in large-scale violence in areas where Christians, Buddhists or Hindus are located. They have inhuman ways and violent means to express their opinion and their brutal activities in Mindanao (Philippines) and Bali (Indonesia) are shocking. Although immediate steps are needed to contain them, to be effective requires a multilateral effort to evolve common policies to deal with them. Indonesian and Malaysian governments are thinking that their security forces are sufficient to pin them down, but recent developments suggest that their strength is limited. Islamic fanatics have increased their political influence at the highest levels. There are important elements in the power politics of those countries and they have taken advantage of the evolving democratic institutions. Islam is increasingly interpreted as an essential element of nationalism is some countries of Southeast Asia and in that context any harsh steps against Muslim fanatics or terrorists cannot be envisaged.

It is in this environment that ASEAN should be referred to for a suitable solution. Australia, India, Japan, China and Korea are important dialogue partners. If they adopt a collective stand and articulate their opinion effectively at ASEAN post-ministerial meetings, and if they display their legitimate concerns against the spread of terrorism, especially Jemaah Islamia, in a concerted fashion, the solution may be found within the ASEAN framework. Such a resolution supported by the ASEAN countries and dialogue partners can contain the rise of terrorist groups. No country should try to intervene unilaterally in sensitive affairs. Moreover, the ASEAN countries have been following the policy of non-interference in the internal affairs of one another using the "Treaty of Amity and cooperation" as one of the basic guidelines for the conduct of its diplomacy in regional politics. Although an explosive situation prevails over the question of sovereignty of the Spratly Islands, and every claimant has a right to protect the areas under its jurisdiction, yet they are searching for a peaceful regional solution. They are indeed concerned about the rise of the terrorist networks and they may be looking for a peaceful regional solution.

Trade

The ASEAN is an organisation with 10 members and 10 dialogue partners, encompassing many powerful countries in the Asia-Pacific region. Southeast Asia has 500 million people with US$37 billion of income and US$720 billion of external trade (Sharma and Mehta, 2000; 5). If the dialogue partners are included, the volume of income and external trade of the association is larger. ASEAN is endeavouring to accelerate economic growth, social progress, cultural development and regional peace and stability. All these aforementioned issues are important for the development of the region. Although the issues of democracy, human rights and terrorism are pertinent, and there are compelling circumstances to attend to them, ASEAN will not tolerate an imposed solution.

India attaches the utmost importance to ASEAN, under the framework of its "Look East Policy". Hence, India's economic, cultural and security understanding and partnership is growing. Indo-ASEAN trade grew from US$2.9 billion in 1992 to US$6.5 billion in 1996. Bilateral trade grew further to US$7.35 billion 1999 but came down subsequently to US$6.96 billion in 2001 (Ministry of External Affairs, 2002; 13). India considers its partnership with ASEAN as an important step towards globalisation and free trade. It is through ASEAN that India can aspire to promote its interest in the Asia-Pacific region. It is also through ASEAN that India would like to promote its interest in Australasia. It is desirable on the part of Australia to understand the emerging paradigm and framework for possible intervention in the region and trust India for its regional strategies.

Conclusion

To conclude, it may be observed that if Australia, India and ASEAN coordinate their regional policies and diplomacy in evolving a common consensus on growing threats to regional stability, peace and development, it may prove immensely beneficial. Territorially Australia is closely linked to Asia, but its mindset has yet to cope with the geo-political realities of Asia in letter and spirit. Its 20 million population, dominated by people of European origin, and its alliance with the Western world may prove an asset if they are viewed as an important Asian link with the Western World (Fitzgerald, 1997; Keating, 2000; McGillivray, 1998). Australian endeavours to promote democracy, human rights and free trade are the ideals of a civilised society and they may be meaningful only in tune with Asian realities, however.

REFERENCES

Australian High Commission (1988), Australian High Commission, News Release, 'Indian Nuclear Tests', New Delhi, 14 May.

Australian Information Service (1986), News Release, Australian High Commission, New Delhi, October.

Department of Foreign Affairs and Trade (1994), *India's Economy at the Midnight Hour: Australia's India Strategy*, Canberra.

Department of Foreign Affairs and Trade (2001), *India: New Economy, Old Economy*, Canberra.

Fitzgerald, S. (1997), *Is Australia an Asian Country?*, St. Leonards, NSW.

Gopal, D. (2002), "Australia and Southeast Asia", in D. Gopal, ed., *Australia in the Emerging Global Order,* New Delhi: Shipra. pp. 159-166.

Government of India (1988), Press Information Bureau, 'India to withdraw Defence Attache from Australia', New Delhi, 28 May.

Keating, P. (2000), *Engagement: Australia Faces the Asia-Pacific*, Sydney.

McGillivray, M., ed. (1998), *Australia and Asia*, Oxford, 1998.

Mequeen, A.E. (2002), 'Australia and Asia', Far East and Australia, Hong Kong.

Ministry of External Affairs (2002), Government of India, Annual Report, New Delhi 2001-2002.

Rumley, D. (2004), 'Geopolitics of Australia-India trade', in D. Gopal and Dennis Rumley, eds., *India and Australia: Issues and Opportunities*, New Delhi: Authors Press, pp. 1-25.

Rumley, D. (2006), 'The French geopolitical project in New Caledonia', in

Dennis Rumley, Vivian Louis Forbes and Christopher Griffin, eds., *Australia's Arc of Instability: The Political and Cultural Dynamics of Regional Security*, Dordrecht: Springer, pp. 229-246.

Rumley, D., Vivian Louis Forbes and Christopher Griffin, eds., *Australia's Arc of Instability: The Political and Cultural Dynamics of Regional Security*, Dordrecht: Springer.

Sharma, A. and Pradip Kumar Mehta (2000), 'ASEAN as a Regional Bloc', *Foreign Trade Review*, Vol. 35, no. 2 & 3, New Delhi July-December.

13

Information Technology and the Prospects for Indo-Australia Bilateral Relations

MADHU BALA

Information Technology (IT) has brought about a fundamental change in the modern world. The importance of IT has been increasingly recognised as a cogent force for modern economic growth and development. It offers a number of services, products and technologies in order to augment the productivity of states. By increasing the process of information exchange, reducing the price of information processing, converging communication and computing technologies and growth in network computing (Pohjola, 1998), this all-pervading technology has been instrumental in increasing productivity, efficiency, competitiveness and growth in almost all spheres of human activity, both in developed and developing countries. The potential benefits, however, can be harnessed only if the technology diffuses across the different sectors of the economy (Joseph, 2001). This is particularly important for less developed economies where market failures are more prevalent and these failures are commonly associated with information problems (Stiglitz, 2002; 483). Therefore, developing countries in recent times have depended heavily on information technology as a driving force to help them cross certain conformist stages of development.

In the era of globalisation, it is increasingly believed that persistent poverty in developing countries is predominantly caused by the lack of widespread knowledge or information. It is argued that, in the present day world, information is becoming a factor like income or wealth, which categorises not just people but countries into rich and poor (Pohjola, 1998). It is also believed that the inability on the part of developing countries to exploit this new source of wealth will widen the gap with developed countries, which already possess the knowledge needed for an assured standard of living. This will therefore result in less developed states becoming more insecure.

The developing countries have therefore taken a keen interest and high hopes are therefore attributed to information technology as a shortcut to prosperity (World Bank, 1999). By transforming the existing social and economic relations into information relations, a paradigm shift is already taking place from *competitive* to *information*. "Traditional competitive paradigms, that have dominated economic theory for two centuries, did not explain key economic phenomena and led to misguided policy prescriptions. The new information paradigm, on the other hand, is about acquiring information that was traditionally incomplete, extremely costly, obstructive and uncertain in developing countries" (Stiglitz, 2002; 486). Therefore, under such circumstances, there arises the need for policies which encourage greater information and communication flows not only between but also within countries in such a way that spillovers and linkages are generated.

India has been one of the prime developing countries to take initiatives and promote this sector by recognising the potential of IT. The rise of IT software and service industry, over the 1990s, is one of the spectacular achievements of the Indian economy (Kumar, 2000). Despite limited diffusion, it has emerged as one of the fastest growing sectors with unprecedented rates of growth and vast potentialities. Australia, on the other hand, is one of the important developed countries with advanced IT resources, which, if tapped reasonably and carefully, may help India in many ways. Therefore, the present chapter looks into IT and its prospects for Indo-Australian bilateral relations in the Asia-Pacific Region. It may be pointed out here that while there is a great deal of literature on different macro economic dimensions of IT growth in India, there is hardly any research associated with this particular dimension.

Information Technologies and the Asia-Pacific Region

India and Australia are important members of the Asia-Pacific Region. IT, including Internet and e-commerce, has influenced the region enormously in the past decade. However, despite economic disruptions in this region, renewed IT opportunities have generated the interest of researchers. It is not out of place to mention here that the Australian economy that was not severely affected by the economic upheavals like Asian Crisis which is presently one of the strongest IT performers in the Asia-Pacific Region (Koch, 1999).

Table 1: GDP and IT Spending in Asia Pacific Excluding Japan

Country	*Share of IT spending in GDP (%)*		*Compound average annual growth rates*			*Average of annual ratios of IT Share*
	1991	*1995*	*GDP*	*IT spending*	*IT share*	*1989-95*
Australia	1.9	2.6	5.3	12.3	7.0	0.0208
China (PRC)	0.5	1.0	15.4	29.3	13.9	0.0034
Hong Kong	0.7	1.3	11.7	24.2	12.4	0.0089
India	0.3	0.6	6.9	24.3	17.4	0.0037
Indonesia	–	–	–	–	–	0.0049
Korea (Rep.of)	0.7	2.3	10.0	33.6	23.6	0.0105
Malaysia	0.9	1.8	14.9	29.8	14.8	0.0097
New Zealand	2.2	2.9	8.9	14.6	5.7	0.0244
Philippines						0.0063
Singapore	1.4	2.6	15.4	27.3	11.9	0.0158
Thailand	0.5	1.0	12.7	26.2	13.5	0.0054

Source: IDC and World Bank, 1998 *as quoted in* Pohjola, 1998 and 2000.

During the 1990s, the world IT market was globally concentrated, with North America, Western Europe and the Asia Pacific respectively amounting to 96 per cent of the total. The two dominating countries were the USA with 41 per cent and Japan with 17 per cent share of the world market. The growth rate was, however, the highest in the Asia Pacific (19% per year) during 1985-95 (Pohjola, 1998). Within the Asia Pacific, however, there were noteworthy differences in the share of IT spending in GDP (Table 1). The table shows that there were countries like Australia, Singapore, New Zealand and Republic of Korea that were spending more than 2 per cent of their GDP on IT. However, other countries like China, India, Indonesia, Philippines and Thailand were spending less than or equal to 1 per cent of their GDP on IT.

Among others IT services are an important component of the IT sector, especially in the Asia Pacific region. Australia leads in IT services as the financial services, banking, retail, and utility sectors are promising growth. Given its large proportion of SMEs, the middle market in the Asia Pacific region is destined to emerge as an increasingly important market opportunity for IT services companies.

A glance at the data provided in Table 2 reveals that, while Australia continues to dominate the scene, India is emerging as an important player in the region. It is China that recorded the highest rate of growth during

1996-2002. Moreover, except India, Taiwan and New Zealand, the figures in the table show for themselves the story of the Asian Crisis as far as the IT services market is concerned. The countries affected by the Asian Crisis, however, recorded signs of a speedy recovery in 2002.

NOIE Australia, in its report "Current State of Play: Australia's Scoreboard", submitted in April 2002, ranked the countries of the world based on a very wide range indicators relating to information technology. According to the report, Australia ranked 3rd in the emerging information economy, only after US and Sweden. Other countries of the Asia Pacific that were ranked among the first ten were New Zealand (5th), Hong Kong (6th), Singapore (7th), S. Korea (8th) and Taiwan (9th). Thus, the report clearly points out the importance of Asia Pacific Region in the emerging information economy.

Table 2: Asia-Pacific Excluding Japan Services Market Forecast by Country, 1996-2002 (percentages)

Country	*1996*	*1997*	*1998*	*1999*	*2000*	*2001*	*2002*	*CAGR(%) (1997-2002)*
Australia	39.8	43.1	54.0	54.7	54.6	54.2	53.9	17.1
Hong Kong	4.4	4.4	3.9	3.6	3.3	3.0	2.6	1.2
India	7.8	8.17	7.6	7.5	7.4	7.8	8.1	11.8
Indonesia	1.4	1.21	0.3	0:3	0.4	0.4	0.4	–8.9
Korea	7.8	12.92	5.1	4.5	4.8	4.7	4.7	–8.3
Malaysia	2.9	2.63	1.7	1.7	1.7	1.7	1.6	1.8
New Zealand	8.1	9.58	10.3	9.9	9.1	8.6	7.7	7.3
Philippines	1.1	1.05	0.6	0.6	0.5	0.5	0.4	–6.3
PRC	2.5	3.17	4.3	5.3	6.5	8.3	9.9	40.7
Singapore	5.4	5.3	4.4	3.8	3.5	3.2	2.9	–0.8
Taiwan	5.8	6.7	7.0	7.2	7.4	7.0	6.6	11.7
Thailand	2.7	1.7	0.7	0.7	0.7	0.9	0.9	–1.4
Total Services	**100**	**100**	**100**	**100**	**100**	**100**	**100**	**12.0**

Source: Calculated from International Data Corporation GIT Survey, 1998, as given in, Ernest and Young, 2000.

Information Technology and India

Over the last decade, the Indian IT software and service industry has grown by leaps and bounds. According to the IDC, Nasscom, the share of the IT industry in GDP has risen from 0.59 per cent in 1994-95 to 2.87 per cent in 2001-02. Today, India is acknowledged the world over as an important base for *offshore IT services*, with more than one third of the Fortune 500 companies outsourcing their software requirements to India.

In addition, the global and financial community is showing considerable interest in the Indian Software and service sector, and sustaining the growth of the software industry is at the forefront of the government of India's agenda.

The Indian software industry has been built predominantly on an export driven model. India has emerged as an important player in the global IT industry recently despite its 1 per cent share of the world export market. According to the World Bank, India's share in the global cross-country customised software development market has grown from 11.9 per cent in 1991 to 19.5 per cent in 2000. IT penetration in Indian commercial establishments and government is, however, still well below international standards. The Indian IT industry has evolved, in scope and capabilities and has moved from a perceived low-cost model to one that is internationally acclaimed for its excellent quality and high reliability.

Growth and Trends

The IT industry in India has witnessed incredible evolution and explosive growth over the last decade. Compounded annual growth rates since 1990 have been over 50 per cent; almost twice the growth rate experienced in the US software sector during the same period. However, in 2001, similar to the trend worldwide, the Indian IT industry also witnessed a lower growth rate of 32 percent. The International Data Corporation (IDC) expects the market to firm up and the industry to grow from Rs. 61,000 crores to Rs. 2,24,600 crores in 2006 at a compound annual growth rate of 30 per cent (IDC, 2002). Broadly speaking, there are four sectors-IT services, software products; IT enabled services and e-businesses-that are creating a number of opportunities for Indian companies. Over 1000 IT companies have mushroomed, especially in the software sector. The total value of business generated in the software sector during 2001-02 was estimated to be Rs. 5100 crores as against Rs. 3630 crores in the previous year, indicating a growth by 40 per cent (IDC, 2002).

According to the NASSCOM survey, there has been a structural shift in the delivery models of the Indian IT Industry in the last decade. In 1991-92, offshore services accounted for 5 per cent and on site services for 95 per cent of total exports. However, during 2001-02, offshore services contributed more than 49 per cent of the total exports. The main destination of Indian software exports in 2001-02 was the United States (63%) followed by Europe (26%) and Japan (4%). This trend is similar to the direction of India's exports in other commodities (Bala, 2002). Companies like Wipro, Infosys Technologies, NIIT, Tata

Infotech, Satyam Computers and Pentasoft Software have excelled over giants such as Telco, Tisco, Grasim, ACC, Hindalco and Mahindra & Mahindra.

Table 3 shows the share of software exports and domestic software market in the Indian software industry from 1995-96 to 2000-01. The table shows very distinctly that the share of software exports in the Indian Software Industry has increased over the years and clearly portrays that the Indian software industry is software driven.

Table 3: Share of Domestic Software Market and Software Exports in the Indian Software Industry (percentages)

Year	*Domestic Software Market*	*Software Exports*
1995-96	40	60
1996-97	38	62
1997-98	35	65
1998-99	32	68
1999-00	30	70
2000-01	28	72

Source: NASSCOM Reports

Researchers have noted this mutually conflicting phenomenon where industrial growth and overall exports were declining despite increased export earnings from IT in the Indian economy during the 1990s. This phenomenon has been attributed as evidence of an IT export-induced Dutch Disease in India (Mukherjee, 2001; Van Wijnbergen, 1984). The argument given is that increased IT exports would lead to increased exchange reserves and money supply. The consequent appreciation of money following inflation would make the domestic producers of trading goods more competitive. The overvaluation of money, in turn, will impede exports, imports, investments and ultimately economic growth.

Unlike the IT export market, which is completely software and service segment driven, the Indian IT domestic market has a strong hardware component, which includes peripherals, networking and hardware services. According to the data provided by IDC, India limited, in 1999-2000, the domestic IT market grew by 30 per cent per annum. Out of the total domestic market, hardware had a major share of 56 percent, followed by IT services with 24 per cent share and packaged software with 10 per cent share in the total. The domestic IT spending, slowed down substantially and the growth rate recorded were 10 per cent per annum.

Notwithstanding that India's inherent competitive advantage in terms of software exports lies in the largest pool of IT manpower, which is second in the world accompanied by high growth rates, India's share in the world software market is still comparatively low. However, the high quality and relatively low cost of Indian software provides the country with a strategic opportunity in the world market. As per NASSCOM reports, IT created 92,000 new jobs and 2,50,000 indirect jobs in 2001-02 and it continues to rank among the fastest growing sectors in the economy.

The challenges faced by the Indian IT industry are several which are detrimental to its growth. One of them has been the lack of adequate IT infrastructure that includes unreliable power supply and bandwidth costs. With a low PC dispersion and even lower Internet diffusion, domestic opportunities for web-based applications and e-commerce have not yet matured. Computer dispersion is mostly restricted to English-speaking cities. There are efforts to develop applications and peripherals in local languages, but they are haphazard. Poor access to venture capital has also hampered the development of entrepreneurial growth companies (EGC) in the IT sector. Moreover, despite offshore services being concentrated in big companies so far, efforts need to be put in developing a model in such a way that second tier companies are ready. Moreover, the immediate need is that software professionals with Ph Ds aim for the application software programming field, which requires coordination between industry and academic institutions. Capturing a major share of international markets requires success in two areas – the development of a global distribution network to respond to clientele needs and standards and the setting up of after sales service shops to provide support maintenance and upgrades for product lines. The software product exports profile shows that the ratio between the major software services and software packages (including data entry) constituted a ratio of 90 : 10, respectively, in the mid-90s. However, in other Asian and South American countries, the ratio was just opposite (Heeks, 1996). Furthermore, in order to reap the opportunities provided by expanding IT markets, Indian software developers need to shift the thrust of their production from contractual programming to indigenous packaged software products (Heeks, 1996).

Many global companies have already sourced IT-enabled services from India like GE Capital, British Airways, Swiss Air, Air France, American Express, Lufthansa and Citibank. More companies are planning to enter India to set up such services. The global market for IT-enabled services is estimated to grow by more than twenty times in the coming decade (Austrade, 2000). The telephone-based service industry is growing approximately at about 23 per cent per annum. Similarly, other IT-enabled services such as back-office management, transcription and content development are growing at more than 20 per cent annually (Austrade, 2000).

Two key elements of IT-enabled services are outsourcing and out-location. A third element-web-based services – is also emerging as the Internet energises newer business models and allows companies to centralise services and/or operations at an optimal global location, and to enhance customer reach. India's strengths as mentioned earlier, are based on the availability of a large pool of English-speaking and computer literate people power at a per capita cost that is quite attractive when compared with developed markets.

Internet Service Providers in India

Internet Service Providers (ISPs) form the backbone for providing internet-related services. While their core services are providing connectivity and access to end-users, the market is rapidly growing for other value-added services such as website hosting and virtual private networks (VPN). VSNL is the dominant service provider and had achieved a strong customer base of approximately 2,00,000 by December 1998. According to the India Internet Log Book, 2000, there were over 1.8 million internet subscribers (and more than 5.5 million users) and the estimated figures for the same are a huge 50 million by 31 December 2003 (IDC, 2002).

The main ISPs in India VSNL, which is the largest ISP, Mahanagar Telephone Nigam Limited (MTNL), Satyam Infoway, Mantra Online, Wipro Net and Dishnet. Of these, MTNL, like VSNL, is a public-sector organisation and provides basic telephone services in Delhi and Mumbai. Corporate giants such as AT&T, Microsoft, Compuserve, BT-MC, and so on, are also planning to become ISPs. The list of companies, which have recently been issued national licenses, include BPL Telecom, Manipal Control, India Internet and Pacific Internet (Austrade, 2000).

Electronic Commerce in India

Electronic Commerce (or e-commerce) includes all kinds of commercial transactions that take place via an electronic medium or network, that is, the internet. E-commerce covers three main types of transactions-business-to-commerce (B2C), business-to-business (B2B), and business-to-government (B2G). Thus, e-commerce is more about strategy and management than about technology, which requires a dynamic approach. Consequently realising this and to create a regulatory environment favouring the development of e-commerce and to harmonise the national approach, the Indian government took the initiative by setting up a National IT Task Force in 1998. The main objective of this Task Force was to suggest ways to increase internet access and to strengthen infrastructure access. A study by Goldman Sachs anticipated nine million (Internet) users in India by 2003, thus signalling the fastest growth in Asia; 76 per cent compounded and annualised. The study said that the value of e-commerce transactions would proliferate in India from US$3.5 million in 1998 to over US$1.7 billion in 2000.

One of most popular portal e-commerce websites in India is Rediff.com. and Bababazar.com, which is an Indian online grocery store. It has developed a unique business model for facilitating e-commerce, circumventing the inadequacies of payment infrastructure with a cash-on-delivery payment system. Initially, B2C Indian web companies focused on products such as books (indiabookshop.com), music (cdbazzar.com), film tickets (delhitickets.com), flowers, cakes and chocolate (indiagiftshop.com). A second wave of Internet companies is now emerging in computers, groceries, and products. Another emerging area in India is the e-auction. B2C e-commerce is expected to flourish once reformed telecom policies and e-commerce laws are introduced. Apart from this there are IT and Management consultancy organisations such as Tata Consultancy Services (TCS), Infosys Technologies Ltd, Wipro, Satyam Computers Services and Gray Cell Inc. There are a few successful software companies providing managed software solutions and products to clients worldwide. Their offices are in Asia, Australia, UK, Europe, Far East, Africa, Canada and USA.

For the success of e-commerce, however, certain specifications need to be fulfilled and India is lacking in some of these. A modern telecommunications infrastructure, a satisfactory distribution of electricity along with access to computer hardware, plus software and servers are the fundamental requirements for electronic transactions. As Singh (2000) puts it, what we need is *info-structure* – that is, the framework and environment for e-commerce that includes the appropriate legal and financial framework; the political and business environment conducive to its development; and the capacity or human resource to deal in it (Singh, 2000). This involves issues of security and payments which need to be sorted out. Banking laws and regulations need to be adjusted to new formats where electronic fund transfers and credit card culture sets in India. Future tax policies on e-commerce not only need to be consistent with principles of international taxation that are transparent, predictable and simple, but also need to ensure that e-commerce competes with traditional commerce on a level playing field.

For this, India must evolve its strategy as a developing country on the global implications of e-commerce. It must become e-compatible in e-commerce and e-trade in order to preserve its existing market share in international trade, which in fact requires research in areas studying the relevance of e-commerce in different product groups including services and chalking out strategies to e-enable Indian trade and Industry. However, an important issue here is security in such transactions, particularly in banking and finance that must be taken care of while evolving any strategy on e-commerce. Communications security is an especially important and evolving consideration in the globalised world.

Information Technology and Australia

As explained earlier, Australia is an important player in the emerging information economy. Especially in the Asia-Pacific region, it is the most important player in the field of IT. According to the IDC, Australia's total IT market in 1998 reached US$11.7 billion and is forecast to increase to a total of US$19.3 billion by 2003. The IT services and software markets are growing at the fastest rates, with five-year compound annual growth rates of 14 per cent (versus on overall IT growth rate of 10 per cent). SME business segments are expected to have the highest growth rates of 12.7 per cent. By 2003, the small business segment is expected to account for over 24 per cent of Australia's IT market.

In a study entitled *The IT Engine Room: SMEs in Australia's IT&T Industry*, DCITA addressed some of the issues that SMEs are encountering in Australia. According to the study, Australian IT SMEs with a strong vision and innovative product and service offerings are expected to capitalise on the window of opportunity in the global IT sector. It maintained that Australian SMEs have been the 'IT engine room' of innovation in developing new products and creating new strategies. Key Australian IT SMEs, which have gained considerable global recognition over the past several years, include Sausage Software, Key Corp, ERG Group, and Creative Digital Technology. The study felt that the IT assistance programmes have been under-utilised in Australia because the specific needs of Australian IT SMEs are not being met. It sought to identify those needs and suggest possible solutions – or specifically formulated government programmes. It suggested that the IT SME could deliver a combination of innovation, technology awareness, competence and dexterousness needed to implement and reach the market quickly. However, this requires the support of the local, regional and corporate offices of IT multinationals, RDOs (Research & Development Organisations), financiers and the many bodies, which provide services to the SME (Austrade, 2000).

According to the Department of Communications, Information Technology and the Arts (DCITA), approximately 50 per cent of all households had home Internet access in Australia in 2001 as against 37 per cent in 2000. Some 63 per cent (56% in 2000) of Australian households used a computer in 2001 and approximately 82 per cent of shoppers paid online. A considerable 91 per cent of Federal government organisations were expected to have appropriate government services online, and, in July 2000, 526 of a total of 714 identified government services were already provided with online access by the Federal government. Presently, eAustralia specialises in Internet marketing and business development and e-commerce solutions (DCITA web site).

Content Developers and It Professional Services

As consumers increasingly gravitate to the Internet to hook up in e-commerce, demand is rapidly increasing for programming and content development skills in the business world. The Australian web design industry is expanding rapidly. At the same time, however, technological opportunities within the industry are diverging. Many Australian web design companies are debating over the selection of technology in the coming years. The debate is between concentrating on e-commerce as the most lucrative business focus and looking to the promise of broadband technologies and media development. Whatever the outcome, it is generally agreed by web developers that the design industry is poised for major changes and rapidly building competencies in order to offer 'end-to-end' services.

As mentioned earlier, at present Australia is well placed to grasp international e-commerce market opportunities. First, with over 20 per cent of its population online, Australia's e-commerce market is the most mature in the Asia Pacific region, and among the top five in the world (DCITA web site). Australia has also been relatively aggressive in relation to its readiness to adopt information technology. Second, the country has a strong IT infrastructure. In a survey conducted by IDC of 55 countries, which together account for 97 per cent of the global Gross Domestic

Product (GDP) and 99 per cent of the IT expenditure worldwide, Australia was ranked in eighth position for IT investment. Other studies have noted similar comparisons. Third, the country has an open and competitive telecommunications market. Finally, Australian economic conditions are both comparatively stable and favourable. These combined factors have helped move Australia to the leading edge in e-commerce in the Asia Pacific region.

Internet Service Providers (ISPs) in Australia

Strong competition and many large players have made the Australian ISP market one of the most mature markets in the Asia Pacific region. The industry is home to at least 700 ISPs, but is dominated by only a handful of well-established players. OzEmail and Telstra BigPond are dominant players, accounting for nearly half of the dial-up subscriber market. The smaller major players competing aggressively for market share include AAPt, OneNet, Primus, and Optus.

The Australian ISP sector is experiencing a phase of consolidation. The major players, primarily telecommunications providers (or telcos), are actively acquiring SME ISPs in order to increase the provision of connectivity options for their customers. Recent acquisition activity has included the entry of several major foreign companies, including MCI WorldCom with the purchase of OzEmail, and Singapore-based Pacific Internet (PacNet) with the purchase of local SME ISPs Mira Networking and Zip World. Other aggressive new-entrant foreign players include iHug of New Zealand, and AOL of the United States. Local players that are quickly gaining a fair market share include TPG Internet, OneNet, and discount service provider, Primus, while Optus is also moving aggressively into the retail Internet space. SME ISPs with 5000 to 15,000 subscribers are emerging and growing rapidly in the Australian marketplace. Some of these SMEs are offering value-added services such as commercial wiring to raise their profiles. Over the next few years, many of Australia's small ISPs are destined to become acquisition targets.

Areas of Synergy: India and Australia

A close look at the facts and the above discussion shows that both the countries have relative strengths and weaknesses. In fact, these countries are quite complementary to each other in many ways in the field of information technology; what one country lacks in particular strengths or capabilities the other country enjoys them in abundance. While Australia has a strong IT infrastructure, an environment conducive to e-commerce; strong Internet usage and aggressive development of e-commerce, especially B2B; strong government commitment towards IT; strong, creative and innovative niche in software development capability; rich SME sector and forte in areas like banking and finance, public sector administration, mining, transportation, retailing, telecom, it has certain weaknesses such as a conservative investment culture with a lack of entrepreneurship skills; not so growth-oriented and enterprising SMEs; traditional domination of IT by branches of multinationals; small size of economy and not very good volume of IT manpower. On the other hand, India possesses capabilities of an entrepreneurial society; a rich and strongly export-oriented SME sector with strong links to the USA; strong technical potential in software development and programming; large domestic economy with enormous potentialities; large supply of low-cost, high quality IT manpower. On the other hand, India needs to overcome poor basic networks and infrastructure; weak diffusion to the internet; problems in the field of e-commerce, banking and finance; unfavourable political environment to international business. These relative strengths and weaknesses or synergies of Australia and India, however, are unique and may be appropriately used by both the countries to reduce competitive barriers and increase the likelihood of business success, particularly to the advantage of India (Bala, 2002; 246).

For this purpose, India and Australia had already signed a MOU in October 2000 for a period of four years, the aim of which is to encourage cooperation between both the countries. It identified the main areas of common interest and cooperation as software and multimedia content development, advanced communication technologies, e-commerce and information industries security and Internet applications. It envisaged that cooperation between both countries would be prompted through bilateral regional and international dialogues in areas of e-commerce, matters relating to removal of trade barriers and standards and conformance issues. Thus, it envisaged translating relative strengths into opportunities, particularly in the areas of IT outsourcing, joint IT ventures, and IT investment and development.

Together with its strong commitment towards IT, the Australian marketplace offers a very favourable and conducive environment for Indian companies to establish their presence. Early adoption of new technology, combined with its strong and stable trading environment, Australia is an ideal country for e-commerce compared to other countries in the Asia Pacific region. It is also recognised that e-commerce, particularly in health, engineering, legal and accountancy is in India's favour and it must take advantage of such links with Australia.

Conclusion

Both countries working together can tap considerable opportunities not only in the existing bilateral relations through outsourcing, but also in dealing with countries having potential markets for Indo-Australian joint ventures – for example, the United States, Canada, Germany, France, the United Kingdom and Japan. As mentioned earlier, dealing with e-commerce issues involves a discussion on security, particularly in the case of IT applications in areas like banking, finance and e-commerce for India. Foreign government laws (particularly US) have restricted their companies that are developing security technologies to export such technologies. Both countries can address this issue together in international forums for their respective growth and development.

REFERENCES

AUSTRADE and Ernst and Young (2000), *Emerging Opportunities in Information Technology for Australia and India*, A Report Jointly prepared by AUSTRADE and Ernest and Young, March.

Bala, M. (2002), 'India-Australia Trade and Investment Relations in the 1990s', in D. Gopal, ed., *Australia in the Emerging Global Order: Evolving Australia-India Relations*, Shipra Publications: Delhi, pp. 235-248.

DCITA web site at http://www.dcita.gov.au

IDC (2002) *Indian it Industry to Cross $45 B by 2006*, A Report, International Data Corporation.

Joseph, K.J. (2001), 'ICT Boom, Economy and Labour', *Labour and Development*, Vol. 7, No. 2, December 2001, pp. 1-36.

Koch, Gary (2000), International Data Corporation, Report No. 20560, September 1999 as quoted in, "Emerging Opportunities in Information Technology for Australia and India", A Report Jointly prepared by AUSTRADE and Ernest and Young, March 2000.

Kumar, N (2000), 'Small Information Technologies Services, Employment and Entrepreneurship Development: Some Explorations into Indian Experience', *The Indian Journal of Labour Economics*, Vol. 43, No. 4, pp. 935-48.

Mukherjee (2000), *as quoted in* Joseph K.J. 2001, 'ICT Boom, Economy and Labour', *Labour and Development*, Vol. 7, No. 2, December, pp. 1-36.

Pohjola, M. (1998) 'Information Technology and Economic Development: An Introduction to Research Issues', *Working Paper No. 153*, UNU/WIDER.

Singh, A.D. (2000), *Electronic Commerce: Some Implications for Firms and*

Workers in Developing Countries, International Institute for Labour Studies, Geneva.

Stiglitz, J.E. (2002), 'Information and Change in the Paradigm in Economics', *American Economic Review.* Vol. 92, No. 3.

Van Wijnbergen (1984), 'Inflation, Employment and Dutch Disease in Oil Exporting Countries: A Short Run Disequilibrium Analysis', *Quarterly Journal of Economics*, Vol. 19, No.2, pp. 233-250.

World Bank (1999), *World Development Report 1998-99*, OUP: New York.

14

India and Australia: Partners for Peace and Prosperity

CHINTAMANI MAHAPATRA

This chapter argues that, despite any outstanding differences, an India-Australia partnership can enable both states to play a constructive role in international affairs, especially in terms of maintaining peace and stability. The chapter discusses the evolution of the relationship since Independence and is divided into four main sections – Cold War India-Australia relations, Post-Cold War Australia-India relations, convergences in the India-Australia relationship and managing differences in the Australia-India relationship. It is concluded that there are at least six broad overlapping areas in which the India-Australia partnership might develop further in the 21st century – defence, terrorism, combating drugs trafficking, political cooperation, educational exchanges and economic cooperation.

When we discuss relations between any two countries, it is always useful to first outline the profile of the countries concerned. What is India's international profile today? India is a country of about one-third the size of the United States. It has a GDP of about $390 billion-a little more than that of Australia, but with about a billion people. India has come a long way since its independence, a little more than half century ago. It was then a newly-independent country with a massive population burden and it was faced with major problems of nation-building in the midst of the Cold War. It was dependent on food aid from abroad and it did not possess a strong military. It had to face external aggression five times in fifty years of its independent existence.

Today, India is not only self-sufficient in food production but also ranks among the top three of the world in the production of rice, wheat, tea, tobacco, ghee and butter, milk and sugar. It has a strong military with a nuclear capability. It has the 12th largest GDP in the world. Unlike in the past, its economic growth is impressive since the institution of reforms in the early 1990s and it is one of the big emerging markets of the world. India has emerged as a global player and is recognised as such by Australia and the major powers of the world.

Australia has been an independent democracy for a little more than a century. It is about the size of the 48 continental states of the United States of America. It enjoys a GDP of about $350 billion with a population of about 20 million. It has been dependent on external actors for its security for a long time. Economically, it was an inward-looking country until the reforms began to take root about two decades ago. Today, it is a vibrant economy, is a strong military power of the South Pacific and an important actor in international affairs. Australia has a very modern military with sophisticated fighting equipment. It has never fought a war directly with any neighbouring enemy (it has none!), but the Australian armed forces posses fighting experiences abroad-in Korea and Vietnam and Australian special forces are still in Afghanistan and Iraq as part of the US-led coalition to fight the terror networks. It has been an active participant in UN peacekeeping and peace enforcement operations; the most recent example being in East Timor. Australia plays a substantial role in most of the international regimes related to arms control and disarmament. It is an aid donor to about 60 countries in the world. South Asia receives about 6 per cent of its foreign aid.

Cold War India-Australia Relations

India's relations with Australia during the prolonged Cold War years were neither friendly nor adversarial. The relationship during these years mainly symbolised political differences. Although Australia was a member of the South-East Asia Treaty Organisation (SEATO) and India was critical of SEATO, New Delhi did not consider the organisation to be an anti-Indian group. However, as Australia joined the US-led anti-Communist alliance-the South East Asia Treaty Organisation (SEATO), it came to share a common security platform with Pakistan – India's adversary. Furthermore, the political differences between Canberra and New Delhi became accentuated. Actually, differing foreign policy priorities led India and Australia to adopt different national security strategies. India sought to maximise its foreign policy gains by adopting a strategy of non-alignment, but Australia decided to join the US alliance. India, a newly-independent country, did not consider it appropriate for its national interest to join the Cold War conflict by taking sides. The challenges of nation-building, domestic political consolidation and economic growth dissuaded India from playing Cold War politics. Australia was not a newly-independent country when World War II ended and the Cold War spread to different regions of the world. However, Australia had become dependent on an external power, especially Britain, to ensure its national security. What it saw in the post-war period was the decline of the British Empire and British power. It looked for a new 'protector' and quickly discovered one in the United States-the new superpower. Australia sought security through alliance politics.

One of the sacrifices that a smaller ally in the alliance network has to make is to share the threat perceptions of the dominant ally without raising critical questions. While Australia neither had communist movements within its territory nor in its neighbourhood, it shared the United States' perception of the communist threat to international peace. India, on the other hand, was not as much concerned about the ideology of communism as was Australia. Although India had experienced communist movements for decades even before it achieved independence and soon after its independence it witnessed one of the biggest communist movements in neighbouring China, the liberal leaders in India viewed communism differently and dealt with it differently. Had the Indian political rulers feared communism or had the Australian leaders of the day no fear of communism, the course of Indo-Australian relations perhaps would have been different and a major area of political divergences between the two countries could have been avoided.

Secondly, India was not as much concerned about the ideology of communism in its neighbourhood as was Australia. While Australia neither had communist movements within the country nor in its neighbourhood, it shared the American perception of the communist threat.

Thirdly, India sought to champion the cause of the developing world, but Australia threw its lot on behalf of the developed world. India's role in the Afro-Asian region and the Non-Aligned Movement, its championship of the cause of the Least Developed Countries in the Group of 77 and its participation in the demand for a New International Economic Order and New International Information Order did not converge with Australian foreign policy. Although Australia itself has been an aid donor country, its foreign aid policies were similar to those of the European states and the United States. However, one major difference is that Australia's ODA is very much directed towards its region, the Asia-Pacific (Rumley, 1999; 179-192).

Last but not the least, there was not enough ground for India and Australia to come together to establish closer economic relations. Australia's economy was largely inward looking and its external engagement was primarily with Europe. As and when Australia developed closer economic ties with East Asian and Southeast Asian economies, India's engagement with that region was minimal. Although the Indian and Australian economies have never been competitive, a lack of politically compatibility and India's economic policies before the reforms were instituted in 1991 prevented closer Indo-Australian economic ties.

Post-Cold War Australia-India Relations

While Australia and India found themselves on different sides of the Cold War divide, neither country perceived the other as an enemy or adversary or a rival. A non-aligned country could pose no threat to the partner of a military alliance. In addition, India faced no threat from Australia, despite the latter's closer security ties with the United States. Moreover, neither competed for political influence or economic presence in the Indian Ocean or the Asia Pacific regions. As a result, by the time the Cold War came to an end, there was enough room for both countries to contemplate an improvement in mutual ties. In fact, the Soviet collapse, the end of communism in Europe, Communist China's economic engagement with the capitalist world and the end of the Cold War confrontations induced every country in the world to re-design its foreign policy objectives and priorities. India and Australia were no exceptions to this trend. Furthermore, the lack of enmity during the Cold War years provided a relatively easy ground for the two countries to improve political and economic ties. Contrast this to the Indo-Pakistan relationship or even the India-China relationship.

There was a quick realisation after the end of the Cold War in Australian governing circles that India had not received the adequate attention it deserved. Senator Gareth Evans in his Ministerial Statement stated that India was the "most under-rated likely great power of the 1990s" (Kaul, 2002; 227). Soon after, the Australian Senate Standing Committee on Foreign Affairs and Trade produced a detailed report on Australia-India relations which pointed out that the relationship was "neglected, underdeveloped" and suffered "a high state of ignorance" (Gurry, 1992; 510).

Before long, India came to be sighted on Australia's national security radar screen. Today, Australia engages four Asian countries in formal political-military dialogues, and India is one of them, the others being China, Japan and South Korea. Australia's Foreign Minister Downer is quoted as saying: "We must not fool ourselves that terrorism has somehow erased the other daunting concerns in our region. The Asia-Pacific region is home to the world's six largest armies (China, the United States, Russia, India, North Korea and South Korea) and, after the Middle East, the world's three most volatile flashpoints-the Taiwan Strait, the Korean Peninsula and Kashmir. Australia will need to use its influence, as part of broader international efforts, to help ease tensions in these places" (Downer, 2002).

However, Australia had almost lost an opportunity to "help ease tensions" in South Asia by taking a hard line position on Indian nuclear tests. There was a serious rupture in the relationship which was mended before it was too late. Canberra took the first step to revive the relationship. The Australian Prime Minister visited India in July 2000. It was the first visit by an Australian Prime Minister in eleven years, but it constituted a milestone in the relationship. While the first step was taken by Australia to break the ice it created, the visit of the then Indian Foreign Minister Jaswant Singh to Australia in June 2001 was a significant development in the restoration of friendly ties between the two countries. This was the "first ever stand alone visit" by an Indian Foreign Minister to Australia! Foreign Minister Jaswant Singh held the first bilateral Ministerial Framework Dialogue with his Australian counterpart, Alexander Downer, during this visit. Recognising the importance of India and Australia as factors for regional stability, the two sides agreed to initiate a security dialogue at the senior official level.

In the meantime, Indian economic reforms encouraged increased trade and investment interactions between Australia and India. India's membership in the ASEAN Regional Forum, the elevation of India's status as a full dialogue partner of ASEAN and the rising trend in US-Indian cooperation provided the right kind of political atmosphere for Indo-Australian cooperative initiatives. It is noteworthy that the first important visit by a high level official to Australia after the Pokharan II nuclear tests was by the Minister of Commerce, Murasoli Maran, in April 2000, followed by that of the Textile Minister, Kashi Ram Rana. These visits were milestones; given the abysmally low level of economic ties between the two countries. India then ranked 13th in Australia's export markets and 26th as an import source.

Convergences in the India-Australia Relationship

It is interesting to note that a common political background, a shared history, similar economic systems and Commonwealth partnerships did not bring India and Australia together. In fact, political differences between these two democracies were wider than, for instance, Sino-Australian political differences in the last few decades. Diverse political systems, value systems and economic structures did not prevent China and Australia in establishing stronger bilateral ties. As Australian Foreign Minister Alexander Downer said: "…it would be a mistake to see differences in national experience, economic structure, political system and cultural outlook as immutable and unchanging. It would be equally wrong to cast such differences in purely negative terms-after all, diversity can be a very positive and dynamic factor in a relationship" (Downer, 1999). However Sino-Australian trade is about five times larger than Indo-Australian trade.

Today, India and Australia share similar worldviews and foreign policy orientations and goals:

- Both India and Australia emphasise closer ties with the world's sole superpower, the United States, as a functional necessity.
- Both consider the USA, the EU, China, Japan and Russia as important power centres and wish to establish cooperative ties with them.
- Both regard the Asia-Pacific region as a significant centre of economic activities and are trying to engage their respective economies with the region.
- Both share common views on non-military security concerns, such as drugs trafficking, small arms proliferation, illegal migration, international crime, environmental degradation, among others.
- Both are engaged in combating terrorism and view this menace as a significant threat to democratic societies.
- Both view WMD proliferation as destabilising and seek to play a role in preventing further proliferation and in efforts towards nuclear disarmament.

However, holding similar worldviews is not enough to establish a closer working relationship. Necessary steps in this direction need to be taken. Both India and Australia, in recent years, have taken steps to establish cooperative ties, better reflected in rising trade and investment relations, high-level exchanges of visits and consultations between officials in forums where both the countries are members, such as the ARF, the Commonwealth and the United Nations.

Managing Differences in the Australia-India Relationship

However, the real challenges for both countries are in terms of dealing with the differences, even as cooperation in other fields is maintained. Certain differences over political and security issues have continued to haunt Indo-Australian relations.

First of all, the nuclear proliferation issue remained fundamental to Indo-Australian political differences. The Pokharan II series of nuclear tests by India froze bilateral ties for quite some time. Although a normal relationship has now been restored, differences continue. The short-term goal should not be to allow the differences over WMD issues to dictate and dominate the overall relationship. Indians become sentimental over people not showing an understanding of their security compulsions. Australians seem sentimental about their non-proliferation mission and role. How best to deal with the sentiments and the respect of each other's views is a long-term challenge. The views expressed by Australian Foreign Minister Downer on sentimental issues in China-Australia relations are indeed instructive. He said: "At various points in time, Australia's relations with China have assumed an overly emotional character, with a tendency to succumb to excesses of opprobrium or enthusiasm.... But there is no doubt that [today] emotionalism has mitigated against a more level-headed and durable policy" (Downer, 1999). One would expect a similar maturity in Australia-India relations in years to come.

The two countries have also different approaches to regionalism, particularly in the context of issues related to Asia-Pacific Economic Cooperation (APEC) group and the Indian Ocean Association for Regional Cooperation (IOARC). Australia was not in favour of making APEC an inclusive body and, in the end, opposed the inclusion of India as a member in that organisation. India did not favour the idea of making IOARC an inclusive body, especially in terms of keeping Pakistan out of it. Although it did not harm Australian interests directly, what Canberra failed to understand was Indian opposition to the discussion of security issues within IOARC and Indian eagerness to join the ARF. Australia should look at India's economy-larger than its own-in the new light of the liberalisation policy and proactively support India's membership of APEC. India should not have any opposition to the discussion of security issues in the Indian Ocean forum.

Conclusion

Australia today perceives itself as a strong state destined to play a role around the world. So does India. The development of science and technology and the evolution of modern weapon systems have no longer kept India and Australia as distant neighbours. The distance between the two is shrinking with every passing day. The two neighbours have enormous potential to work together for the maintenance of stability, promoting peace and achieving prosperity. Australia is geographically a large state, scientifically advanced and economically prosperous. It is a small state in terms of the size of its population. However, its social demography and economic geography are much better than that of India. It no doubt may have the problem of a small population in terms of its power profile, but India will continue to have the problem of an overly-large population in terms of its own power profile. The partnership can enable both to overcome the difficulties and play a constructive role in international affairs.

Today, both India and Australia aspire to play a constructive role in Asia and a global role as well in maintaining peace and stability. Australia perceives itself as "a country with a prosperous and diverse economy, a technologically advanced society, and a long history of strong commitment to liberal democratic values" and "looks beyond the region to play an active role in the development of solutions to global economic, social and strategic problems" (Department of Foreign Affairs, 2000). India perceives itself as a vibrant democracy in the world, which can easily "fit into a world being shaped by the realities of the 21st century". As Foreign Minister Jaswant Singh had stated: "Learning the lessons of the Cold War and drawing from the experiences of the Nonaligned Movement, we believe that a stable global political equilibrium can only be achieved through a multipolar and cooperative world order. We are actively developing our relations with the broader world on this basis...." (Sinha, 2002). These self-perceptions of India and Australia clearly indicate that these two countries can be partners for peace and prosperity in the coming years of the 21st Century.

Future areas of Cooperation can encompass the following:

- **Defence**: training, intelligence sharing, regular dialogues between defence officials.
- **Terrorism**: political, economic and military cooperation in combating terrorism.
- **Combating drugs trafficking**: It is a multi-billion dollar illegal trade that affects international stability and peace.

- **Political cooperation**: Promoting democracy and democratising international organisations.
- **Educational exchanges**: About 12,000 Indian students are currently studying in Australia (Department of Foreign Affairs, 2002). This number can be increased considerably. With passing days, more and more Indian students are going abroad for higher studies. In terms of distance and expenses, Australia can be a more attractive place for them. However, the reverse trend can also be encouraged by marketing Indian education in Australia.
- **Economic cooperation**: One of the most important areas of cooperation, however, is trade along with investment, technology transfer and other fields of economic activity, such as the knowledge industry. The economies of India and Australia are not competitive but complementary. A solid ground should be built for a durable friendship. The durability of the overall relationship, in fact, will depend on the intensity of economic ties between the two countries. Although Indo-Australian economic cooperation has been improving fast in recent years, it has a long way to go. It is important to know that Australia's exports to countries like Saudi Arabia grew by 95 per cent, to Egypt by 71 per cent and Mexico by 46 per cent, during 1998-99. The figure for India would be considerably less. Australia, of late, has developed a new competitive edge in high technology areas, such as scientific and medical equipment, tele-communications and aerospace products. It is a supplier of advanced goods and services among our neighbours. India should try to take advantage of this and has to improve its export performance in Australia. It is significant to note that China has become an important trading partner of Australia and its trade with China is about five times larger than that of India. According to statistics released by the Chinese Government, the total trade between China and Australia was more than $5 billion in 1998 and growing very rapidly. More importantly, Australia had by then become China's biggest overseas investment destination (Chinese Embassy Web Site). Can India learn from these facts? There is little to celebrate for India when Australia became the 8th largest foreign investor in India. What is the state of India's investment in Australia? Clearly, Indian investors need to do more to develop a closer economic relationship.

REFERENCES

Chinese Embassy Web Site, http://www.chinaembassy.org.au

Department of Foreign Affairs and Trade (2000), 'Australia in Brief', Department of Foreign Affairs and Trade, Government of Australia, http:/ www.dfat.gov.au/aib2000part_1/a.html

Department of Foreign Affairs and Trade (2002), *Pioneer,* 29 April 2002. http:/ /www.dfat.gov.au/aib2000/part_1/d.html

Downer, A. (1999), 'Australia and China—Partners for Progress', Speech by the Hon Alexander Downer, Minister for Foreign Affairs, at the 1999 China Oration of the Australia-China Business Council, Sydney, 25 November.

Downer, A. (2002), "Australia's Foreign Policy Challenges," Speech by the Australian Minister for Foreign Affairs, National Press Club, Canberra, 7 May 2002, *http://www.foreignminister.gov.au/speeches*

Gurry, M. (1992), 'Leadership and Bilateral Relations: Menzies and Nehru, Australia and India, 1949-1964', *Pacific Affairs*, vol. 65, no. 4, Winter.

Kaul, M.M. (2002), 'Australia-India Relations: a critical survey', in D. Gopal, ed., *Australia in the Emerging Global Order*, Delhi.

Ministry of External Affairs Web Site, http://meadev.nic.in/govt/parl-qa/loksabha/ jul25-565.htm

Rumley, D. (1999), *The Geopolitics of Australia's Regional Relations*, Dordrecht: Kluwer.

Sinha, Y. (2002), Address by Yaswant Sinha, Foreign Minister of India, at the International Institute of Strategic Studies, London, 30 October.

15

Globalisation and the New Security Agenda

Developing a Regional Paradigm

DENNIS RUMLEY AND D. GOPAL

It was argued in the first Chapter of this book that both India and Australia have been subject to the emergence of a "new security agenda" which all states inevitably have to confront due to globalisation (Coker, 2002; 8). This concluding Chapter takes up this point and contributes further to the debate over the need to broaden the security discourse (Thakur and Newman, 2004). It argues in favour of a move of the regional security agenda away from a sole concern with traditional security thinking and identifies some of the directions that this shift might take. It is the belief of the authors that both India and Australia are in a unique position to undertake a leading role in facilitating this very challenging new orientation. We begin and end the Chapter with a quotation from the UN Secretary-General's Report to the General Assembly of 21 March 2005 entitled, *In Larger Freedom: Towards Development, Security and Human Rights For All*:

> The threats to peace and security, in the twenty-first century, include not just international war and conflict but civil violence, organized crime, terrorism and weapons of mass destruction. They also include poverty, deadly infectious disease and environmental degradation since these can have equally catastrophic consequences. All of these threats can cause death or lessen life chances on a large scale. All of them can undermine states as the basic unit of the international system (Annan, 2005; 25).

To elaborate the above stated position, the Chapter will reiterate the view that both the threats and (in)security have constructed meanings and thus both are inevitably contested and, second, to re-emphasise the

UN Secretary-General's view that since security can no longer be seen just as a traditional military concept, that regional security thinking and policies need to fundamentally change in order to guarantee sustainable security. Of course, from what we have just said, our construction of these issues will inevitably be as an outcome, not only of our own bias and predispositions, but also as a result of our perception of the Indian Ocean Region from different locations.

The Chapter will revisit some old issues (as well as some new ones), but more to attempt to reinterpret them in order to raise a number of questions about Indian Ocean security which require further regional debate and which will, in turn, require appropriate regional forums. The Chapter argues that states construct geopolitical categories that emphasise 'the other' as threatening partly in response to an outmoded concept of state function. Resultant analytical categories are thus contested, and, in order to develop appropriate regional security policy to meet 'real' threats, states need to make themselves aware of the nature and direction of contestation. Furthermore, whether regional states like it or not, ultimately much of the responsibility for constructing Indian Ocean security lies in their own hands. In our view, in the final analysis, sustainable regional security can only be guaranteed regionally.

On the face of it, outside observers may argue that the Indian Ocean region is inherently insecure. For example, from a geopolitical perspective, the region does not comprise a "true security system"; rather, it comprises a set of highly diverse sub-systems (Bouchard, 2004). Furthermore, the region has been characterised as being akin to an "arc of crisis", since it contains many poor, unstable states which are beset by bilateral land-based and/or maritime disputes (Gordon, 1996). This view is similar to an earlier characterization by Brzezinski of the region as an "arc of crisis" through the Middle East into Africa (House, 1984; 6). However, it has been recently argued that the Indian Ocean Region has now entered a new geopolitical era which comprises an Indian oceanic order characterised by heterogeneity, fragmentation into sub-regional systems, an emergent regionalism, subordination to large regional powers and realisation of the actual importance of the Ocean itself both as highway and environment (Bouchard, 2004). In this new "order", many regional states are as much concerned with the problems of internal stability as they are with the Indian Ocean regional issues or questions related to a security threat from another state.

The Chapter is organised into five major sections. First, the question of what is a regional security threat will be considered and various ways of constructing such threats will be reviewed. Second, the Chapter will describe the nature of conventional security threats in the Indian Ocean Region. Third follows an evaluation of extra-regional security interests, especially the United States and China. Fourth, the structure of regional economic *insecurity* will be considered. Finally, the Chapter identifies a range of well-known 'non-conventional' security threats and discusses in more detail the regional variations in the quality of *human* security since this is regarded by the authors as the principal source of regional insecurity. Underpinning all of this is an argument in favour of an increase in the "democratisation of security" around the Indian Ocean Region in order to maximise 'real' security.

What is a Security Threat?

Constructing Security

It is well-known that security is both a contested and a multidimensional concept – it can embody traditional concerns over military security which are generally evident at the scale of the state and it can also encompass concerns over other aspects of security such as economic and environmental security. In addition, a broad definition of security would include other non-state forms of 'non-traditional security', such as terrorism, money laundering and drug trafficking. Thus, security threats can take many forms – from armed conflict to sexual violence against women (Commission on Human Security, 2003; 49). Policies designed to meet traditional security concerns have generally been enacted at the state scale, but, with increasing globalisation and technological change, policies associated with economic and environmental security and with all forms of non-traditional security increasingly necessitate inter-state cooperation. This is a significant policy concern for most Indian Ocean regional states since the nature of non-traditional security threats is becoming increasingly more important, and since, in a globalising world, states will wish to portray themselves both as being secure and as being of no threat. Constructing Indian Ocean security in the broadest sense in the 21st century requires regional cooperation.

Manufacturing Threats: Imaginings and Warnings

Among other factors, threat perceptions are a product of structural, geopolitical, historical, socio-cultural and economic considerations (Tilman, 1984). While a fundamental consideration in the formulation of security policy is a threat assessment, threat perceptions and assessments will vary over time both in terms of content and in terms of accuracy

(Dupont, 1991). However, threats may not be "real"; they may be manufactured. Many in the West possess a range of fears about the world and especially about Asia and the developing world. In addition, many Westerners are God-fearing and have a fear of the other. Western perceptions of the developing world, in particular, have been heavily influenced by 'orientalism' – a Western concept which sees Asia, for example, as comprising a mixture of savagery, exotica and despotism – descriptions which would be considered by most Westerners to be the very opposite of those attributable to themselves (Said, 1991). The East is thus invariably demonised and marginalised in the West. Perhaps this is a function of the uncertain environment or perhaps it is an innate characteristic of Western society?

As Rajaram (the hair collector) put it to Om (the tailor) in Mistry's *A Fine Balance*:

> Foreign women enjoy wearing other people's hair. Men also, especially, if they are bald. In foreign countries they fear baldness. They are so rich in foreign countries, they can afford to fear all kinds of silly things" (Mistry, 1997; 172).

In Australia, there has been a long-standing "red scare" and a "fear of the north". India, too, has felt regionally vulnerable. In Australia's case, a "sense of vulnerability" has characterised much of its modern history (Dalrymple, 2003; 4). Fear has also been a key feature of Australian domestic politics in recent years (Gale, 2005). Perhaps we all share some imagined fear and a fear of the unknown. Some might even fear freedom itself. The UN Secretary-General, however, has argued strongly for the global realisation of a fundamentally different goal – that is, "freedom from fear", as part of a broader vision of collective security. However, as Kofi Annan has recently pointed out: "Collective security today depends on accepting that the threats which each region of the world perceives as most urgent are in fact equally so for all" (Annan, 2005; 24-5). Prioritising and securing the strategic agenda of the North compared to the South is not part of this vision. There is therefore an urgent need to "democratise security".

The imaginings of fear can also be both constructed and manipulated. They can be constructed by the governments, by intelligence agencies, by the media and by education systems. Indeed, fear is often a function of a lack of knowledge. Fear can also be manipulated by governments at election times, for example. In addition, government warnings about other states can also reinforce fear based on inadequate knowledge. In this sense, 'real' security threats are invariably seen to be those which are officially sanctioned by states and *not* those which are perceived by its citizenry. Thus, HIV/AIDS was declared a security threat by the UN Security Council in 2000 (Commission on Human Security, 2003; 99). As the recent US Commission has shown, if intelligence agencies and governments wish to find a threat, they will, irrespective of the data (Davis, 2005).

However, and perhaps not surprisingly, various facets of security can be in conflict and result in contradictions. In potentially conflictual environments between states, the involvement of other states in security matters – for example, in arms supply – can potentially exacerbate the situation. The extent to which such involvement is seen to be acceptable can produce what might be regarded as a kind of "security hypocrisy". Some commentators might therefore be forgiven for perceiving a 'double standard' in the US condemnation of possible European arms sales to China while itself being in the process of deciding to supply F-16 fighter planes to Pakistan. The latter decision naturally led to "great disappointment" in India and perhaps contributed to the timing of an announcement of a significant upgrading in its military hardware (Agence France-Presse, 2005). However, from an Indian perspective, such a decision must also be interpreted in the context of India's approach to security matters which has been characterised as "modified structuralism" – that is, on the one hand, India seeks to maximise its own conception of power based on military strength, economic development and internal order, while being willing to yield concessions to rival interests, on the other hand (Bajpai, 1998).

Even in 'non-threatening' state-state relations, fear of reprisal will often govern the nature of interstate interaction. Unspoken threats can therefore arise due to asymmetrical relations between more powerful states and those wishing to guarantee their own economic security. Guaranteeing a state's economic security (or even a politician's re-election) in these circumstances may result in states jettisoning principles related to human security. Particular dilemmas can arise when there is a contradiction between maximising traditional security and maximising a state's economic security.

Geopolitically-Constructed Security Threats

In the 21st century, geopolitically-constructed security threats have been ascribed by the West, both to states and to regions. Thus, both "rogue states" and "failed states" have been portrayed by the West as being located outside of the civilized world in a way which echoes the Cold War good-versus-evil rhetoric of the conflict with the Soviet Union (Rumley, 2003; 321). However, it is clear that there is a tendency for international crises to be centred around weak or failing states (Fukuyama, 2004; 93). The characterisation of Iran, Iraq and North Korea as being part of an "axis of evil" was not only based on the *belief* that such states were developing WMD but that they were intending to use these weapons against Western interests.

Geopolitically-constructed security threats are inevitably contested. The term Cold War, for example, which was popularised in the United States, has been interpreted as comprising four different but related conflicts – USA vs. European states, economic centre vs. economic periphery, freedom vs. totalitarianism and USA vs. USSR (Rumley *et al.*, 1996; 3).

Another well-known global geo-political construction, of course, is the clash of civilizations hypothesis (Huntington, 1996). For the Indian Ocean Region, this construction predicts an ongoing set of conflicts among African, Islamic, Hindu, Buddhist, Sinic and Western 'civilizations', with permanent 'fault lines' being located where these six civilizations connect. However, Huntington would have us believe that Australia will be in permanent conflict with most of its Indian Ocean neighbours, including India, since the primary dimension of conflict is seen as between so-called Western civilization and the rest. As has been pointed out, not only is Huntington's concept of 'civilization' conceptually and operationally flawed, his analysis seems to ignore the fact that, in recent years, most violent conflicts have actually occurred within civilizations and more particularly within states (Rumley, 1999; 27).

An alternative construction of a primary dimension of conflict which has implications for the Indian Ocean region is provided by Tariq Ali in which he sees the main source of global conflict as being a "clash of fundamentalisms", especially between Islamic fundamentalism and what he characterises as "the mother of all fundamentalisms: American imperialism" (Ali, 2002; 281). This characterisation has some fundamental implications for real and perceived security threats within the Indian Ocean region, given the locations of the land and sea based presence of the United States.

Most of the West Asian portion of the Indian Ocean Region has been characterised as "the global zone of percolating violence" and "is likely to be a major battlefield, both for wars among nation-states and, more likely, for protracted ethnic and religious violence" (Brzezinski, 1997;

52-3). In addition, most of the Northern half of the Indian Ocean Region, including India, has been incorporated into a US-designated "Southern Belt of Strategic Instability" which stretches from southern Japan in the East to northern Italy in the West (Flanagan, Frost and Kugler, 2001; 17). Not only do such constructions tend to be self-reinforcing and self-fulfilling, they can also come to be regarded as rigid templates for policy-making.

From an Australian perspective, much of the eastern portion of the Indian Ocean Region has been characterised as an "arc of instability". This arc of instability, which is located within Australia's region of primary strategic interest, has emerged since the end of the Cold War in response to globalisation, the history of colonialism, problems of social and political viability, poor governance, economic instability, aid dependency, ethnic tension and religious fundamentalism (Rumley, Forbes and Griffin, 2006). The most recent government White Paper points out that, in Southeast Asia, for example, "extremists.......target not only Westerners, but also seek to destabilise the region's secular governments" (Commonwealth of Australia, 2003; 40). On the other hand, the contested nature of the 'arc of instability' appellation has prompted one influential Australian commentator to refer to this region as an "*alleged* 'arc of crisis'" and to argue that its characterisation is being used as a mechanism for increasing Australian government military spending or as a rationale for an outdated regional strategic orientation (Dupont, 2003).

While threats can be geo-politically-constructed, the opposite can also be true – that is, security can potentially be enhanced by geo-political constructions. In this sense, Indian Ocean economic regionalism, in the form of IOR-ARC, though still relatively weak, is potentially an extremely important mechanism for enhancing regional security (Bajpai, 1998; 172). One of the more obvious reasons for this is based on the interaction-stability thesis – that is, the greater the degree of social, economic and political interaction among states, the lower the probability of inter-state conflict. However, the current status of Indian Ocean regionalism, as expressed through IOR-ARC, is something of a self-defeating vicious circle, since one of the principal reasons for its weakness lies in the existence of relatively weak bilateral linkages within the Indian Ocean Region. Furthermore, such weak bilateral linkages militate against Indian Ocean regionalism both from being fully inclusive and also from being preoccupied with matters other than a very narrowly-defined form of *economic* security.

Threats and Legitimate Interests

Most states will pursue their legitimate interests in order to maximise their economic security. However, in situations of competition and resource scarcity, states are likely to be in conflict with others and these conflicts may well be 'developmental' – that is, they are based on a developed state static concept of 'developmental order' which requires economically less developed states to pose no significant economic challenge. A threat to a developed state's *economic* security and economic dominance may well be portrayed or characterised by it as a threat in the traditional use of the term. Furthermore, challenges to the 'developmental order' may also be portrayed as challenges to regional hegemony and thus resisted. From a traditional security perspective, the identification of hegemonic 'no-go spaces', such as the Indian Ocean, for example, constructs a security threat both to the hegemon and to the 'invading power' which has legitimate regional interests. As in the Cold War period, the identification of and propagandisation of such spaces to some degree results both in potentially conflictual competition and uncertainty.

Conventional Security Threats in the Indian Ocean Region: Measuring Security

Attempts to objectively measure security and to precisely define security threats are fraught with difficulty, compared with, for example, the measurement of insecurity outcomes – such as the number of deaths in battle, or the number of piracy attacks. Threat assessment, at best, is an imprecise science, and, dependent on its policy impact, runs the risk of exacerbating insecurity, especially between states.

In terms of the most basic indicator of traditional security-defence expenditure-the Indian Ocean region contains two of the world's top ten spenders-Saudi Arabia (US$21 billion) and India (US$13 billion) (Commonwealth of Australia, 2003, 20;). In addition, both Australia (US$7.5 billion) and Indonesia (US$6.2 billion) possess very substantial defence budgets, as do Iran (US$4.9 billion), Kuwait (US$3.3 billion), Malaysia (US$3.3 billion), Burma (US$2.8 billion), Oman (US$2.7 billion), United Arab Emirates (US$2.7 billion), Pakistan (US$2.5 billion) and South Africa (US$1.7 billion). As a proportion of GDP, it seems that few states have significantly increased their defence expenditures, 1990-2000, however (Table 1).

Table 1: Some Conventional Security Indicators in the Indian Ocean Rim

	Armed Forces (total force)	*Militarisation (force as % pop)*	*Arms Imports US $M 2001*	*Defence as % GDP 1990*	*2000*
India	1,303,000	0.1	1,064	2.7	2.4
Pakistan (L)	612,000	0.5	759	5.8	4.5*#
Iran	513,000	0.8	335	2.7	3.8#
Egypt	448,000	0.7	486	3.5	2.3
Burma	344,000	0.8	N.A.	3.4	1.7*#
Thailand	301,000	0.5	162	2.2	1.6
Indonesia	297,000	0.1	38	1.3	1.1#
Saudi Arabia	202,000	1.0	143	12.8	11.6*
Bangladesh (L)	137,000	0.1	180	1.0	1.3
Sri Lanka	115,000	0.6	40	2.1	4.5*#
Malaysia	96,000	0.4	20	2.6	1.9#
Yemen (L)	66,000	0.4	33	8.5	5.2
UAE (H)	65,000	1.7	288	N.A.	N.A.
South Africa	63,000	0.2	17	3.8	1.5
Singapore (H)	60,000	2.0	141	4.8	4.8*#
Australia (H)	51,000	0.3	687	2.2	1.7
Oman	44,000	1.8	30	18.3	9.7*#
Tanzania (L)	34,000	0.1	N.A.	2.0	1.3
Kuwait (H)	15,000	0.6	34	48.5	8.2*#
Mozambique (L)	6,000	0.04	N.A.	10.1	2.5
	Average	**0.6**	**262.2**	**7.3**	**3.8**

All states have medium human development levels unless otherwise noted (H or L)

*military expenditure higher than on health

\# military expenditure higher than on education

*# military expenditure higher than on health and education

Source: Rumley and Chaturvedi, 2004; p. 28.

While the Indian Ocean Region contains considerable variation by state in terms of the size of the armed forces, the level of militarisation does not necessarily correspond. Thus, while India has the region's largest armed forces of more than 1.3 million, its militarisation index is well below the regional average at 0.1. Kuwait, on the other hand, with armed forces of 15,000, has a much higher level of militarisation (Table 1). However, the regional arms trade is significant and there are considerable regional arms imports, especially to India, Pakistan, Australia, Egypt, Iran and United Arab Emirates, which, to a considerable degree, reflect internal regional conflict and/or instability.

Unfortunately, given the developmental context of many Indian Ocean states, international as well as domestic realities ensure that human development often takes second place to military development. There are at least six regional states – Burma, Kuwait, Oman, Pakistan, Singapore and Sri Lanka – in which government military expenditure exceeds government expenditure on health and on education (Table 1).

Regional Nuclear Proliferation

The extent of regional nuclear proliferation can be seen both as a regional security threat and as a guarantor of peace, depending on one's perception and point of view. The standard arguments can be opposed – that is, the "more will be better" school of Waltz and others versus the "more will be worse" perspective of Sagan and others. On the one hand, while Waltz has argued that nuclear proliferation will lead to greater stability through deterrence, Sagan has argued that proliferation induces greater instability because of the potential for deliberate or accidental conflict and thus there is a need to enhance the global non-proliferation regime (Howlett, 2001; 428-9).

Others have argued that the inevitability of nuclear proliferation has resulted in a fundamental shift in global geo-politics as a result of the onset of the "second nuclear age" (Bracken, 2000). While the "first nuclear age" began on 16 July 1945 with the US testing of the atomic bomb in the New Mexico dessert, the "second nuclear age" – an "Asian nuclear age" – arguably began with the Chinese nuclear tests in 1964, with India's nuclear test of 1974 being the first example of what one American commentator refers to as an "outlaw bomb" (Bracken, 2000; 95-124). Among other things, this characterisation assumes that some (other) nuclear bombs are 'legal' and thus available for 'legitimate' use, if necessary.

While some regional states, such as South Africa, had them but gave them up, and others such as Iran may have them but say they do not and are not developing them, yet others, like Australia, seek shelter under a nuclear umbrella. The Australian state appears to be comfortable with not having any nuclear weapons of its own on the one hand, yet it is content with exporting substantial quantities of uranium on the other (admittedly under treaty safeguards). Furthermore, when Australia chastised India, when it tested a nuclear device in 1998, this had a negative impact on the economic security of both the states, since the relative importance of inter-state trade declined almost immediately (Rumley, 2004).

Many Western commentators find it difficult to conceive of a state like Iran, with such enormous fossil fuel reserves, taking the pathway to nuclear energy. One obvious interpretation of Iranian nuclear behaviour is that it is in direct response to that of Israel, and, earlier, to an Iraq which *did* possess WMD. In the case of the latter, this same rationale lay behind the US invasion, now designed in part it seems, to design a new democratic map for the Middle East, the basic structure of which is yet to be determined. In the meantime, traditional security in Iraq is to be guaranteed by a Western coalition, and the US, with its 1,50,000 troops, is obviously the dominant force. Australia is the only Indian Ocean state which is a part of that coalition and its original 400 troops is now bolstered by a further 450 in Al-Muthanna Province in southern Iraq to guard "Japanese engineers" (Kerin and Bita; 2005). This may well change in the near future. Furthermore, the actual or planned exodus of other members of the coalition – for example, Italy, The Netherlands and Ukraine-is likely to place greater strain on the Australian Defence Force, and, consequently on Australian public opinion.

If we were to accept the arguments of Waltz that more is better, then India, Israel, Pakistan and potentially Iran are no regional nuclear threats. Accepting the arguments of Sagan, on the other hand, results in the opposite conclusion. Equality of nuclear security would necessitate that *all* regional states or that *no* regional state should possess nuclear weapons. Inequality of state access to nuclear weapons is arguably the 'real' security threat.

Security Dilemmas and 'Real Threats'

There is still a certain degree of resistance to the removal of Cold War conceptions of security that led to a global spatial structuring into a set of excluded spaces that were to be feared. What this helped to facilitate was a self-perpetuating "security dilemma" – that is, the production of a 'security threatening' situation for one state or region which arises as a result of the perceived consequences of another state or region's behaviour in attempting to guarantee its own security (Rumley, 1999, 16). The security dilemma possesses three essential characteristics; benign intent (actions are defencively motivated), uncertainty of intent (they did not know that the others were acting for defensive reasons) and paradoxical outcome (their actions only made matters worse) (Collins, 2000; 24-5). State policy responses designed to meet potential threats can fall into a similar category.

Uncertainty of intent, of course, may also be a reflection of a lack of understanding over a state's regional geo-political orientation. As has been noted, for the Indian Ocean Region, there is a general dearth of published material concerning the geopolitical orientation of regional states (Rumley and Chaturvedi, 2004; 24). This lack of information means that the regional states have to rely on perceptions of actions and their intentions and it may well be that these intentions change or are perceived to change. Thus, some regional states might be forgiven for perceiving some ambiguity in how Australia sees its regional role – is it an "honest broker" or is it a "deputy sheriff"? In the case of the latter, some commentators might then perceive Australia to be potentially threatening, especially if it is seen to be associated with a doctrine of "pre-emption", which itself is an offensive posture based on perceived threat.

For the Indian Ocean region, one could develop a simple hypothetical Indian Ocean state threat index (HIOSTI) based on conventional security data. For example, we would expect any regional state to pose a 'real threat' to be above average on all of these indicators – that is, we would expect a 'real' state threat to be above average on militarisation, on arms imports and on per cent expended on defence in 1990 and in 2000. When we examine the data we find, in fact, that no such 'real threat' exists. Several states are above average on one or more of these categories, but no state is above average on all the four. Indeed, only one state is above average on three of the categories (militarisation and above average spent on defence in 1990 and in 2000) and that is Oman, and most strategists would not regard the state of Oman as an Indian Ocean regional threat. On the other hand, according to Chalmers Johnson, the apparent US military build-up in Oman could be seen as a possible security threat to Iran (Johnson, 2004; 252). However, in general terms, 'real' security threats in the traditional sense of the term are intra-state and invariably do not emanate from other states (UN 2004; 24) and war data since the Second World War demonstrate this.

Extra-Regional Security Interests

The Indian Ocean Region has had a long-standing history of extra-regional influence and perhaps it could be argued that some of the many remaining legacies of this, which are evident around the region, are potential sources of stability. Apart from Indian Ocean states, all major industrial powers and all major energy suppliers have an innate interest in Indian Ocean security and stability (Rumley and Chaturvedi, 2005).

An important question is the extent to which any extra-regional security presence, while aiming to guarantee regional as well as its own security interests, is also perceived by other states as a source of *insecurity*. On the one hand, it should be recognised and accepted that both the United States *and* China, as well as other extra-regional states, possess legitimate regional security interests. On the other hand, while some commentators might accept this view, what many would have difficulty with, however, are those contexts when US and Chinese regional 'interests' are enforced 'illegitimately'.

The United States Regional Presence

In recent years, there appears to be a growing United States traditional security interest in the Indian Ocean Region (US Defence Report, 2001; 27). There are at least three general arguments that have been canvassed regarding the rationale for this extra-territorial presence of US military personnel (Rumley, 2003). The first is that a US military presence is necessary for the good of the region in the sense that it functions as a 'regional stabiliser'. Thus, according to this view, a US military presence in the Indian Ocean is a kind of guarantor for the security of regional states. Whether this view is perceived to be the case by all Indian Ocean states, however, is highly debatable. A second view is that a US military presence is essential for the enhancement of US economic interests. In this view, therefore, the US presence is designed to maximise its own national economic security. According to Chalmers Johnson, one of the several explanatory reasons for the more than 725 US military bases around the world is to provide protection for American dependence on imported energy supplies (Johnson, 2004; 167). A third view is that a US military presence is unnecessary, since, not only has there been a basic shift in the security environment since the end of the Cold War, but that, in addition, the very existence of US military personnel constitutes a regional security threat.

Apart from its very substantial Ocean naval presence, the regional distribution of US *land*-based personnel is highly variable but with the highest security priorities being in Saudi Arabia and Kuwait (Table 2). Overall, these data demonstrate a correlation between the US land-based presence and the presence of substantial volumes of oil and gas and thus provide some support for the second view noted above.

Table 2: United States Indian Ocean Land-Based Military Personnel 2001*

Army	*Navy*	*Marines*	*Air*	*G. Force*	*Total*
Australia	8	61	663	71	803
Diego Garcia	4	557	0	29	590
Egypt	341	30	57	72	500
Kuwait	2150	7	41	2010	4208
Oman	0	122	7	544	673
Qatar	97	3	2	14	116
Saudi Arabia	285	29	47	4444	4805
Singapore	8	92	16	44	160
Thailand	42	9	30	32	113
UAE	0	7	7	190	209

* In East Asia and Pacific 12,578 afloat; In ME 13,546 afloat
Source: Johnson, 2004, pp. 158-9

Diego Garcia, however, which was seen as a pivotal node in the US Cold War "strategic axis" policy with its 'flanks' in South Africa and Western Australia (Rumley, 1999; 171), contains by far the largest proportion of land-based navy personnel. In the 21st century, however, Diego Garcia has served as a major base for B-52 bombing in Afghanistan as well as the bombing attacks on Baghdad. Issues of human security on the part of Diego Garcia's deported indigenous population still remain to be resolved (Johnson, 2004; 221-2). In 2000, a British High Court ruling invalidated the local immigration order that had excluded indigenous people from the archipelago, but upheld the special military status of Diego Garcia (CIA, 2005).

Chinese Threat: Myth or Reality?

China would like to portray itself as being of no actual or potential threat to Indian Ocean states. From a Western perspective, however, China is often portrayed as possessing the greatest potential threat to Western and other interests (Tang, 1997; p. 82). Five sets of factors appear to have contributed to this Chinese threat perception – China's rapid economic growth, its authoritarian political system, its increasing military capability, concern over internal instability and rising Chinese nationalism (Yee and Storey, 2002; 1-19).

China's introduction of an anti-secession law into the National People's Congress in March 2005 has been perceived both as a threat and as a reaffirmation of the status quo. The law was described by the US Press Secretary as an example of "unilateral" action that should have been prevented. To the United States, it is seen as being "unhelpful" and thus "should be reconsidered". On the other hand, others see the law as "a legalisation of current policy". To these observers, China is content with Taiwan to continue as an independent democracy so long as it does not proclaim itself to be so. In this sense, the legislation is perceived to be an "empty law" (Taylor, 2005). China says the anti-secession law is aimed at peace, however, that is not quite how Taiwan sees it.

From an Indian Ocean standpoint, China has been portrayed as being "potentially more assertive" and having the "ambition and strategic requirement to project power" into the region and that these events are "now becoming reality". Among other things, part of this power projection is the adoption of a "string of pearls" strategy of bases and diplomatic ties from southern China to the Middle East, including the construction of a naval base at Gwadar in Pakistan and a strategic commitment to the current Iranian regime (Pickford, 2005). To some commentators, such developments threaten Western SLOCS. However, since four-fifths of China's oil comes through the Straits of Malacca, China is faced with what has been referred to as a "Malacca dilemma" – that is, the problem of developing a non-threatening security strategy for its oil supplies and dilemmas over whether the Chinese navy can become involved in this process (Singh, 2005).

From another perspective, the size and importance of the Chinese state and thus its market inevitably ensures an almost insatiable demand for a wide range of commodities. For example, it has been estimated that, by 2010, China's demand for imported oil may reach an amount equivalent to half of Saudi Arabia's daily production (Asia Yearbook, 1997; p. 23). To some in the West, therefore, China is seen as an *economic* threat and as a global rival. However, China's increasingly market orientation and thus regional and global interdependence plus its developmental imperative combine to create immense opportunities for regional states to help guarantee food and resources security and to provide technical and service expertise of various kinds. Perceptions of China as a threat are therefore subject to change. For example, in a relatively recent assessment, it has been argued that, in the case of Malaysia, perceptions of China have moved from "hostility" to "cordiality" (Baginda, 2002). However, the most recent Australian Government report on Malaysia notes that even though Malaysians generally view China "as an economic opportunity, rather than a threat", nonetheless, "the threat of China's industrial rise is real" (Australian Government, 2005; 27-8). In the case of Australia, China's rapid economic growth is now also seen as a great economic opportunity and one that is very beneficial to the Australian stock market. However, an alternative US perspective, and one "that is assumed to have been correctly proven", is that China's establishment of long-term high-value resource contracts with Australia is merely a mechanism for driving a wedge into the Australia-US alliance (Pickford, 2005).

Economic Insecurity in the Indian Ocean Region

It has often been said that a Post-Cold War global North-South division is replacing the former East-West division as one of the principal dimensions of global conflict. In this new paradigm there is a danger of prioritising the security agenda of the North at the expense of the South. Regional security threats can arise because of the instability of states with problems of economic, social and political viability. In addition, resources scarcity and resources competition constitute threats, especially when they are linked to food and energy insecurity. Indeed, it has been argued that, in the years ahead, "resource wars" will become "the most distinctive feature of the global security environment" (Klare, 2002; 212). Furthermore, states which 'fail' due to basic problems of good governance and corruption, are incapable of asserting authority within their own territories and are seen to be "troubling to world order" since they may become sources of instability, mass migration and terrorism (Rotberg, 2002).

One of the important common characteristics of Indian Ocean states is that the majority of them are members of the developing world indeed some regard the Indian Ocean region as the heart of the developing world. By far the highest proportion of regional states (48%) has a low human development index (HDI), concentrated principally in the North and East African and SAARC sub-regions. On the other hand, only 11 states of the IOR possess a high HDI; Australia, Bahrain, Brunei, Kuwait, Malaysia, Mauritius, Qatar, Seychelles, Singapore, Thailand and the United Arab Emirates. In this sense, the Indian Ocean Region is a global focus not only for North-South conflict, but also for external intervention and potentially for South-South cooperation. Problems of underdevelopment, poor governance, internal political instability and conflict are thus common to many regional states (Rumley, 1999; 228).

Africa is the continent that is the hardest hit by poverty, and, while life expectancy has been decreasing, at the same time, there has been an increase in food and energy insecurity. The annual HIV/AIDS deaths in Africa exceed the total number of battle deaths in all civil wars fought in the 1990s (United Nations, 2004). If we take, for example, the eight states which constitute the Western Indian Ocean Littoral (WIOL) – Kenya, Madagascar, Mozambique, Oman, Somalia, South Africa, Tanzania and Yemen – only two – the northern and southern 'anchors' of Oman and South Africa – do not possess low human development indices and Somalia has been classified as a "failed state". Furthermore, of these WIOL states, only the latter is not a member of IOR-ARC.

Since food insecurity has now reached a crisis point in some of these WIOL states, addressing their problems necessitates confronting the causes of economic insecurity and also requires the *implementation* of a "shared vision of development" (Annan, 2005; 8-23). The eight goals outlined in the 2001 UN Millennium Declaration – to eradicate extreme poverty and hunger, achieve universal primary education, promote gender equality and empower women, reduce child mortality improve maternal health, combat HIV/AIDS, malaria and other diseases, ensure environmental sustainability and develop a global partnership for development – are central components of this "shared vision". The "special needs" of Africa were referred to in the Millennium Declaration and the UN Secretary-General has recently called for a green revolution in Africa and a new global partnership for Africa's development (Annan, 2005). Among other things, this means that richer Indian Ocean states have a special regional developmental responsibility in order to enhance regional security. An analysis of the bilateral disbursement of ODA to the 21 Indian Ocean littoral states is instructive in this regard (Table 3).

The only significant Indian Ocean ODA donor contribution in 2002 was of Australia to Indonesia. Furthermore, Japan is the largest ODA donor to 8 regional states; France is the largest donor to an additional 5 states; the United States is the largest donor to 3 states; the Arab states are the largest donors to 2 states and the EC, Germany and the UK each donate the most to one regional state. Donor state ODA priorities are fairly well-defined with Japan giving the largest amount to Indonesia; France gives the largest amount to Mozambique; the United States gives the largest amount to Pakistan; the Arab states give the largest amount to Yemen; the UK and Germany give the largest amounts to India; and, the EC gives the largest amount to Tanzania (Table 3).

Donor states appear to have fairly well-defined sub-regional priorities, with Japan giving the largest amount of ODA to every state surrounding the Bay of Bengal. France has concentrated its ODA mainly in the southwestern Indian Ocean, the USA in the Horn of Africa and Pakistan and the Arab states have their highest priorities in Oman and Yemen.

Table 3: Indian Ocean Littoral States: Bilateral ODA Recipients 2002 (US$M)

	Three Largest State Donors	*Indian Ocean Donors in the top 10*
Bangladesh	Japan (262), UK (188), USA (95)	–
Burma	Japan (54), EC (10), UK (9)	–
India	Japan (768), UK (346), Germany (159)	–
Indonesia	Japan (891), USA (219), Germany (120)	Australia (79)
Iran	Germany (35), Japan (32), France (9)	–
Kenya	USA (108), UK (70), Japan (54)	–
Madagascar	France (99), EC (69), USA (42)	–
Malaysia	Japan (187), Denmark (18), Germany (6)	Australia (1)
Maldives	Japan (8), Norway (1)	Australia (1.3)
Mauritius	France (19), EC (16), Japan (3)	–
Mozambique	France (240), Italy (231), USA (148)	–
Oman	Arab states (53), Belgium (6), Japan (3)	Australia (0.1)
Pakistan	USA (656), Japan (284), France (250)	–
Seychelles	France (4), EC (3), Japan (1)	–
Singapore	France (3), Japan (2), Germany (2)	Australia (0.2)
Somalia	USA (35), Norway (33), EC (32)	–
South Africa	EC (125), USA (98), UK (87)	–
Sri Lanka	Japan (249), Germany (25), Norway (25)	–
Tanzania	UK (208), EC (136), Netherlands (117)	–
Thailand	Japan (651), USA (36), Germany (20)	Australia (9)
Yemen	Arab states (188), Netherlands (35), Germany (31)	–

Source: Development Assistance Committee web site

Regional Non-conventional Security Threats

In the globalised world of the 21st Century, what is becoming increasingly clear is that the traditional realist model of security – principally embodied in the view that threats emanate from one state, are aimed at another state, and are of a military nature-has increasingly come into question (Commonwealth of Australia, 2003b). Furthermore, the specific nature of these 'non-traditional' security threats — for example, people smuggling, drug trafficking, piracy and terrorism-require 'non-traditional' responses by state security agencies (Dupont, 2003). At the Indian Ocean regional scale, these new security threats essentially require a new approach to regional security thinking and cooperation at various levels. Questions of human security, environmental security (Doyle, 2004) and food security are central regional issues for the 21st century, and India and Australia can take a leading regional role in confronting them.

Overall, there exists a fundamentally different mindset when comparing traditional and non-traditional security from the perspective of policy planning for potential threats. In the case of the former, there tends to exist a mindset of "planning for conflict". In the case of the latter, on the other hand, there is more likely to be a mindset of "planning for cooperation". Both, of course, can be self-fulfilling. In this sense, there is good reason to believe that Indian Ocean cooperation to meet a range of non-conventional security threats will actually lead to a minimisation of traditional security threats. For the sake of the present discussion, only one type of 'non-traditional security threat' – human security – will be considered here since it is considered to be the most important threat to regional as well as global stability.

Human Security

The Commission on Human Security has argued that the current global war on terror is deficient in at least two ways. First, much state-sponsored terrorism is not addressed. Second, some legitimate groups have been labelled as terrorist organisations in order to stifle any opposition to authoritarian government policies (Commission on Human Security, 2003; 23). While the state still remains the central purveyor of security, it often fails to properly discharge its security obligations and at times can even be a threat to its own citizens. As a result, attention must now shift from the security of the state to the security of the people – that is, there is a need to shift the focus to human security (Commission on Human Security, 2003; 2). This shift will involve greater attention being given to human rights and to assure the "freedom to live in dignity" (Annan, 2005; 34).

One can examine this issue another way by attempting to differentiate between threats to the state and threats to people. One of the changes, consequent upon the end of the Cold War, is that there was an important change of scale and differentiation in threat reality and threat perception. In the 21st century, while threats to the economy and the natural environment of states tend to be global, 'real' threats to *people* are more likely to be intra-state and even intra-urban. In short, 'real' threats to the state are global and 'real' threats to people emanate from within the state. The "democratisation of security" is thus essential to address 'real' needs.

The existence of authoritarian regimes in the Indian Ocean Region is not uncommon. Authoritarian regimes not only threaten their own people, but they also threaten regional and even global resources security given their general coincidence with the distribution of hydrocarbons.

According to Freedom House, over the past thirty years, states which are classified as "free" in the Indian Ocean Region are in a small minority (consistently less than 20%), although it is clear that the overall pattern of states which it classifies as being "not free" and "partly free" has changed since 1972. Nonetheless, in 2002, states in the "not free" category comprised the highest percentage with several new states being placed in this category compared with 1992 (for example, Egypt, Maldives, Oman, Pakistan, Swazhiland, UAE, Yemen and Zimbabwe).

In its 2004 global survey, the state ranking of press freedoms provided by the organisation, *Reporters Without Borders*, shows that the worst offenders are to be found in East Asia (especially Mynamar, China, Vietnam and Laos) and in the Middle East (particularly Saudi Arabia, Iran, Syria and Iraq). Of all of the Indian Ocean states, only two (South Africa and Australia) were in the ranking's upper quartile and the largest group of states was located in the ranking's lowest quartile.

Kofi Annan talked recently of the global need to strive for "larger freedom"-that is, a view of freedom which "encapsulates the idea that development, security and human rights go hand in hand" (Anna, 2005; 5). Among other things, international and regional pressure and public and private dialogue are needed to encourage larger freedom and to enhance the process of democratisation.

In March 2005, a government move was initiated in Malaysia to pressure Myanmar to implement democratic reforms. Parliamentarians from the ruling *Barisan Nasional* coalition were to table a resolution calling for Myanamar to be stripped of its chair of top regional grouping, ASEAN in 2006, unless its military regime changes its dismal human rights record.

Perceived Security Threats from Indian Ocean People

Western-style democratisation, however, is not unproblematical. One of its greatest flaws is that of a legitimation crisis in which citizens of the West have generally lost faith with their politicians and subscribe increasingly to a civil society model or to non-participation (Castells, 1997; 309-353). Furthermore, its strict application around the Indian Ocean Region, especially to large states still in the process of nation-building, will likely induce spatial instability. Presumably those who argue that greater democratisation will enhance regional security would nonetheless agree that 'real' security threats are actually those that are perceived by people living in the Indian Ocean region. This is an important issue for the future security of the Indian Ocean Region, and it is an issue on which there is a need to engage in more collective research.

A recently-launched study of such issues from an Australian perspective lends some interesting insights into such 'real' security threats (Cook, 2005). The majority of potential threats, which worried more than 50 per cent of the Australians, sampled were 'non-conventional'. Australians worried equally about Islamic fundamentalism and US foreign policies, and the latter were seen to be much more worrying than China's growing power. Furthermore, even though most Australians value the ANZUS alliance, only a small minority would support Australian involvement with the United States in the event of any Chinese conflict over Taiwan. Indeed, Australians generally felt more positively towards four Asian states – China, Japan, Malaysia and Singapore-than the United States, and also believed that the Australian government was taking too much notice of the views of the United States in constructing Australian foreign policy (Cook, 2005; 1-7).

Conclusion

In a very real sense, there was no necessity for regional states to devise a security regime during a period when the Indian Ocean was dominated by outside powers. The combination of colonialism and the Cold War ensured that regional states were insufficiently emancipated to collectively decide their mutual destinies. In any event, internal interaction was relatively weak and this ensured a weak regionalism. Just as security threats and insecurity are constructed, so security itself also needs to be constructed. As it stands at present, apart from the role of the United Nations and a few second track groups, ultimately, much of the responsibility for constructing security in the Indian Ocean region lies in the hands of regional states, whether they like it or not.

There are at least four implications of this security environment. First, there is no regional security regime for the Indian Ocean. Second, sub-regional security regimes are relatively weak. Third, security arrangements are essentially Western-oriented and are principally orchestrated by the United States. Fourth, there is an emphasis on stronger bilateral rather than multilateral security relationships in the Indian Ocean Region.

There is considerable scope to construct security regimes around areas of common interest and concern – for example, the ocean environment, SLOCS, piracy and so on – the majority of which are 'non-traditional' (and perhaps less threatening?) security concerns. Minimising insecurity requires greater mutual knowledge, education and understanding among Indian Ocean governments and peoples. Indeed, it has been argued that civil society will likely be a primary location for political struggle and political change during the current century (Schecter, 2000). Such struggles will be an outcome of the refusal by social movements to accept the 'taken-for-granted' communication boundaries of established systems of domination such states and because such groups will also offer resistance opposition to neo-liberal globalisation (Routledge, 2000). On the other hand, while another common assumption of the emergence of a global civil society is that new political organisations structurally converge around a common global agenda. In reality it seems that the convergence of world views is highly fragmentary (Heins, 2000). *Regional* opportunities currently exist around the Indian Ocean for "second track" actors to make an important contribution to regional security. Other areas of concern, such as environmental security and many other non-traditional security threats such as those noted above, might well form the basis of an increasingly strong civil relationship among people living around the Indian Ocean Region in the future.

In the final analysis, creating "freedom from fear" in the Indian Ocean Region requires all regional states to:

> "Commit themselves to implementing a new security consensus based on the recognition that threats are interlinked, that development, security and human rights are mutually interdependent, that no state can protect itself acting entirely alone and that all states need an equitable, efficient collective security system; and therefore commit themselves to agreeing on, and implementing, comprehensive strategies for confronting the whole range of threats, from international war through weapons of mass destruction, terrorism, state collapse and civil conflict to deadly infectious disease, extreme poverty and the destruction of the environment" (Annan, 2005; 57).

Overall, increasing interdependence due to globalisation implies greater inter-state cooperation. It also implies the increasing importance of non-traditional security threats. The logical outcome of the interaction of these processes is a decline in regional inter-state conflict. Regional states such as Australia and India are in an important regional position to facilitate such outcomes by initiating a new regional security agenda along the lines conceptualised above and discussed throughout this volume.

REFERENCES

Agence France-Presse (2005), "India goes on weapons spree", *The West Australian*, 31 March, p. 31.

Alagappa, M., ed. (1998), *Asian Security Practice: Material and Ideational Influences*, Stanford University Press.

Ali, T. (2002), *The Clash of Fundamentalisms: Crusades, Jihads and Modernity*, London: Verso.

Annan, K. (2005), *In Larger Freedom: Towards Development, Security and Human Rights For All*, New York: United Nations.

Australian Government (2005), *Malaysia: An Economy Transformed*, DFAT, Economic Analytical Unit: Canberra.

Baginda, A.R. (2002), "Malaysian perceptions of China: from hostility to cordiality", in Yee, H. and Storey, I., eds. (2002), *The China Threat: Perceptions, Myths and Reality*, London: RoutledgeCurzon, pp. 227-247.

Bajpai, K. (1998), "India: modified structuralism", in Alagappa, *op. cit.*, pp. 157-197.

Bergin, A. (2004), 'The proliferation security initiative – implications for the Indian Ocean Region', paper delivered to the second IORG conference on 'Energy Security and the Indian Ocean', Tehran, February.

Blackwill, R.D. and Dibb, P. eds. (2000), *America's Asian Alliances*, Cambridge, Mass: MIT Press.

Bouchard, C. (2004), "Emergence of a new geopolitical era in the Indian Ocean: characteristics, issues and limitations of the Indianoceanic order", in Rumley and Chaturvedi, *op. cit.*, pp. 84-109.

Bracken, P. (2000), *Fire in the East: The Rise of Asian Military Power and the Second Nuclear Age*, Perennial: New York.

Buzan, B., Wæver, O. and de Wilde, J. (1998), *Security: A New Framework for Analysis*, Boulder: Lynne Reinner.

Brzezinski, Z. (1997), *The Grand Chessboard: American Primacy and its Geostrategic Imperatives*, New York: Basic Books.

Castells, M. (1997), *The Information Age: Economy, Society and Culture, Volume II, The Power of Identity*, Oxford: Blackwell.

CIA (2005), *The World Factbook.*

Club de Madrid (2005), web site at: http://www.clubmadrid.org

Coker, C. (2002), 'Globalisation and insecurity in the twenty-first century: NATO and the management of risk', ISSS, *Adelphi Paper,* 345, Oxford University Press.

Collins, A. (2000), *The Security Dilemmas of Southeast Asia*, Singapore: ISEAS.

Commission on Human Security (2003), *Human Security Now*, New York.

Commonwealth of Australia (2003), *Advancing the National Interest: Australia's Foreign and Trade Policy White Paper*, Canberra, DFAT.

Cook, I. (2005), *Australians Speak 2005: Public Opinion and Foreign Policy*, Sydney: Lowy Institute.

Council for Security Cooperation in the Asia-Pacific (CSCAP) web site: http://www.cscap.org/

Dalrymple, R. (2003), *Continental Drift: Australia's Search for a Regional Identity*, Aldershot: Ashgate.

Davis, J.H. (2005), "Report faults US spy community, challenges strategy for overhaul", *The Baltimore Sun*, 1 April.

Development Assistance Committee (DAC), website: http://www.oecd.org.countrylist

Doty, Roxanne Lynn (2003), *Anti-immigrantism in Western Democracies: Statecraft, Desire and the Politics of Exclusion*, London: Routledge.

Downer, A. (2005), "Securing Australia's interests – Australian foreign policy priorities", *Australian Journal of International Affairs*, Vol. 59 (1), pp. 7-12.

Doyle, T. (2004), "An agenda for environmental security in the Indian Ocean Region", in Rumley and Chaturvedi, *op. cit.*, pp. 154-171.

Dupont, A. (1991), "Australia's threat perceptions: a search for security", Strategic and Defence Studies Centre, ANU, *Canberra Papers on Strategy and Defence*, No. 82.

Dupont, A. (2001), *East Asia Imperilled: Transnational Challenges to Security*, Cambridge University Press.

Dupont, A. (2003), 'Transformation or stagnation? Rethinking Australia's defence', *Australian Journal of International Affairs*, Vol. 57 (1), pp. 55-76.

Dupont, A. (2005), "Neighbours back on track", *Australian Financial Review*, 31 March, p. 63.

Eizenstat, S., Porter, J.E. and Weinstein, J. (2005), "Rebuilding weak states", *Foreign Affairs*, Vol. 84 (1), pp. 134-146.

Flanagan, S.J., Frost, E.L. and Kugler, R.L. (2001), *Challenges of the Global Century: Report of the Project on Globalization and National Security*, Washington DC, National Defense University.

Freedom House (2005), *Freedom in the World Country Ratings: 1972 through 2003,* Freedom House web site at: http://www.freedomhouse.org/

Fukuyama, F. (2004), *State-Building: Governance and World Order in the 21st Century*, Ithaca: Cornell University Press.

Gopal, D. and Rumley, D., eds. (2004), *India and Australia: Issues and Opportunities*, New Delhi: Authors Press.

Gordon, S. et al (1996), *Security and Security Building in the Indian Ocean Region*, Canberra: Strategic and Defence Studies Centre, ANU.

House, J.W. (1984), "War, peace and conflict resolution: towards an Indian Ocean model", *Transactions*, Institute of British Geographers, New Series, Vol. 9, pp. 3-21.

Howard, J. (2005), "Australia in the world", address to the Lowy Institute, Sydney, 31 March.

Howlett, D. (2001), "Nuclear proliferation" in Baylis, J. and Smith, S. eds., *The Globalization of World Politics*, Oxford University Press, pp. 415-439.

Huntington, S. (1996), *The Clash of Civilizations and the Remaking of the New World Order*, New York: Simon and Schuster.

Johnson, C. (2004), *The Sorrows of Empire: militarism, Secrecy, and the End of the Republic*, New York: Metropolitan Books.

Kerin, J. and Bita, N. (2005), "Diggers could go in as Italy quits Iraq: PM", *The Australian*, 17 March.

Klare, M.T. (2002), *Resource Wars: The New Landscape of Global Conflict*, New York: Henry Holt.

Mistry, R. (1997), *A Fine Balance*, Vintage International: New York.

Mohan, C.R. (2003), *Crossing the Rubicon: The Shaping of India's New Foreign Policy*, Viking: New Delhi.

Nyman, P.N. and Morrison, J.S. (2004), "The terrorist threat in Africa", *Foreign Affairs*, Vol. 83 (1), pp. 75-86

Pickford, A. (2005), "Australia-PRC relationship hampered by contradictions and lack of contextual view", Future Directions International, *Weekly Global Report*, Vol. 1 (5), pp. 1-5.

Proliferation Security Initiative (PSI) web site: http://www.state.gov/t/np/c10390.htm

Rao, P.V., ed. (2003), *India and the Indian Ocean in the Twilight of the Millennium*, South Asian Publishers: New Delhi.

Reporters Without Borders (2005), web site at: http://www.rsf.org

Rotberg, R.I. (2002), "Failed states in a world of terror", *Foreign Affairs*, vol 81.

Rumley, D. (1999), *The Geopolitics of Australia's Regional Relations*, Kluwer, Dordrecht.

Rumley, D. (2003), "The Asia-Pacific region and the new world order", *Ekistics*, Vol. 70, no. 422/423, pp. 321-326.

Rumley, D. (2004), 'Geopolitics of Australia-India trade', in Gopal, D. and Rumley, D., eds., *India and Australia: Issues and Opportunities* (Delhi: Authors Press), pp. 1-25.

Rumley, D. and Chaturvedi, S., eds. (2004), *Geopolitical Orientations, Regionalism and Security in the Indian Ocean*, South Asian Publishers, New Delhi.

Rumley, D. and Chaturvedi, S., eds. (2005), *Energy Security and the Indian Ocean Region*, South Asian Publishers, New Delhi.

Rumley, D., Forbes, V.L. and Griffin, C., eds. (2006), *Australia's Arc of Instability*, Dordrecht, Springer.

Sachs, J. (2005), "The development challenge", *Foreign Affairs*, Vol. 84 (2), pp. 78-90.

Said, E. (1991), *Orientalism*, Harmondsworth: Penguin.

Shiva, V. (2002), *Water Wars: Privatization, Pollution, and Profit*, Cambridge, MA: South End Press.

Singh, S. (2005), "China's expanding energy deficit: security implications for the Indian Ocean Region", in Rumley and Chaturvedi, *op. cit.*, pp. 166-188.

Stares, P.B., ed. (1998), *The New Security Agenda: A Global Survey*, Tokyo: Japan Center for International Exchange.

Taylor, J. (2005), "China's anti-secession law 'empty': experts", Australian Broadcasting Corporation (ABC) online, 9 March.

Thakur, R. and Newman, E., eds. (2004), *Broadening Asia's Security Discourse and Agenda: Political, Social, and Environmental Perspectives*, Tokyo: United Nations University Press.

Tilman, R.O. (1984), "The enemy beyond: external threat perceptions in the ASEAN region", ISEAS, *Research Notes and Discussions Paper*, No. 42.

United Nations (2004), *A More Secure World: Our Shared Responsibility*, Report of the Secretary-General's High-level Panel on Threats, Challenges and Change.

United Nations Economic and Social Commission for Asia and the Pacific (UNESCAP) web site: http://www.unescap.org/

US Defense Report (2001), *US Department of Defense Quadrennial Defense Review Report*, 30 September.

Yee, H. and Storey, I., eds. (2002), *The China Threat: Perceptions, Myths and Reality*, London: RoutledgeCurzon.

Index

Contributors

Prof. D. Gopal is Australian Studies Programme Coordinator and Professor of Political Science, School of Social Sciences, IGNOU. A scholar in International Relations, he obtained his Ph.D. from Jawaharlal Nehru University, New Delhi.

Prof. Dennis Rumley is Adjunct Professor, Edith Cowan University in Perth and Associate Professor, School of Social Studies and Cultural Studies, University of Western Australia. He gained his Ph.D. at the University of British Columbia and has been Professor of Australian Studies at the University of Tokyo.

Dr. Suparna Karmakar, Trade Policy Consultant, affiliated with ICRIER, New Delhi. She obtained her Ph.D. from Jawaharlal Nehru University, New Delhi.

Prof. Kamal N. Kabra, Professor of Economics in the Indian Institute of Public Administration, New Delhi. He has authored several books and articles. He obtained his Ph.D. from Delhi School of Economics.

Sharad Joshi is a Research Scholar at the Graduate School of Public and International Affairs, University of Pittsburgh. He has a Master's Degree in International Relations from Jawaharlal Nehru University, New Delhi.

Dr. Pankaj Kumar Jha is Associate Fellow, Indian Institute of Defence Studies & Analysis, New Delhi. He obtained a PhD from Jawaharlal Nehru University, New Delhi.

Dr. Pushpita Das is Associate Fellow, Institute for Defence Studies and Analysis. She obtained her doctorate from Jawaharlal Nehru University, New Delhi.

Dr. Vivian Louis Forbes, Adjunct Associate Professor, Curtin University and Map Curator, University of Western Australia, Perth.

Dr. H. S. Prabhakar, Associate Professor, Chairperson of the Centre for East Asian Studies, School of International Studies, Jawaharlal Nehru University, New Delhi.

Dr Anthony S. Bergin, Associate Professor, School of Politics, University College, Australian Defence Force Academy, Canberra, Australia

Dr. Ganganath Jha, Associate Professor, Centre for South, Southeast and Southwest Pacific Studies, School of International Studies, Jawaharlal Nehru University, New Delhi.

Dr. Madhu Bala is Associate Professor in Economics at Indira Gandhi National Open University, New Delhi, India. She obtained her Ph.D. from Jawaharlal Nehru University, New Delhi.

Dr. Chintamani Mahapatra is Associate Professor at the School of International Studies of Jawaharlal Nehru University, New Delhi. He was a Commonwealth Scholar at the University of London. Dr. Mahapatra obtained his Ph.D. from Jawaharlal Nehru University, New Delhi.